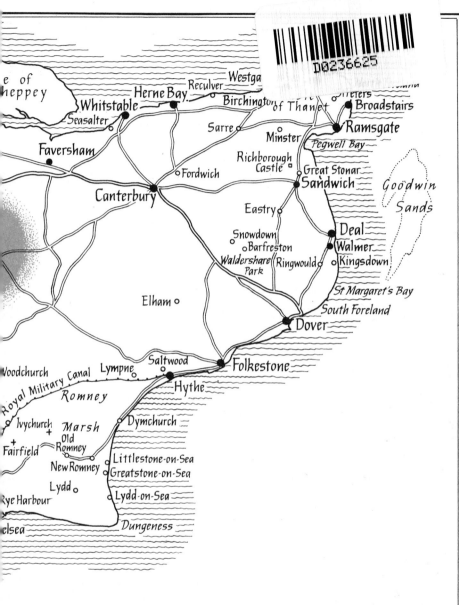

The Bulwark Shore

Miles
0 2 4 6 8 10
0 5 10 15 20
km

NSH

DEREK INGRAM HILL
M.A.
F.S.A

Canon of
CANTERBURY
CATHEDRAL.

1980

The Bulwark Shore

The Bulwark Shore

Thanet and the Cinque Ports

CAROLINE HILLIER

with photographs by
John Mosley

Eyre Methuen · London

First published in 1980 by
Eyre Methuen Ltd
11 New Fetter Lane, London EC4P 4EE
Text copyright © 1980 Caroline Hillier
Photographs copyright © 1980 John Mosley
Printed in Great Britain by
Richard Clay (The Chaucer Press) Ltd
Bungay, Suffolk

British Library Cataloguing in Publication Data

Hillier, Caroline
    The bulwark shore.
    1. Kent, Eng. – History   2. East Sussex, Eng. –
    History
    I. Title
    942.2'3'00946   DA670.K3   80–40361
ISBN 0–413–39580–4

To the memory
of
Captain John Valentine Wotton CBE, RN
and
Violet Isobel Wotton ARRC

Acknowledgements

We should like to thank all those people who have been kind enough to talk to us about themselves and the places in which they live, and who have allowed photographs to be taken. Although they are too numerous to list, their generous co-operation has played a major part in shaping this book.

I would like particularly to thank Miss Anne Roper MBE, FSA, Mr Ian Gill LLB, Registrar of the Cinque Ports and Chief Executive Thanet District Council, Mr Jonathan Aitken MP, Lord Clark OM, CH, KCB, and Lady Clark, Rear-Admiral T. H. Bradbury CB, RN, The Earl and Countess of Guilford, the Rev. Canon Derek Ingram Hill MA, FSA, Mr Paul Youden, Publicity Officer of Dover Harbour Board, Mr Charles E. Busson, Branch Librarian, Ramsgate Library, Mr Ian R. P. Josephs, The Regency Hotel, Ramsgate, Mr John Bratby RA, Mr Bill Coleman, Mr Terry Pryor, and Mr Sibert and Mrs Peggy Shingleston, of Whitstable, Mr Frank Fishlock of Deal, Mr Ron Miles, Chairman of the Publicity Committee of the East Sussex Branch, NFU, and Councillor Mrs Joan Yates and Mr Tom Finn-Kelcey of Rye. Also the Elder Brethren and members of the staff of Trinity House, London; the Royal Marines of 41 Commando and the Royal Marines, Deal; RAF Manston; and the staff of Shoreham Library, Shoreham-by-Sea, for their unfailing help during research.

We are also most grateful to Bob Woodings, our editor, and to Giles Gordon, our agent, for their enthusiastic help and encouragement, and for their expertise.

Extracts from *Kent* by Richard Church are reproduced by kind permission of the Estate of the late Richard Church, of Laurence Pollinger Ltd and of Robert Hale Ltd; the extract from *The Last Enemy* by Richard Hillary is by kind permission of

7

Macmillan, London and Basingstoke; extracts from *Kipps* by H. G. Wells are by kind permission of A. P. Watt Ltd; extracts from *The War Speeches of Winston S. Churchill* compiled by Charles Eade are by kind permission of Cassell Ltd; the quotations from Caesar: *The Conquest of Gaul*, translated by S. A. Handford, from Chaucer: *The Prologue to the Canterbury Tales*, translated by Nevill Coghill, from John Newman's *North East and East Kent* and *West Kent and the Weald* and from Ian Nairn and Nikolaus Pevsner's *Sussex* are reprinted by permission of Penguin Books Ltd; and the quotation from 'The Little Church on the Marsh' is by kind permission of the author. The publishers have made all effort to trace copyright holders; any omissions will be corrected if possible in future editions.

Our book is dedicated to my uncle, Captain Wotton, and to my aunt, Miss Violet Wotton, with great affection. My uncle returned from retirement to serve in the Navy in the Second World War in the exacting task of Staff Officer Minesweeping on the staff of the Commander in Chief the Nore, and (I quote from his obituary) 'His chief responsibility in the early years was to keep the Thames Estuary and East Coast clear of mines ... That the Port of London was never closed bears testimony to the way he carried out his job'. My aunt served as a VAD in the First World War, and was awarded the Royal Red Cross. She was the first Ramsgate VAD nurse to volunteer to go to the Front, and was accepted as a member of one of the first VAD units to serve there. I mention these details (although they never did so), because they seem to me to sum up the, often quiet, courage, of the people of the Bulwark Shore, to so many of whom we are all indebted.

Shoreham-by-Sea   C.H.
1979

Contents

Maps

Illustrations

'There is no advantage in living on an island unless your navy rides in undisputed sway over the waters that surround it.'

ALFRED THE GREAT

'Let us be masters of the Channel for six hours and we are masters of the world.'

NAPOLEON I

'The frontiers of England are the coasts of the enemy.'

ADMIRAL FISHER

'For what we can foresee, all Europe may form but one great Republic, and man be free of the whole.'

THOMAS PAINE: *The Rights of Man*

'The Channel is no more than a wide frontier.'

TWENTIETH-CENTURY DOVORIAN

and much of their character. Then the Christians who came with St Augustine; the Normans who came with William, making Kent, with its apple-orchards, farms and cathedrals, still more like the Normandy it was once joined to; followed down the years by French pirates, and Protestant refugees. And there were threatened invasions: of armies called upon by the Pope to force Henry VIII back into the fold; of Napoleon's massed troops; of Hitler's war machine. As Winston Churchill once pointed out, 'there has never been a period in all these long centuries of which we boast when an absolute guarantee against invasion, still less against serious raids, could have been given to our people.'[1]

On this vulnerable shore, along the coasts of Thanet, of Kent and East Sussex, massive defences were set up. Iron-age earthworks; the great chain of Saxon Shore forts built by the Romans; Henry VIII's castles; the Military Canal and Martello Towers; the wartime defences of this century. And, manning not only the defence posts, but also the narrow straits of the Channel itself – since Englishmen did not feel supreme unless they owned the waves too – were the men of the Cinque Ports. From an early date – probably before the Conquest – they were active in time of war and controlled the sea passage in peacetime, being both a defence against and a link with the Continent. The peak of their power was in the thirteenth century, but their role did not come to an end then: the Ports consolidated their Confederation; other ports joined; by the time that they no longer formed the nucleus of the Navy, the character of the towns and of their people had long been formed. This character can be seen re-emerging time and again down the years – in Pitt's Volunteers; in some of the bravest life-boat feats on record; in the indomitable courage of the men of the Dover Patrol; in the fortitude of civilians under bombardment, or the dogged spirit of airmen under stress; in local pride and a caring for tradition and for trusted values. It can be seen more colourfully in a streak of individuality and independence that has led men of the area to fight against oppression, or against each other in the past, to become pirates and smugglers, warlike fishermen or rival costermongers, rivals in pageantry; fierce, dogged, reticent or outgoing; but usually kind, always themselves, and more than most aware of change.

Each port and town was, and is, different from the others. The coastline itself has changed, and is still changing, from the days when Thanet was an island and Tenterden had its own port on an inlet of the sea. The people have adapted. They have adapted to newcomers from abroad, and since the coming of the railways, and the introduction of Bank Holidays, to an influx of holidaymakers from all parts of the country and its capital. Today they are adapting to a wave of tourists from abroad, and fruitfully so, since tourism is our largest single source of invisible earnings. Their state now perhaps epitomizes the state of the country as a whole: anxious to keep an identity while belonging to the larger European Community, beleaguered by pollution, heavy lorries, growing urban areas; determined to keep the best of their heritage; grappling with the often warring claims of employment and conservation; bewildered to be no longer entirely islanders. Visually, these places are the best and the worst we have to offer. Nothing can be more English and more drear than a wet day by the bingo hall beside the pier, or more English and more stirring than a fine evening as the tide goes out, or, on a full tide, as the fishing trawlers come home.

In this story, Canterbury plays a leading part, and so has been included in the book. If these coasts are our physical bulwark, Canterbury is our spiritual bulwark. Closely linked to the monarchy, it also had a role in the Confederation of the Cinque Ports. From the days when the Church had an international political role and the Pope could claim supremacy over kings, to the present day when a bond of faith may be arguably the only worldwide bond that can in the last resort defy political barriers and oppression, it has not been logical, far less in a deeper sense true, to play down the importance of this leading theme of our national life. W. G. Hoskins has pointed out that churches have been 'our special contribution to the culture of Western Europe'.[2] Sussex, and even more so, Kent, are counties particularly rich in fine churches.

There are probably as many books about Sussex as there are churches in the county; one wonders if there are more books about Kent than sheep in the fold. The first English topographical book, dedicated to Thomas Wotton of Boughton Malherbe in Kent (the father of the diplomat poet Sir Henry Wotton), was William Lambarde's *A Perambulation of Kent*, first published in

1 Pegwell; Minster; Richborough; Sandwich

> 'Thanet, round Isle, by Water compass'd, reckon'd,
> Fertile and clean, to none on Earth the second.'
>
> Monk's inscription

A wide bay opens like a mouth on the shore where English history began. Beyond chalk cliffs is a calm arc of water, merging into weed-edged land. Low bars of chalk finger into the sea on the northern side, and here winkle gatherers bend against the backdrop of fields and cliff. When the tide has peeled back, laying bare miles of sandflats and shimmering shallows, the sun fills the whole curve with streaks of opaline light.

Into the bay, nowadays, speed the black-red-white slugs of Hoverlloyd's hovercraft, in a cloud of spume, bringing the present-day hordes to our invasion shore. Native horror at their arrival can equal that of the ancient British facing the Vikings. 'They *fill* the shops – you can't go into the town. And you should *see* what they take back – a *half-hundredweight* of butter!' French – and Belgians and other from across the Channel – throng in the streets of nearby Ramsgate, and to see a line of them purposefully pulling their wheeled shopping bags into a café is somewhat like witnessing a military operation. Will we be taken over? Or is their coming, as one can't help suspecting, just what this country needs?

Quite apart from the hovercraft, Pegwell Bay has changed since I first knew it, and people who remember it as it was at the beginning of the century will passionately denounce its loss of charm. There is Richborough power station, for a start, breaking the uniquely flat skyline. Weed has encroached far into the bay. But it is still a magical place, if you catch it in the right mood. It has been depicted in countless prints and on pot lids, and

William Dyce's painting 'Pegwell Bay, Kent – a Recollection of October 5th 1858' (Tate Gallery) catches its essence, with cockle gatherers, children on the rocks, and Victorian girls in red and pink silk shawls gathering shells.

Driving back from Sandwich one evening, John and I saw, on the turfy cliff overlooking the water, cut through by a distant hovercraft with its plume of spray, six gypsy children dancing round a fire in red silk curtains, which they wore like cloaks, with delighted grins. Their grandmother was sitting on an up-ended box sorting dirty clothes to wash in a large bucket which was on the fire. She said they were 'strangers'. 'We may have to move on at any time.' She was fine looking, with a thick plait of blonde hair round her lined face, thin gold earrings. I asked her about this continual 'being moved on'.

'It's the life we're used to ... we don't know any other. Nice on a day like this ...'

'Isn't it rather noisy here?' John asked, eyeing the throbbing hoverslugs.

'No, my darling, we're used to noise,' she smiled, pointing at her six grandchildren.

And when we left, she settled back on her box to light a fag, the washing still not in the pot.

In spite of their modern caravans, and passing traffic, the large family seemed to have an aura of that freedom, that ability to breathe a less trammelled air, that others of us can only catch when looking at a place such as Pegwell.

*

The actual spot where, as the historian J. R. Green put it, 'English history begins'[1], was at Ebbsfleet. Here Hengist and Horsa landed in AD 449. They had been invited by King Vortigern, who was harassed by Picts and Scots, but in driving back Vortigern's enemies, Hengist also strengthened his own position by sending for more warriors from Jutland, and then cunningly got his daughter wedded to Vortigern. He noted the 'voluptuousness of King Vortiger' and 'plied him with pots' and then 'let slippe before him a faire gentlewoman, his owne daughter called Roxena or Rowen', and the king 'pledged her so hartely, that from thence-forth he could never be in rest, until he had obtained her to wife ...' or so Lambarde, our earliest topographical writer, has it.[2] Hengist then overthrew his father-in-law in a series of battles, in one of which Horsa was conveniently killed. Hengist became King of Kent.

The landing of Hengist and Horsa was commemorated in 1949 by some Danes who built the Viking ship *Hugin* and rowed it across the North Sea. The *Hugin*, with its rows of shields, stands beside the road at Pegwell Bay.

'This stone ... was unveiled by H.H. Prince Georg of Denmark ... and commemorates the beginning of English History with the landing at Ebbsfleet in this vicinity of Hengist and Horsa in AD 449 ...'

'Hengist? What's that?' asked a schoolboy, to whom I mentioned the ship at the hoverport.

'I think it's really lovely to see that ship, in this place ...' A woman from another part of the country, photographing the boat from every angle. 'It's wonderful here, lovely ... We haven't been to Kent before ... It's the one the Vikings came in, then? The wood doesn't look old enough, does it?'

'If people have a little time to wait here,' said Mr Roberts, Traffic Controller at the hoverport, who stands in kindly manner by the entrance, 'I send them over there to look at the ship. I say, "The old way of crossing the Channel, and the new way ..."'

The hovercraft speed out beyond the mast and prow of the wooden ship.

I asked Mr Roberts if he was for the old or the new.

'I'm not for rowing.'

*

'We're not allowed to tidy up this bit,' Mr Wright, Duty Officer at the hoverport, told me, pointing to a bramble-covered stream that runs at the foot of the cliff beyond Hoverlloyd's carpark. (The cliffs at Pegwell Bay, being renowned for their fossils, are a geologist's delight. Most of the layers are composed of chalk and flints which were formed on the bottom of a warm shallow sea some ninety million years ago, but an adjoining sandy layer is of the formation called the Thanet Beds which differs greatly in age – by twenty million years, being seventy million years old – so that the site, where twenty million years' worth of deposit is missing, is of international importance.) The cliff he was pointing to is covered with bushes of pink May, which ramble down it unchecked. Hoverlloyd's land ends just before the cliff, and the brambles below the cliff collect litter, although the stream is geologically important. As a stickler for cleanliness, Mr Wright is upset by this patch. I said I rather liked the brambles. A tree enthusiast, he also showed me the trees Hoverlloyd have planted on their own ground and at the approaches to the terminal – Leyland's cypresses, which will grow to thirty feet, to screen the carpark; laurels, tamarisks, interspersed with roses. Hard hit by the weather of recent years, they will be very effective when grown. He assured me that he had known this part of the bay in the fifties, before the advent of the hoverport, and that it was 'a dump', smelling badly; an opinion that several people voiced.

More importantly, Hoverlloyd are providing employment in an area that desperately needs it. A planning application before the Department of the Environment for expansion of the hoverport seems likely to be approved. MP for Thanet East, Jonathan Aitken, said in a speech in the Commons in March 1979:

That expansion will mean not only a £30 million order for the British Hovercraft Corporation, not only £3 million-worth of building works in and around the terminal buildings, not only 200 permanent new jobs in Thanet, but, above all ... an increase in today's already substantial cross-Channel hovercraft traffic to projected figures by 1983 of 448,000 vehicles and 3.1 million passengers annually.

(In 1978 the figures were 233,000 cars and lorries, 1,266,000 passengers, giving Ramsgate the position of Britain's second busiest Channel port.)

Additional seasonal jobs would be likely to add the same number again. At present Hoverlloyd employ approximately 750 people in the winter, with up to 1,100 in the summer; 75 per cent of employees come from Thanet or Canterbury, 90 per cent are local if one includes Herne Bay and Dover in the region. And this is an area – Ramsgate – where there are currently 2,000 out of work, half of them *under* 35 (a total figure of 12 per cent unemployed.) In addition, the hoverport traffic brings tourists to benefit hotels and guest houses in Ramsgate and Margate, although Mr Wright, who lives in Canterbury, said, 'If a tourist is here for two days and wants to see something pretty, I'm not going to send him to Ramsgate.'

Perhaps he should.

Perhaps the East Kent bus service should run better buses to Ramsgate (there are none at all from the hoverport to the station). Perhaps, I suggested, Hoverlloyd should paint green their walkway to the spot where English history began, on the Viking Ship clifftop (even Hengist might have been deterred by the present elephant-grey railings, embellished with a rabies sign), and dragoon Thanet District Council into painting the barrier round the ship and landscaping the grass which is neither long nor short. Perhaps more Ramsgate businesses should buy space in the partly empty advertising windows at the hoverport. It is a two-way situation, but possibly the tide is turning.

Hoverlloyd, an independent company, accountable to the Broströms of Sweden group, has a workforce which is a very happy one. 'The best place I've ever worked at,' said Mr Roberts, who lives in Ramsgate. And he told me how coaches of pensioners or school children call in at the rate of two or three coaches a day, ringing up in advance to ask if they can have a cup of tea, and enjoying the view (anxious drivers also appeal for the use of lavatories for their passengers – a valuable social service).

Stewardesses make travellers welcome; they are introduced to passengers in a magazine, in one copy of which I found the story of an old lady sitting upright in her front seat on arrival at Pegwell, waiting to hover on to London ... or passengers expecting to hover overland to Paris from Calais. Perhaps one day this will be possible, or as Mr Roberts might say, an advance on oars.

*

A more gentle invader also landed at Ebbsfleet, in 597, although he came in the spirit that has perhaps shaped our history more than any other. Augustine came ashore here, with forty monks, to convert King Ethelbert of Kent, whose wife Bertha was already a Christian. Augustine had been a brilliant administrator under Pope Gregory in Rome, and during his seven years as archbishop, Christianity became the official religion (some in Anglo-Saxon Britain were Christians before his mission), in a kingdom that later spread its rule as far north as the Humber. The Romans had left England nearly two centuries before; here once more was a strain of European civilization brought to the people of Kent, whom Caesar in his *Commentaries* had remarked on as being the most full of humanity: 'By far the most civilized inhabitants are those living in Kent (a purely maritime district) ...'[3] (Although Caesar as an anthropologist may sometimes be doubted. All Britons, he said, dyed their bodies with woad, wore their hair long with hair on the upper lip but not elsewhere, and shared wives between a group of ten to twelve men, especially between brothers and fathers and sons ... The last fact questionable, except in primitive communities.)

Augustine was 'a saint in spite of himself' (I quote Dom Hubert van Zeller, author of over fifty books, both religious and secular, to whom I wrote asking about Augustine's character); he was 'pushed into holiness by St Gregory who wouldn't let him come back to Rome when he wanted to. Once launched in England he made a go of it against all odds.' (And Dom Hubert adds, with typical verve, 'St Thomas à Becket was much sterner stuff ...') Ethelbert refused to meet St Augustine indoors, for fear of spells being cast over him, so they met on what is now high ground in the Minster Marshes, inland from Pegwell – at that time it was on the peninsula of Ebbsfleet, jutting into the Wantsum channel. A cross was erected at the spot in 1884 by Lord Granville.

On the opposite side of the road a family are carrying on the tradition of selling lavender – soap, lavender waters and a spicy pomander with oil of orange – although a large field where some of the lavender was grown has recently reverted to farmland. Such an industry is typical of Pegwell, whose great cottage industry of the nineteenth century was potted shrimps. Shrimping at Pegwell was at its height from 1847 to 1875. It was given its accolade in 1837, when Mr Cramp of the Belle Vue Tavern was appointed 'Purveyor of Essence of Shrimps and Potted Shrimps, in Ordinary to Her Majesty', Queen Victoria, as Princess Victoria, having visited the tavern with her mother the year before.

From that time the Belle Vue was a favourite venue for parties who would go there from Ramsgate and Margate to dine or have shrimp teas; the remainder of a jetty can be seen on the beach, where boating parties would land. Mrs Winters, who is 97 and lives in Ramsgate, used to live in the cottages by the Belle Vue which are now demolished. She can remember a Miss Coleman and Miss Adams of Pegwell doing shrimp teas, and the evening crowds at the inn. She also remembers, earlier – and her faded but alert eyes light up at the distant memory – fires being lit on rocks below the Belle Vue by the shrimpers, so that shrimps and mussels could be cooked on the beach.

'I'm sorry I can't remember more, dear, but every little sheds a bit more light, I expect ...' Her smile is eager, and her hands hold the rug on her knees lightly. In her daughter's brightness is the same openness to life that leads to longevity. She gave me a 'Walkers' Guide' (published by the Pegwell Bay Committee) to the clifftop footpath that runs from Ramsgate to Pegwell, and which is still just passable, through a tangle of bushes and butter-flies, despite cliff falls and a sinister area called 'Dead Man's Drop'. I know the path well, and at intervals in my life have pushed past the brambles by the little coastguards' cottages, and through a welter of wildflowers – vetch, field scabious, lucerne, pale flax, cranesbill, cinquefoil, sainfoin, hedge bedstraw, rest-harrow, mignonette and winter heliotrope – the flowers as pretty as their names and typical of Thanet. Down in the bay are cockles and bivalves, which live in the sand and mud, providing food for seabirds and waders – dunlin, sanderling, redshank and oystercatchers. The saltmarshes in front of the power station are composed of rich mud in which millions of tiny snails live, and these too attract birds such as shellduck and even, a few years ago, two Chilean flamingoes, who spent the summer in Pegwell.

In the bay itself, many tons of lugworm, a favourite bait for anglers, are dug up each year and their retail value is estimated to be in the region of a quarter of a million pounds. At low tide you can see the bait diggers far out towards the horizon, bent double over their U-shaped trenches in the sand, with the opening towards the sea so that the water drains away leaving an area in which to dig. As recently as fifteen or so years ago, there would also be a line of professional shrimpers, moving out across the bay at low tide, pushing their ten-foot-wide nets, and re-turning with the tall baskets on their backs laden with shrimps.

Scenes such as these were depicted on the lids of the famous pots in which shrimp paste was 'purveyed' – shrimpers, shells, scenes of Pegwell and the Belle Vue Tavern. Most of the later pot lids came from Staffordshire, and many are particularly successful examples of Staffordshire multi-coloured underglaze printing which was produced for F. and R. Pratt of Fenton. They are extremely decorative, with all the detail of a fine print, and warm colours. A collection of them is in the Local Studies room at Ramsgate Library. My Zig Zag Guide of 1897, illustrated by Phil May, who often stayed in Ramsgate, tells one also to buy a bottle of Samphire pickle from Banger's – the firm of S. Banger of Pegwell who were also famous for shrimp sauce.

Sole, lobsters and mullet were also caught at Pegwell. The whole 'Rutupian Shore' of the Romans had indeed been re-nowned for its shellfish, and Juvenal praised the taste of a Roman epicure by saying: 'The oysters of the Rutupian bay/At the first taste he knew ...' (Among curious exports of the Romans were bears, slaves – and pearls.)

Today, at Reculver when we visited it, was a sharp notice saying that all shellfish caught must be thoroughly boiled, and shrimping at Pegwell is not what it was, although by no means dead.

*

'If someone had registered the Bay as common land for 7s 6d a few years ago, it would have been saved,' says Dennis Gisby, who carries on the shrimping tradition in his spare time. He lives at Ramsgate and is a builder by trade, but the courtyard of his house is full of fuchsias, his thoughts full of shrimps. The season begins in September and October, running on until April or May. When we last visited him he had just caught ten gallons, over in Minnis Bay, where I shrimped as a child. Pegwell, he said, is not as good a ground as it was, with the hoverport and its busy traffic, although he shrimps there still and in fact the hovercraft have 'done shrimpers a favour in a way', because shrimps feed in the channel they cut in the sand. However, there are inclined to be deep pits into which the unwary shrimper plunges, and Dennis Gisby feels the new harbour works at Ramsgate may be to blame, by changing the flow of the tide. His father took up shrimping when the price rose to 1s 6d a pint, and his mother worked at the Belle Vue, just after its paste-making days. The old shrimpers didn't tell their secrets, but 'kept it in the family. They went by the tides and equinoxes ... and plankton. They did it for a living but they also got eels and cockles across the river (in Sandwich Bay).' One of the old shrimpers, Fred Streeter, gave Dennis his pint pots and basket; he wears the basket and transfers shrimps from the net into it with a sieve, then cooks the shrimps to sell to pubs. He has various nets, all large – one about nine feet across – and heavy. He thought the last one of the old guard must have died, because he hadn't seen him recently round the town. 'You could tell him if you saw him, by his walk ...' Old shrimpers walked with a hunching gait, their shoulders thrusting forward as if they were still pushing their nets through the water, with the rod against their thigh.

Would Dennis Gisby's son continue the line? 'I don't know –' His pink face beams and his sea-blue eyes become even more round – 'but he collects fossils –'

Could another site have been chosen for the hoverport, ten years ago?

Could the 'deplorable decision', as Councillor Derrick Molock called it in his independently owned *East Kent Critic* in 1968 (and which has since championed the cause of Cliffsend residents plagued by noise and the smell of kerosene), have been reversed?

Could 7s 6d have saved the bay?

*

Across the Minster Marshes lies Minster – the heart of Thanet, and appropriately so. A little to the north is Mount Pleasant, from where there is a magnificent view, although I am not sure that it is as extensive as my 1801 guide states:

an extent of prospect from the Queen's Channel to the mouths of the rivers Medway and Thames; on the other, the cliffs of Calais, the Downs, the Straits of Dover, the towns of Deal and Sandwich, part of East Kent, the Earl of Guilford's seat at Waldershare, the spires of Woodnesborough and Ash, the ruins of Richborough castle, the gothic tower of Canterbury cathedral, and a compass of hills of vast extent.

When we visited this viewpoint, there was a mist over the Queen's Channel, and two off-duty irate aircrew from Manston were banging on the door of the pub at Mount Pleasant, which was shut.

In the past, the view would also have been of the wide Wantsum channel, which cut through from Richborough and Sandwich to Reculver, which was then also at the mouth of an open bay. Ships from Boulogne and Calais sailing to London went through the Wantsum channel rather than going round the dangerous North Foreland, and until as late as the fourteenth century, a sizeable creek ran to within a stone's throw of Minster church. The channel itself was navigable by merchant ships as late as the latter half of the fifteenth century. Now the rivers Stour and Wantsum are all that remains of the channel, and at Plucks Gutter, south of Minster, a bridge forms one of the entrance ways to Thanet, with little ceremony, houseboats moored in the muddy river, and a view of the flat land of the old island.

Flat but not infertile. The flatness is accentuated by the fact that the hedges of this outpost land were grubbed up at the time when it was feared Napoleon might invade, but the area has a

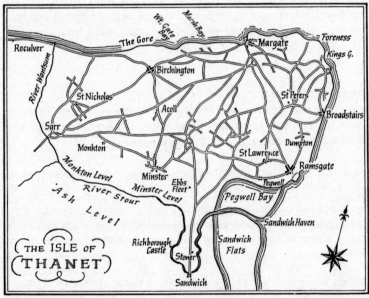

The Isle of Thanet in the nineteenth century (from an 1822 map)

peculiar attraction of its own, which you are aware of as you
drive through blossoming blackthorn of the few hedges left, or
through a blaze of poppies and corn. For the land is some of the
best in the country, and interestingly, it was the monks who made
it so. The subsoil in Thanet is chalk, and much of the natural
soil was thin and poor, but the monks, the richest and best
farmers of their day, manured it endlessly with seaweed, starting
a tradition of efficient farming, with 'clean', tilled land. In other
respects, Thanet, with its sea breezes, is fertile too, and its inhabitants long lived. Out of twenty-three people buried in St Peter's
in 1762, ten were 78 or more, and a writer in 1775 remarked that,
'In some of the Villages you can hardly put one Foot before the
other without tumbling over a child.'[4] The people were noted for
being temperate, thin and healthy.

More corpulent, probably, were the monks. There is a carved
head of Christ on a misericord of 1401 in Minster church. It has
the realism and power of a Renaissance portrait. Beside it are
two gross faces of monks. Originally, there was a nunnery at
Minster, one of the earliest centres of Christianity in Kent. It
was founded by the noblewoman Domneva, whose two young
brothers had been murdered at the order of King Egbert in
AD 669. He compensated her by giving her what she asked for,
which was as much land as her tame deer could run over 'at a
breath', despite the counter advice of Thunor, the murderer, who
was, so the tradition goes, swallowed up alive when the earth
opened at his evil words – at the place called Thunor's Leap.
Domneva's daughter was St Mildred, patron saint of Thanet,
who performed many miracles, among them lying in a hot oven
for three hours without feeling the flames, and imprinting the
permanent impression of her foot in stone at Ebbsfleet, when
she came from France. The abbey was later sacked by marauding
Danes, and its land given by Canute to the monks of St Augustine's Abbey at Canterbury, who began the existing church in 1027.
The chancel and transepts are thirteenth century; in the small
east window is brilliant blue glass, over 700 years old, the secret
of whose indigo has now been lost. At the south-east corner of the
church is a Saxon stair-turret, with a pointed cap of flints, which
was probably used as a watch tower for enemies stealing in from
Pegwell Bay.

A ruined tower with part of a herringbone wall at nearby Minster Abbey are also probably Saxon; the house itself, now a Benedictine convent, incorporates parts of the old manor house used as a grange by the monks of St Augustine's. The garden is serene and tree-filled; under a small tiled flint arch sits a strange sculpted figure with upraised arms – a thirteenth-century Doomstone.

Among other treasures in Minster church, my favourite is a window, showing horses ploughing a field, to Thomas Young Chapman, 'who loved God's earth and tilled it faithfully for many years in this parish . . .'

Minster was a prosperous market town when Ramsgate and Margate consisted of a few fishing huts. Today it seems a quiet village, in spite of vandals who tore up a 300-year-old book, destroyed a font, and did other monstrous damage in the church (most Thanet churches are now kept locked), and coachloads descending on the Abbey and the nearby courteously frantic café, who have tea and fruit cake at the ready. Why so many vandals in Thanet? Is it the quietness itself, the unemployment?

Thanet people still feel themselves to be islanders. During floods they say with pleasure, 'We're an island again.'

Up the road is Monkton village, a country hamlet, with pleasant old houses, some light industry. On the wall of the long-backed church there, an early monk inscribed his verses to his round Isle, 'to none on Earth the second.'[5]

*

A map in Minster church, a replica of an old script, shows a drawing of a beacon, shown at 'Berchington'. There were beacons throughout Thanet, to be lit when an enemy was sighted, and it was the Saxon word *tene* – fire – or the older British word *tan*, which probably gave the island its name. The beacons could also serve as a guide to shipping, and through the centuries one notices again and again this double use of monuments along our invasion shore. Perhaps the grandest of these, possibly the grandest England has known, was the vast monument built in the late first century, in AD 80–90, at Rutupiae – Richborough – by the Romans. Richborough was then a peninsula or island escarpment overlooking the Wantsum channel, and here the Roman legions of the Emperor Claudius landed in AD 43. It became our first great port, and the Roman administrative centre for the whole of Britain. From here the last legions were evacuated in the early fifth century.

The monument was a towering quadrifons, or four-way arch, faced and paved with Carrara marble, on top of which were bronze statues, probably similar to those on the reverse of a Roman coin, which shows chariots drawn by triumphal elephants. On one side the arch looked out to sea, providing a landmark for shipping; on the other, it opened on to Watling Street. The legions could march, ten abreast, inland to Canterbury, London, and on to Viroconium – Wroxeter – and so to Chester.

Richborough is the most notable Roman monument south of Hadrian's Wall, and has been extremely well tended by the Department of the Environment – I see that in the eighteenth century it was overgrown with ivy. The day we visited it was one of the rare days it is shut, but some friendly Germans showed us where we could crawl under the wire – we had come from Shoreham to see it and no doubt they from Stuttgart, and none of us were in the mood to be brooked. A heavily-built Englishman in white shirt and black suit roamed disconsolately outside the wire, not chancing his luck.

Of the central monument only the concrete foundation remains, but round the site are immense encircling ditches, covered with close-cropped grass; inside these are walls, five feet thick, with the typically Roman horizontal lines of red tiles dividing layers of stone with an impressive regularity. These were the walls of the fort that had to be built in the mid-third century to combat Saxon raiders, and they were the headquarters of the Count of the Saxon Shore (*Littoris Saxonici Comitem*), who had nine great fortresses, among them, in Kent, Reculver, Richborough, Dover, Lemanis (at Lympne), and in East Sussex, Pevensey.

The place fills you with an electric sense of history, of the transience of civilizations. A cloud of gulls rises screaming from the direction of Richborough power station, which looks insubstantial beside the great walls. The view stretches over to Pegwell in one direction, Sandwich in the other, Europe across the sea which in those days came right up to where the Stour winds round one wall; and inland the country reaching away, full of promise, flat, peaceful and green, with a haze of heat or mist, the gentle patterns of later civilizations pinpointing the scene – the spire of a church, an old white windmill, farms with sheep, poplars. Larks sing dizzily above the daisied grass, and over the soft turf of the circling ditches, under which lie forgotten fragments of gleaming marble and slivers of bronze. The era, like all other eras, leaving its certain answers buried in the chalky earth.

On the seaward side, holding their own with the rest, are the foundation stones of a small Saxon chapel dedicated to St Augustine.

*

Between Richborough Castle and the sea is flat marshy ground, then Richborough Port. In 1916 a canal was cut and the Stour widened, to relieve the war traffic through Dover. The railway line was also extended to the new wharf, so that besides barges bringing supplies for the troops, trucks could be shunted straight on to ships with railway lines on their decks – an early form of roll-on, roll-off loading. During the Second World War units of the Mulberry Harbours for the Normandy invasion were secretly built here. Now the area forms an industrial estate, with Great Stonar, where Pfizer Ltd, the multinational manufacturer of pharmaceuticals and chemicals, has a factory, with about a third of the personnel engaged on research. In 1979 they won the Queen's Award for Technological Achievement, for the development of a drug used in the treatment of a disease affecting at least fifty million people in the Third World. Petbow also have a factory here, and again are a firm with Queen's Awards to Industry to their credit. Haffenden's is another large employer. Tankers use the waterway to carry oil for the power station, which opened in 1961.

Sandwich has been clever in banishing industry from the town. The whole place is a Conservation Area, the only town wholly so in Kent. A ring road is to be built, which is extremely necessary, because Sandwich's chief enemy today is traffic.

'It must be open for the Open,' we were told, concerning the ring-road. The Open Golf Championships will be held at Sandwich in 1981, at the famous Royal St George's Golf Course at

Sandwich Bay. This is one of three courses between Sandwich and Deal: the Prince's and the Royal Cinque Ports being the other two. Sandwich Bay is perhaps the only stretch of coastline, now, in the south-east that has an air of being exclusive. Large, thirties-style houses stand behind their villa gateways; a toll is paid to drive along the beach road, and the road closed when it is considered that enough cars have driven in; the bay is a mecca for sailing and water sports, with the Sandwich Bay Sailing and Water Sports Club. The air is breezy and the beach uncluttered; yellow poppies, sea flowers, even orchids, grow along the shingle verges, and the Sandwich Bay Nature Reserve is known for its rich flora, and for birds, among them the little tern, which breeds there. The Sandwich Bay Bird Observatory has its headquarters at Old Downs Farm.

It was at the Royal St George's that Ian Fleming, whose fondness for golf never tired, used to play. He referred to it as the 'best seaside golf course in the world', and in the 1950s he bought Noël Coward's house at St Margaret's Bay, where he erected a telescope on the terrace to watch the shipping, and from where he could go round to Sandwich. The negotiations over the sale led to a spirited exchange between Coward and Fleming. The latter accused Coward of leaving patches on the walls after removal of shelves, and asked him for a cheque for just over a hundred pounds, or an article on the most scandalous things he knew about his most intimate friends, in payment.[6] James Bond's battle with Goldfinger takes place at St Mark's (St George's). Ian Fleming was to be the next Captain of the Royal St George's, when he died. It was an honour that meant more to him than all the success of his books.

*

Meanwhile, until the new road is open, the traffic thunders, lorries narrowly missing houses or knocking tiles off walls.

Sitting in the low Sixteenth-Century Tea House in the market place, the sky was suddenly obscured and I thought Doomsday had come; a lorry was entirely blocking the window.

Sandwich has known many Doomsdays – has been laid waste by Angles, Jutes, Saxons, Danes and the French. The last came in 1457, from Honfleur, under the command of Marshal de Brézé,

pillaged the town and murdered the mayor. The Mayor of Sandwich still always wears a black robe in mourning; recently the
Mayor of Honfleur, which is now Sandwich's twin town, tried to
persuade him to come out of mourning and change to a red robe,
but to no avail.

I was waiting in the sixteenth-century café to see round the
Guildhall. The method is to ring a bell at the side door of the
Guildhall, and the Town Sergeant will reveal its treasures. He
happened to be away, and I rang a ghostly peal by pulling the
iron chain, which echoed into a fastness of polished corridors
and lady councillors.

Later, I was shown round. In one of the panelled rooms in the
Guildhall there are two precious relics of the Cinque Ports –
the Charter of Charles II, decorated with a border of clover
flowers, strawberries and bees, and a quarter of the silver and
gold thread canopy borne by the Barons of the Cinque Ports at
the coronation of King George III in 1761. This privilege, the
highly prized Honours at Court, was one of the original privileges
of the ports. The canopy was held above the monarch's head as he
walked to his coronation, and was shared out afterwards among
the Barons – or Freemen – of the Ports, together with the silver
bells and silver staves which went with the canopy. Samuel Pepys
was one of the Barons who carried the canopy of James II. George
IV's coronation was the last at which the canopy was used – and
there was an unseemly scuffle to try to rob the Barons of it afterwards – but at the most recent coronations, places of honour
have been reserved for the Barons in their uniforms.

Anne Roper, the authority on the Cinque Ports, has a copy of
*The History of the Coronation of King James II and Queen
Mary* by Francis Sandford, Leicester Herald of Arms, a day-by-day
account published in 1687, and fully illustrated. How Sir William
Throckmorton 'claimed' to build scaffolds, but was not allowed
to; pictures of the crowns, swords, sceptre, of the 'sandalls' and
buskins still worn by the monarch at the coronation; of the
procession which started with herb strewers, followed by a man
weighted down by kettledrums, aldermen, dignitaries, a choir
and baronesses carrying their coronets, earls, countesses, other
nobility, then thirty-two barons of the Cinque Ports carrying
their canopies over the king and queen. There is a picture of

34

the champion throwing down his gauntlet in the West Hall at Westminster before the coronation banquet, and of the hundreds of dishes set at each table, listed by number: cheese-cakes, trouts souc'd, pettitoes hot, nine pigeon pies cold, twelve leverets, pistach cream, and every imaginable delicacy.

The first charter, setting out the duties and privileges of the Cinque (pronounced Sink) Ports as a confederation, was in the reign of Edward I, in 1278, but the history of the ports dates back to the eleventh century and the reign of Edward the Confessor, or earlier. He had established his residence in Sandwich in 1049 and made the harbour a base for his fleet, being troubled by Danish raiders and an ambitious father-in-law, Earl Godwin. (There are many earlier references to Sandwich haven in the Anglo-Saxon chronicle: 1012 'in the same year ... came king Swein with his fleet to Sandwich.' 1015 'At the same time king Cnut came into Sandwich ...' 1049 'earl Godwine sailed from Sandwich with forty-two ships to Pevensey ...' 1052 'Then king Edward had forty small vessels fitted out which lay at Sandwich...')

The five original Head Ports were Sandwich, Dover, Hythe, Romney and Hastings, and the 'Antient Towns' of Winchelsea and Rye were later added. In the thirteenth century the Confederation was enlarged to include Limbs or Members of the Head Ports; at various times over thirty places were recognized as Corporate or Non-corporate Members.[7]

The grouping of ports was in the tradition of the Saxon Shore forts of the Romans, and the first 'Wardeine' of the Ports, in William the Conqueror's day, was no doubt modelled on the Count of the Saxon Shore, with his nine forts. In their early beginnings therefore, the ports were literally a bastion against invaders, and, their ships becoming the nucleus of the royal fleet, they set the foundations of England's naval supremacy in the centuries to come. Their role has always been deeply rooted in tradition, with the resonances of the past, and of the sea, of which we as an island race are always aware.

The office of Lord Warden is now an honorary one. Many great men have filled the post, including Sir Winston Churchill. He always flew the Lord Warden's standard from the bonnet of his car. At his funeral, one of the most awe-inspiring and

poignant moments of an era, a banner of the Cinque Ports preceded the coffin, and the flag of the Lord Warden was flown in
that last journey up the Thames, from the jackstaff of the launch
Havengore, as it bore his body from Tower Pier to Waterloo
Station.

*

The main duty of the Ports was to provide fifty-seven ships between them, fully manned, for fifteen days a year. Each crew was
to consist of twenty men and a boy, or 'grummit'. Fifteen days
was the time allowed for a crossing to the Continent and back, in
Edward the Confessor's day, and as enemy raids by Danes for
instance, were short and sharp, this period of service was ade-
quate. As the Portsmen owned all the strategic harbours, no one
could cross to the Continent without their consent, and this, with
their privileges, sowed the seeds of their high-handedness and
independent character, which can be seen down the ages. They
could be counted upon to fight to the death, and to kill the
crews of French ships 'quicker than it takes to eat a biscuit',[8] but
were not especially discriminating between friend and foe and
were not above attacking a ship carrying the Queen (in 1252); or,
according to Matthew Paris, 'cruelly exceeding the limit pres-
cribed by the King and robbing and killing English as well as
French.'

Their privileges, besides the Honours at Court, included freedom from various taxes such as Lastage (duty by weight) and
Tallage (duty by number), from a tax on landing (Passage) and
from bridge and wharf tolls with the strange sounding names
of Rivage and Ponsage. Another important privilege was the right
of wreck. Portsmen could claim all that the sea washed up; elsewhere the King claimed anything that came ashore. Or this was
the theory anyway. I see that the people of Thanet used to call
a shipwreck a 'God-send', and made the most of what they could
get, just as they indulged in acquiring 'a few Articles in the Way
of private Trade', or smuggling. As Lord Warden, Sir Robert
Menzies made a practice of visiting the beach each time he came
to England, to pick up flotsam, which was his by right. Also his
was the whale which came ashore one year in Thanet.

Portsmen also had the right of Den and Strond in Yarmouth,

which meant that they had the right to sell their fish and dry their nets there, and to control the annual Herring Fair. This led to much trouble, as may be imagined, and was one of the privileges defended by the Courts of Shepway, Brodhull and Guestling, which were created to handle the affairs of the Ports.

The arms of the Cinque Ports are three demi lions joined to three castellated ships' hulls, so that the effect is of three satyr-like creatures, half lion, half ship, perfectly depicting England's might at sea and the men who were as much at home at sea as on land.

There is a fine example of the arms on the fifteenth-century stone font in St Clement's Church at Sandwich. The church has a Norman tower with three tiers of arcading on each side, both strong and delicate. It is a quiet church inside, one in which you feel compelled to pray. The floor has old red and yellow tiles as well as bricks and stone, and there are sea blue windows. You sink back into the past of this once hugely important town, which lies in layers all around you. Layers as above the chancel arch in St Clement's, where you can see the gables of the original Norman roof and of the Early English roof; layers as in timber-framed houses with later (but still old) brick fronts; in Roman tiles used in flint walls; in a house for sale down by the Old Custom House in Upper Strand Street, where I saw builders had uncovered a cellar with its oven and placed on the window sill their finds – oyster shells, a piece of old ceramic tile, mouthpieces of clay pipes. Alleyways wind among houses; rooms open off rooms; lofts open off stairways, are beamed with ships' knee timbers; a lead angel is set in a wall; gardens are sheltered by the stones from monastic buildings; under the plaster of a room a brick and painted stone panel of a thistle and rose was discovered with initials commemorating a wedding in a weaver's house in 1611; on a brick in Strand Street a bricklayer has cut his name in fine early script – Richard Paramor; through part of the town the Delf stream runs, emerging at Horse Pond Sluice. Each stone and brick in Sandwich tells a piece of history. As one woman there said, 'You could live your life in Sandwich and still not know it all.'

The outlines of the oldest part of the town, which was the Saxon 'Sandwic' or village on the sand, were different then, because the river was wider, and the sea often swept in over what is now dry land. (But which flooded disastrously again in the winter of 1978-9 bringing river mud into many houses.) The town was prosperous until well into the fourteenth century, but the river was gradually silting up and by the sixteenth century, when ships were bigger also, the harbour was in decline.

The town is ringed by grassy ramparts: Ropewalk, Millwall, the Bulwark, the Butts. ('There's nothing for visitors to do in Sandwich except walk round,' a disenchanted townsman told me.) It was from the Butts that Henry V's archers of Agincourt fame were said to have practised. Henry V set sail from here, as did Thomas à Becket; Richard Coeur de Lion landed here on his return from the Crusades in 1194, and the Black Prince in 1357. Queen Elizabeth I visited the town amidst great pomp and courteously tasted many of 160 dishes, tactfully asking for the remaining dishes to be taken to her lodging (the magnificent King's Lodging which can still be seen). Queen Catherine of Braganza was less gracious in 1672 and had food brought to her carriage as she refused to get out.

From the number of sorties against France that were made from the Cinque Ports, it is not surprising that Marshal de Brézé made his bloody reprisal. Warfare was ruthless on both sides. The first major engagement won by an English fleet at sea, off Sandwich, was won by a mixture of cold-bloodedness and cunning. Eustace the Monk, a renegade from holy orders, was in command of the French fleet and was said to be a dabbler in witchcraft. The Cinque Ports ships, under Hubert de Burgh (Regent for the young King Henry III), put to sea as though to attack Calais, then veered round and threw quicklime in the air, blinding the French crews. The English archers set to work and a swift ramming of the French boats completed the victory.

But peacetime was equally brutal. At times one has to suppress a shiver in Sandwich. In the Guildhall are a thumbscrew and branding irons. A narrow alleyway under an arch, called Holy Ghost Alley, winds from the old town jail to the site of the prisoners' treadmill and is full of an acrid atmosphere, in spite of the scent of flowers drifting over garden walls. Less lucky prisoners were drowned in the Guestling Stream (witches in particular) or buried alive in Gallows Field. There is almost too much dust, too many stifled memories in Sandwich.

Yet one would not say, with Celia Fiennes, 'this sad old town all timber building, you enter by a gate and so you go out of it by a gate ...'[9] To get to know the town, you have to stay there, to be invited into some of the houses, which behind their dusty walls (from the traffic), and deceptively un-ornate exteriors, are perhaps more full of character than any I know, often opening on to walled gardens where roses thirty feet high climb to the sun. In these houses the ghosts, echoes of family voices, are warm and lusty, as friendly as their modern counterparts, who will say, 'Don't bother to lock the door, we don't bother with that here...'

Or go to Sandwich market, on a Thursday, where all the town will be, bartering, bantering, exchanging the week's gossip, buying the week's food.

'Come on now, you were all left standing last week ...' cries the auctioneer at the egg market (eggs and plants are still auctioned here). Trays of eggs, thirty in a tray, start at £1.50 and slowly descend in size and price to £1. Pensioners lovingly carry off boxes of bean plants or pinks; housewives haggle over the size of grapefruit and crisp apples; a cut of pork is held high for all to inspect. The faces are honest, and beaming. There may be, as one resident told me, two populations in Sandwich – those who work at the factories, miners, unemployed, and those who live in the larger houses, or at the Bay – but the two seem to mingle without rancour, and they are certainly all at the market, jostling among the stalls.

*

The town's lowest ebb was in the sixteenth century. In Saxon times, trade was, as for most Saxon towns, with the Rhine (hence the carved interlace on the tympanum in St Clements, showing the Saxon stylistic link via the Rhine with that of Northern Italy, which in turn came from Byzantium). Later, in medieval times, ships unloading at the quays brought merchandise as varied as wax, figs, almonds and grain, casks of oil, honey and hog's lard, fish, coals, iron from Spain and Normandy, pepper, wine, salt, tallow, saffron, leather, whalebone, onions, wool-fells, quicksilver, lead and ginger. The wine trade, particularly with

Gascony, flourished in Sandwich, and from the thirteenth century onwards, ships laden with wool were sent from London or elsewhere to Flanders from the port. During the fourteenth and fifteenth centuries, Sandwich was the last port of call for the 'Flanders Galleys', the ships of the Venetian merchants, who with those from Genoa, traded between ports, bringing, for England, sugar and molasses, comfits and coral beads, cotton, and silk yarn.

When the harbour silted up, petitions were made to the Crown to remedy matters, but to little avail. However, on her memorable visit, besides the junketings, Elizabeth I did much good. She had allowed Protestant refugees from the Netherlands to settle in the area, and while in Sandwich expressed her concern for their welfare. They were artisans – workers in serge, baize and flannel – and market gardeners, and through their skills Sandwich became a thriving market town. (They introduced market gardening – and several new vegetables – into England.) A sensitive act of integration.

Another legacy of the immigrants is the beautiful Flemish architecture, which can be seen on many of the most striking buildings in Sandwich. In the cupola of St Peter's church, which is the landmark one sees from outside the town (the tower was rebuilt by Dutch refugees, who were allowed to worship there, with bricks from the sand of the harbour; Thomas Paine, author of *The Rights of Man*, who lived in the town for a while, was fittingly married here); in the design of the Dutch House with its curlicued brickwork; in the stepped gables of Manwood Court; on the fine carved gables of Arthur H. Lock (bicycles) and many other buildings. Architectural styles form a composite whole here. The black-and-white Barbican was until 1977 a toll gate ('For every Chariot, Landau, Berlin Chaise, Chair, Calash or other vehicle drawn by 6 or more horse or other beasts. 2s 6d ...'); gas lamps are lit with gas; 'The Sandwich Weavers' sells clothes in its old premises; there are bookshops and printshops and a remarkable toy collection, jostling modern enterprises such as the pottery shop run in The Chain by Nicola Morriss, who produces traditional ware and fine white earthenware, and the equally traditional Sandwich Tanneries, producing leather and suede. There are few tourist gimmicks, fewer tourists than you would expect.

On a June weekday, you can be alone on the ramparts. The oldest church, St Mary's, is large and empty. When open, birds fly in and out, over an ancient Peter's Pence Box, or trunk. The church was ravaged by the French and, amazingly, by an earthquake in 1578. In 1956 the Mayor and Friends of St Mary's collected £7,000 to repair the wooden beams of the timbered roof, which makes a fine contrast to the whitewashed walls. Another piece of history was saved from extinction.

And the famous sandwich itself? Everyone knows that it was invented by the (Fourth) Earl of Sandwich. I didn't know, or had forgotten, that he was an inveterate gambler, and it was because he couldn't bear to leave the game that he called to his servant to bring some slices of meat and bread, which he then put together.

*

Round about Sandwich are many places to visit, with or without sandwiches. One town has vanished, however, that of Stonar, the landing place of King Canute, and across the Wantsum channel from Sandwich. It was of considerable importance, but was submerged by the sea in 1365, and anything remaining burnt to the ground in a French raid twenty years later. An equally legendary place is Eastry, where in the seventh century was the royal palace of King Egbert of Kent and where his two young cousins, brothers of Domneva, were slain. Thomas à Becket hid here from his enemies in 1164, waiting to escape in a fishing boat from Sandwich.

Market gardening, which has moved outside Sandwich, flourishes at Ash-next-Sandwich, and the hamlet of Marshborough has land which is probably the longest cultivated in the country, and highly fertile. Worth also has some of the finest soil in England and was originally cultivated by the Lords of the Manor of Eastry. Woodnesborough is again steeped in history, being 'Woden's hill', a high spot from which the Woden-priests could have seen St Augustine landing at Ebbsfleet. From here you can see the Goodwin sands off Deal and the white cliffs of Ramsgate and inland, the hub of the area, Canterbury.

We went to a concert in Woodnesborough church, on a hot Sunday evening in June. The Schubertians, the men's chorus

2 Ramsgate; Broadstairs; St Peter's; Sarre; Manston

'... a most beautiful marine promenade, much frequented in the season, and not to be surpassed, if equalled, by any watering-place in the United Kingdom ...'

1810 Guide (Ramsgate)

Ramsgate – a gate or gap[1] in two gently sloping cliffs of chalk, in the V of which lies Ramsgate harbour, a natural haven used from Roman times onwards – has assimilated the energetic engineering works of the eighteenth and nineteenth centuries and today's new marina without losing its charm. It is a visually supreme harbour, which lies below you as you walk down the East or West Cliffs, and from whose piers you can look back at the town, Royal Parade and Nelson Crescent sloping up to the Regency buildings of the Paragon and the West Cliff, the balconied buildings of the East Cliff leaning over the inner basin – houses which are in need of paint but none the less attractive, attractive despite Tesco's yellow bricks towering in the centre of the V. From the East Pier you can look across the West Pier with its small red-capped lighthouse, towards Pegwell Bay, the shore and skyline of Sandwich shimmering bluely in evening light, or half-hidden by mist, a line barely discernible on the horizon, like that other mystical line half-seen on a clear day from Ramsgate – the coastline of France.

This view, taking in the town silhouetted in half-light, St George's church with its lantern tower like an incandescent fretwork cutout, the pier light-tower graceful on its rounded pier end, fishermen and boys hurrying their catch off the boats, is reminiscent of a Canaletto painting, and is still hard to surpass.

The town is barely mentioned in some modern guidebooks,

passed over as vulgar and ugly, dismissed by even those who love Kent, in half a sentence, as if the smell of whelks and fish teas were in their nostrils as they hurry on to the more acceptable charms of Broadstairs – acceptable to the literati because Dickens worked there, indeed visited so many houses in Broadstairs that the owner of one cottage in desperation pinned a notice to his walls: 'Dickens did *not* stay here.' Yet in the first half of the nineteeth century, guidebooks to Ramsgate and Margate abounded, the former town being the more fashionable of the two.

There are several good coffee-rooms near the sea, and some excellent billiard tables. Warm, cold and shower sea-water baths on a superior construction have been completed here ... The great numbers of the nobility and gentry who frequent these baths prove their great utility ... The bathing is excellent, and upwards of twenty machines are employed every morning during the season ... The sand which at low water extends to the northward towards East Cliff, a distance of near a mile, forms a most beautiful marine promenade ...[2]

Jane Austen was a visitor to the town, which is mentioned in *Pride and Prejudice*, and where Tom Bertram in *Mansfield Park* experienced difficulty in knowing whether girls were 'out' or not. Coleridge, a keen bather, was a summer visitor. The coming of the railway brought a more motley crew, but Ramsgate still held its social lead:

All London quits London ... Russel-square sends its plate to the banker's, and, leaving word that it is on the Continent, bargains for a first floor and double-bedded rooms at Ramsgate: Cadogan-place buys itself big-brimmed hats, and commences bathing at Broadstairs; and Camden-town and Kennington, rush off to shrimp teas at Margate.[3]

By the beginning of this century, the discovery of coal in Kent had brought a different crowd of visitors; according to one resident: 'It was the coming of the miners that spoilt Ramsgate, as I see it ...'

It is difficult to re-see a town that one knows well. I have approached Ramsgate so many times. Along the dead-straight Roman roads, poppies blazing on the verges, bucket and spade clutched between my feet. Later, by train, along the coast of Kent, past Rochester's ancient cathedral, and the Medway towns; then the flat north coast of Kent, travelling – in recent years as if making a journey towards one's youth – through a level warm countryside, with budding fruit trees and blackcurrant bushes, oasts, hop-poles, new corn shoots like combed hair, unhedged plough, white caravans, white sheep, white sky. The sudden appearance of the sea – flats of sand, chalk rocks; then bathing huts (the sharp smell of tar and decaying seaweed in one's nostrils as one rummaged behind them for shells), golf links, villas, and on the long, flat, unbroken line of sea wall, die-straight for miles, the silhouette of Reculver, upright in the distance, twin-towers in a solitary landscape, poignantly outlasting tides and time. Birchington with its wooden balconies, Westgate with white painted woodwork, shops gaudily guttered, with curved corrugated iron awnings; Margate, and Dreamland funfair – in memory large and monstrously lit; Dumpton – Ramsgate –

I began afresh at the station. Ramsgate once had two stations, one almost on the beach; the present one is dignified with a coat of arms and vaulted ceiling, and has photostats of old prints in the buffet – 'Shower and Dowse Baths Ramsgate, Patronized by HMG Majesty King William the Fourth ...' (the Dowse cost 3s or ten for a guinea). As the girl in the buffet said, eyeing the Victorian matrons in the prints in their voluminous gowns, walking on the sands which have changed little since then, 'The people look so strange – it's weird, like time standing still ...'

Near the station is St Lawrence, the original settlement, with its church of St Laurence-in-Thanet, its fine tower having windows and arcading, with Norman interior arches. From here the long High Street slopes down to the harbour. Past flint walls and Gothic villas, with the cry of seagulls overhead. 'The Cottage', flint, 1560, a Salvation Army hall, the Eagle Inn with iron canopies, the Odd Fellows Club and Institute 'Loyal Isle of Thanet Lodge', and in the basement the 'Evergreen Old Time Dance Club' ... Skylighted cottages in 'Paradise', 'Howards Teas Please!' painted over an empty corner shop; off to the left up Chatham Street, beyond the 'Ancient Order of Foresters' Friendly Society, the graceful white portico of Townley House, where Queen Victoria stayed as a child – a house designed by Mrs James Townley, a brilliant pupil of Sir Joshua Reynolds and one of the earliest women architects, who also planned much of Albion Place and started the Royal Crescent. She was a noted hostess, entertained William IV, and gave balls and masquerades; she was also a King's Proctor, keenly interested in politics, and on one occasion presented colours painted by herself to the Ramsgate Volunteers. As Mr Farley, whose firm now owns Townley House, told me, the Duchess of Kent would leave her daughter the young Princess Victoria at Townley House in the 1820s, while she went off on a boat to the Continent.

The ghost of Victoria haunts Ramsgate – on the sands painted by Frith – she bought his painting 'Ramsgate Sands' in the 1860s and it is now in Buckingham Palace; at Albion House, and at East Cliff Lodge, where Sir Moses Montefiore, the outstanding Jewish figure who was a benefactor to those of all faiths, gave Victoria and her mother a golden key to the grounds. A gravestone was found at Townley House, to Fox, her 'favourite dog and friend'; her white donkey is said to be buried on the land which adjoined my aunt's garden – a legend I have not investigated for fear of disillusionment.

On the other side of the High Street the gilt and glass lettering of a pharmacist on the corner of Chapel Place, where the 'lodgings' were new in 1810, now surrounded by alleyways of cottages dated to the 1880s. Farther down, the High Street runs into souvenir shops with china dogs and shell vases, 'Rowlands' home-made confectionery – rock, and sugar false teeth – ugly small branches of giant chain stores, the tiny Kings Theatre cinema, and on to the harbour and the Royal Victoria Pavilion – 'Ramsgate's Family Fun Centre' which unexpectedly also houses the 'Liberius Casino'. There seem to be a great many Friendly Societies, Building Societies and Quaker meeting places in Ramsgate; the town has an air of goodheartedness and frugality, an innocence about it that may at times be glum but which has prevented it becoming spoilt. Outside the Parish Church of St George the Martyr, on the memorial to servicemen of two wars, is the added sentence: 'In Remembrance of all who lost their lives in Ramsgate through enemy action, 1939-1945.' A durable innocence. Sparrows chatter round the pierced hexagonal tower of the church in the deserted evening High Street. Trinity House contributed to the lantern, so that it would be a landmark for

46

shipping. Inside the church stained glass commemorates Dunkirk. Sun catches the gold weathervane of the tower.

*

Down at the harbour, next to the red custom house with its cupola, is the Queen's Head pub, ornately tiled and gilt balconied. Here I talked with Arthur Verrion, who I had been told was 'as old as Ramsgate'. I recognized him at once, although he didn't look old. He has a sturdy short figure, smiling weather-beaten face and saltrimmed eyelids, and talked to me with that straightforwardness that is typical of the Thanet man – who will meet you on an equal footing with none of the grins intended to ingratiate or hoodwink that strangers may encounter elsewhere. Here men look you straight in the eye and if you ask the way of one pushing a dustcart, he will reply as if directing you to his own estate.

Arthur Verrion insisted on buying me a drink – I immediately became his guest. I tried his own favourite, which is rum and blackcurrant. 'You can drink three times as much of that' (without smelling of it, he indicated, clearly a useful trick on board). It's also very good. He possibly picked up the secret in the West Indies or America, during his early days in the Navy. His voice becomes wistful as he speaks of Bermuda, the bananas and tomatoes, and sleeping in a grass hammock – 'it was paradise'. On a pay of 1s 8d a day. He had left school at 13 and left his first job, which was polishing pianos, after a week. 'I didn't like guvnors ...' He served in the Navy during the First World War, although he has never learnt to swim and used to cry as a child when he got cramp in the sea. But his father encouraged him: 'Well, if you're born to be hung, son, you'll never drown.'

'I've had a wonderful life ... Sometimes I was worried, but I didn't show it.' He found the people in Canada and the States, during the First World War, wonderfully friendly.

After the war, he joined the Ramsgate life-boat crew, in the days when life-boats still had sails. The first motor life-boat was the *Prudential* in 1926. He was bowman, and later the second coxswain, and fishing all the while when not out with the life-boat. There was a trawling limit of three miles during the Second World War – 'We used to go out ten miles.'

47

He was coxswain of a later life-boat, the *Michael and Lily Davies*, for eleven or twelve years. 'The only thing I didn't like was fog ... When you're young you take more notice. You have just as bad journeys when you're older but it comes natural.' He told me of some of the worst wrecks he can remember. In particular when the South Goodwin lightship broke adrift and was washed on to the Goodwins. None of the crew could be saved, but an American birdwatcher who was with them was later picked up by a US helicopter, by some strange quirk of fate.

'You can see sand there today (in the Goodwins), or a wreck – then there's a change of wind (and you can no longer see them). There's a British ship, the *Montrose*, still there. She blew out of Dover.'

The treacherous sands, onetime kingdom of Earl Godwin, which became Lambarde's 'most dreadfull gulfe, and ship swalower'.

Verrion's father, he told me, remembered a ship breaking up on the Goodwins, with one half landing up on the pier at Pegwell and the other at Dumpton, the other side of Ramsgate. In the days of the Pegwell pleasure boats – the good old days, 'before Social Security ... it was better then. My wife didn't have enough to buy her wedding dress, I had to buy it for her ... I'm a lucky man ... If I had my life to live over again, I'd still ... T'aint like it was. I can remember a thousand men and boys employed here. We used to fish day and night with only a couple of hours down. Margate, Ramsgate and Broadstairs were all separate before; now they're all the same. Factory parties coming for the day ...'

When summoned to the life-boat, you drop everything and go. But Arthur was otherwise involved with the Navy when the *Prudential* made her most famous trip, although he wanted to go – to Dunkirk.

The jolly, saucy look leaves his eyes for a moment. 'I can always remember this ... they came off the boats straggling ... But when them Guards came off, they fell in on that pier (it is a very long one) and marched off. Upright as darts. The Castle Hotel barman was corporal – I saw him marching there. Upright as darts they were ...'

*

The discipline that was the secret of Dunkirk. In his both detailed and impressive account of the evacuation, *Dunkirk: The Great Escape*, A. J. Barker has pointed out the methodical planning that underlay what has now become the legend of the 'little ships'. The little ships played a vital role, and it was at Ramsgate that they assembled to make the crossing, and also at Ramsgate that approximately a third of all the troops disembarked. But history has tended to forget that it was the troop carriers, and cross-Channel and Irish ferries, which could carry many more troops in a single voyage, which ensured the success of the operation as a whole. Or perhaps the combination of elements: of the discipline of those who planned Operation Dynamo (Naval Control at Ramsgate, for instance, handed out a thousand charts to the ships taking part in the evacuation), and of those who superbly carried it out, epitomized at one more orderly juncture, described in *Dunkirk: the Great Escape*, by the Royal Navy with white-blancoed leggings and pipe-clayed belts standing with fixed bayonets on the beaches, giving a message of reassurance to the troops who had been lined up waiting under bombardment for hours – all this combined with the selfless spirit of courage typified by the amateurs and yachtsmen who volunteered to help. Not forgetting the miracle of a smooth sea, in the notoriously choppy Channel.

A. J. Barker tells of one clash between the two styles of bravery, from the account of someone who was present.

Captain Bennett was a phlegmatic type when at sea and it took a lot to ruffle him. As the MTB drew near we observed a young officer on the bridge clothed in a peaked cap and vivid striped pyjamas, and with a megaphone to his mouth. After asking the names of our two ships, he ordered us to the Owers lightship until sunrise. This may have been fair enough, but he added that gauche remark 'Don't you know there is a war on?' Bennett, who was leaning on his port bridge rail, removed his pipe from his mouth, picked up a megaphone and shouted 'You won't win it in your f—— pyjamas, will you.' [4]

Of life-boats involved, the coxswains of seventeen said they felt their boats were not suitable for going, as without smaller wherries was indeed the case, and these crews were replaced by the Royal Navy. Only the *Prudential* from Ramsgate and the *Lord Southborough* from Margate were manned by their own crews. They had gone on ahead of Admiral Ramsay's cockleshell navy, on the afternoon of 30 May, the *Prudential* towing a ship's life-boat and eight wherries, loaded with drinking water and rope for hauling small craft from the beaches. Their first anchorage was off Malo-les-Bains, near the charred remains of the *Crested Eagle*, the London-Margate/Ramsgate paddle steamer.

On a board at Ramsgate harbour, which lists the achievements of its life-boats from 1865, is noted that the *Prudential* evacuated 2,800 British and French soldiers from Dunkirk by ferrying them from the beaches to larger craft. She was away from the station for over forty hours, for thirty of those was at the beaches, for nearly all of that time under fire, for two nights her crew without sleep. Coxswain Howard Knight's report reads:

... found naval ratings who manned wherries were not skilled at handling small boats under such conditions [seas breaking in the shoal water]; members of life-boat crew took their boats and places, and although an intensely dark night managed by shouting to establish communication with officer in charge of troops on beach ... when the last three boatloads were being taken from the water, the officer called, 'I cannot see who you are; are you a naval party?' He was answered, 'No, sir, we are members of the crew of the Ramsgate life-boat.' He then called, 'Thank you – and thank God for such men as you have this night proved yourselves to be. There is a party of fifty Highlanders coming next ...'

They continued until the last of their eight wherries was shattered by shrapnel and they themselves almost dead with tiredness. And so back to Ramsgate, through the black pall of smoke, the shell-fire, the sinking ships, the weary soldiers drowning helplessly under the weight of their equipment as they struggled to the boats, the floating corpses of those already dead in the sea around them.

*

The present Ramsgate life-boat is the *Ralph and Joyce Swann*; Margate's the *North Foreland*. After the storm of 11 January 1978 had broken Margate jetty, where her boathouse was, she was moored in Ramsgate harbour beside the *Ralph and Joyce Swann*.

Leading down to the harbour from the West Cliff is Jacob's Ladder, beside which is the peaceful Sailors' Church, where there are paintings of other storms and a photograph of the men who saved the crew of the *Indian Chief* on 5 and 6 January 1881, a legendary exploit. There are model boats in cases, and over a doorway verses from the 107th Psalm:

They that go down to the sea in ships, that do business in great waters;
These see the works of the Lord....

An account of the wreck of the *Indian Chief* was printed in the *Daily Telegraph* on 11 January 1881.[5] The scene was painted by William Broome in oils twice, and his paintings had such a success that he spent the rest of his life painting the event.

The *Indian Chief*, bound from Middlesborough for Yokohama, ran aground on the Long Sand, twelve miles north of Margate. There was a strong easterly gale blowing and the sea was running very high. The life-boat, the *Bradford*, towed by the steam-tug *Vulcan* was out for twenty-six hours, and had to wait overnight before she could locate the ship. Twelve of twenty-nine men were saved, and a crowd of two thousand greeted the boats' return. 'Seafarer's' account in the *Telegraph* is duly dramatic:

Whispers flew from mouth to mouth. Some said the rescued men were Frenchmen, others that they were Danes, but all were agreed that there was a dead body among them ... There was blood on the faces of some, circled with a white encrustation of salt, and this same salt filled the hollows of their eyes and streaked their hair with white lines which looked like snow ...

One young man of the crew told how he had been in the main rigging during the night with eight others, all of whom dropped off one after the other into the sea from cold and exposure. The Chief Mate related that when he saw the life-boat, he cried out,

'She'll never face it! She'll leave us when she sees that water!' for the sea was frightful all to windward of the sand and over it, a tremendous play of broken waters, raging one with another, and making the whole surface resemble a boiling cauldron ... Over and over again the boat was buried, but as regularly did she emerge with her crew fixedly looking our way, and their oilskins and the light-coloured side of the boat sparkling in the sunshine, while the coxswain leaning forward from the helm, watched our ship with a face of iron.

The Captain was dead in the rigging, the Second Mate still alive, but a maniac, and he died on the return journey. The *Bradford's* coxswain later said 'it was more like a flaying machine than a natural gale of wind. The feel of it in the face was like being gnawed by a dog. I only wonder it didn't freeze the tears it brought out of our eyes.' And the Chief Mate concluded: 'Never could I have believed that so small a vessel could meet such a sea and live ... Believe me, sir, it was a splendid piece of service; nothing grander in its way was ever done before, even by Englishmen.' The RNLI's gold medal was given to Coxswain Charles Fish and the silver medal to each of his crew who helped him save the *Indian Chief.* Charles Fish died in 1915, aged 74, having helped to rescue 877 lives. The Ramsgate Harbour Life-boat Station has the record of saving the greatest number of lives of any RNLI Station in Great Britain.

Two pleasing footnotes to the epic. I note that a Charlie Verrion, with the *Bradford* life-boat, was told to measure out the rum and send it round (surely a relation of Arthur's). And a baby son was born to the Mate of the *Vulcan,* whose wife had been pregnant during the storm. The father named the boy after the dead Second Mate of the *Indian Chief,* who had been called Howard Primrose Fraser. The boy, Howard Primrose Knight, grew up to be the Howard Primrose Knight of the *Prudential* life-boat, awarded the DSM for his gallantry at Dunkirk.

'They that go down to the sea in ships, that do business in great waters....'

*

Opinions as to the harbour vary. One man will tell you that it 'was the biggest thing built since the Pyramids', another that 'it's not like it was, look what they're doing to it.' A man who takes people out for a day's fishing will tell you it is full of everything from mullet to eels, but a pensioner from London in a woollen cap, down on the outer basin steps to buy his tea from an incoming boat, told me straight that the harbour was 'only good for seagulls'. But he loved the place, and as we watched the fisherman gut his catch on the boat, he named for me the long, spotted, ugly dogfish, the flounders, whiting, codling, dabs, pouting, sand dabs, crabs and rig, which has no bones – 'what they call rock salmon in London.'

'Lost the bloody net didn't we, off the North Foreland,' smiled the fisherman, chucking a few spare fish into three buckets to be sold for his beer money, or his wife's beer money (the rest of the fish is under contract, to firms such as Ross at Whitstable, or will be sold at Folkestone market in the morning). There are about ten trawlers working from the harbour, and the winter fishing is very good. (But not as good as in the last century, when in 1878 Ramsgate was described as the most important fishing port on the east coast between the Thames and Plymouth, and where in the years before 1914 upwards of 20,000 cwt of plaice passed through the port, with other prime fish.[6])

Besides the fishing boats, another twenty or so boats take out anglers, who come from many parts of the country – from Coventry, or Luton, or London. There used to be prawns in the harbour, but no longer. The biggest joke, which is retold all over the town, is of the Belgians who came over on a hovercraft to go shrimping at Pegwell, at the wrong season, and on the wrong tide.

Prints in the library show the beginnings of the harbour, in the early days nestling between softly turfed cliffs with barely a building in sight, except the custom house and George IV's obelisk. (When asked to name a design for a pillar to commemorate his visit to Hanover from Ramsgate, in 1821, he is said to have held up a toothpick, but was impressed with his reception on his return, bestowing the title 'Royal' on the harbour.) Probably the earliest printed view shows a kiln for burning seaweed to make kelp – used for glazing pottery – and nine-pounder guns that defended the original wooden harbour. There is a hooded bathing machine, and drying towels. 'The Bathing Place at Ramsgate', by Benjamin West RA, a painter patronized by George III, was made into a print and shows bathers also going in from the beach, 'dippers' with struggling children, two naked men, one a cripple presumably drinking the health-giving water, a little farther off a group of girls, one with a naked pretty backview lying in the surf, and beyond them hatted gentlemen surprisingly paying no attention.

The old wooden pier probably dated from the fifteenth century. Ramsgate had become a Member of the Cinque Ports by the fourteenth century, but by the time of Elizabeth I the town had declined. There were only twenty-five inhabited houses, with fourteen boats, seventy men being employed in carrying grain and fishing. Then a revival was brought about by trade with Russia and the east, which by the eighteenth century was flourishing. This continued well into the town's time as a newly fashionable bathing resort, so that between 1780 and 1808, the population nearly doubled in size. One industry which dates to Elizabethan days or earlier was brewing, the first known deed buying land for the brewery at Ramsgate (which became Tomson and Wotton, now associated with Whitbread's), being dated 1554.

The building of a new harbour was begun in 1750. In 1744 the House of Commons presented an address to George I regarding a haven at Sandwich, not for commerce, but for ships in distress in the Downs, and as an anchorage for men of war. But on the night of 16 December 1748, a violent storm caused ships in the Downs to seek refuge in Ramsgate's small harbour. So the position was changed to that town. Planning and construction took many years, John Smeaton (who built the Eddystone lighthouse) being the most famous engineer involved. He had observed harbour works in the Low Countries, and put forward a plan for clearing, by means of a cross wall and sluices, the large quantities of sand and silt which are brought into the harbour by the tide. At low tide, the sluices were opened, and the water drove out the sand far beyond the harbour mouth.

The harbour still silts up very quickly. A dredger is used today, and is 'more expensive', as Mr Pay, Assistant Harbour Manager and Marina Master, told me. The marina is in the inner basin, below the renowned Royal Temple Yacht Club (of which Ted Heath is an Honorary Member), and the Military Road, which was built to facilitate the embarkation of troops during the Napoleonic wars – ten thousand cavalry embarked for Belgium before Waterloo from Ramsgate; in addition all roads to the sea had been fortified with barred gates, and an armed boat 'and six men' cruised outside the harbour in case of invasion by the French (which sounds like an early form of 'Dad's Army' . . .). Completed in 1977, the marina is well planned, with 500 berths, good facilities for yachtsmen, and being the nearest marina to the European coast, has put out leaflets in five languages, describing services offered and places to visit in the area.

It is proving very successful, with well over a hundred per cent increase in traffic.

The harbour reverted back to Ramsgate Corporation in 1934, and is now under Thanet District Council. In the 1930s and 1940s, it was losing £30 thousand or £40 thousand a year, but as I write is breaking even. Mr Pay described present improvements to the harbour as a 'chicken and egg' situation. Reclamation of land to the west of the harbour will provide more space for cargoes and for berthing ships. It is hoped more shipping will be attracted by these facilities, and a new deep water access channel should defeat what has always been the bugbear of the harbour – its depth. Roll-on roll-off facilities can be transferred there from the outer basin in due course; some of the new land has been allocated for a new freight and passenger cross-Channel ferry terminal – planned to open in the early 1980s. There is little export at present; the main importer is Volkswagen, and other imports are steel and timber. The *Ramsgate*, carrying five-hundred VW cars, can turn round in two and a half hours, since Ramsgate stevedores are notedly good workers.

The depth in the outer harbour, with its problem of tide and silting, is indicated by the light at the harbour-mouth, in a strangely converse way. When a red light burns on the West Pier head, this denotes that there is more than ten feet of water in the entrance, and that the bank of mud by the East Pier is covered. Red signified danger in the old days when sailing ships would tear in from the Downs, and if unable to come conveniently to a halt on the mud bank, would crash into the pier. The green light denoted that there was less than ten feet of water at the pier head, and that the uncovered mudbank would provide a safe place to run aground. Today, the red light denotes safety for big ships, which swing round in the deep water.

It seems likely that Ramsgate will attract more shipping trade, which will bring new life to the town, which already has an industrial estate. 'An industrial dormitory'? 'The end of Ramsgate as a holiday place'? Yet the harbour has always been the centre of its life, and what takes place there shapes the town's destiny. If container freight and marina traffic replace the Russian trade and seabathing of earlier centuries, there could be an injection of a more virile and dynamic prosperity than the family holiday and day-tripper trade has brought during recent decades. Preservationists must be, and are, up in arms, however, to protect Ramsgate's remaining architecture.

One who has fought, and succeeded, is the artist Ruth Cousens. One evening in 1973 she was walking past the Castle Hotel on Harbour Parade – which in its present form is a Regency building, but as the Dover Castle was one of only two major buildings facing the old Ramsgate Jetty – when she saw a demolition notice fixed on it. With the 'Artists in Thanet' group she ran a petition and protest, and the building is now a listed one. It was empty and vandalized, but with the support of Thanet District Council's Chief Executive, Ian Gill, and MP Jonathan Aitken, volunteers were enlisted to give financial and practical support (Pfizer's donation paying for dry rot chemicals for instance), to clear the rubble, and to set about restoration work. Holidaymakers were invited to pay for a slate for the roof, and in May 1979, the Castle Trust opened as an arts centre, with a military band, exhibitions and a poetry reading. It was, as Jonathan Aitken, the Honorary President, says, a 'a huge triumph of self-help, self-determination ... a completely new community of artists ... real cultural activity.'

The centre still has many problems, but backed by Thanet District Council, and with Ruth Cousens's dedication, it is hard to see how it can fail. Mrs Cousens has expressed her love for the town in watercolours which have been compared to those of the Italian vedutisti of the seventeenth and eighteenth centuries, with their light-enhanced townscapes. She has exhibited widely, and in 1973 was awarded a Gold Medal at the Tricentenaire of the Paris Salon. She is a member of the Executive Committee of the Thanet Arts Council, and in halting her own work at times when the Castle needed all her attention, has shown that rare generosity which it is hard for most artists to give. It is difficult to have a long talk with her, as she is clearly always rushing headlong towards the next step, but she told me with great candour of the moment when her affection for Ramsgate crystallized. She was born in London, and came to Ramsgate when she was six. She remembers the 'great selfless spirit there was' in the war, and in particular a woman in a shop at St Lawrence who, at the time of Dunkirk, gave away her entire stock to children who were being evacuated. The woman, Ruth Cousens says, didn't survive the war. She herself was given a bar of chocolate, but passed it on to a Frenchman with blood streaming down his face. I would imagine that she has been giving metaphorical bars of chocolate to Ramsgate ever since ...

*

'I'm really quite in love with Regency Ramsgate.' To hear the area's MP say this of a town many people label differently is more than heartening. Newspaper columnists have called Jonathan Aitken the best looking MP at Westminster, but Thanet is likely to be grateful to him for other qualities. He was returned as Conservative MP for Thanet East with more than a doubled majority in 1979. A former foreign correspondent and journalist, he had two books published by the time he was twenty-five, and has had two more published since, of which the last was *Officially Secret*. He has a long-term ambition to write a history of Thanet.

He has championed Ramsgate ceaselessly, pressing in Parliament for better signposting to the town from London. 'I have indicated that the town is moving ahead industrially as well as being on the verge of a massive expansion as a communications centre ... Ramsgate is undergoing a status change,' he said in the House in March 1979. He stresses the town's great natural charms and points out that it has energetic small firms. He would like, he says, to see Ramsgate 'enjoy the kind of status that Brighton enjoys on the Sussex coast', instead of being a 'Cinderella with Brighton the belle of the ball.'

If the status changes, he will have been a great initiator in the change.

Another key factor will be the new hotel to be built in the centre of the harbour front. Initially it was to have been too tall and would have spoilt the lines of East and West cliffs, but now it is to be lower. It will be the centrepiece of the view, instead of Tesco, which as all are agreed, can't be a bad thing. If it succeeds in being attractive and in offering visiting yachtsmen and other visitors a stylishness not seen in Ramsgate since Victoria's day, it could give a feeling of confidence to the whole town. As Councillor Derrick Molock, who together with the Ramsgate Society, deplores past 'depredations of developers', says: 'The town has been used for so long to thinking of itself as a backwater ... Thanet has the opportunity now to attain its full potential ...'

*

'Mind you, this place gets me down ...' The speaker was one of two glaziers from St Albans, working in Pugin's Roman Catholic Church of St Augustine, which is considered Augustus Welby Pugin's finest work. 'I think this is the bloke you've come to see,' his companion up a ladder said. 'He's the one they all come to see.' And his mate went on, 'We're a dying craft, too ... [I was not quite sure to what the 'too' referred. Pugin?] We worked on the stained glass in Coventry Cathedral. It really got me down that job ...' Pause. Then the, 'Mind you, this place gets me down too ...'

Pugin lay shrouded in a dustsheet. They were repairing the window above his tomb. He not only designed but paid for the church himself, and regarded the sea and Christian architecture as 'the only things worth living for'. The exterior is solid with flints, without a spire on the tower because he ran out of money, and curiously unlike the label 'Gothic Revival'; the interior with its outstanding works of early Victorian craftsmanship is ornately gloomy. Pugin lived at The Grange, the house he built next door. From its windows, he watched for ships in distress and his spire, if completed, would have afforded a landmark for them. Having once seen an injured sailor carried ashore, he kept a chest in his hall filled with entire suits of clothes, and would clothe and feed sailors in need. He hired two small houses and engaged nurses to tend fever-stricken sailors left destitute in port; his fellow townsmen then contributed to help him found the Seaman's Infirmary, the forerunner of the present Ramsgate Hospital.

As I left the church it was raining. Ramsgate in the rain can indeed get one down. The word 'dead' was echoed on every lip. 'A bit dead for me,' said a Spanish café owner, and the French students drinking coffee looked at me with glazed eyes. 'A very boring and ugly place,' a German girl said succinctly.

How did it strike Van Gogh, that genius of the sun, when he was a teacher at Mr Stokes's school at 6 Royal Road in 1876? (It was known for a long time that Van Gogh had lived in Ramsgate, but it was Mr Busson, the present Branch Librarian at Ramsgate, who traced the house, by means of a Kelly's Directory and Van Gogh's letters to his brother Theo – 'don't I love Paris and London, though I am a child of the pine woods and of the beach at Ramsgate.'[7] Mr Busson is a most keen and generous local historian and the Local Collection room at the library outstanding. Mr Busson will tell one that it was my uncle who first got him interested in local history, and who lobbied local councillors to get funds to make a back room into the local history room. The prints, china and notes Jack Wotton collected are now mostly in the library and seem to me as notable a legacy as any a man can leave to his town and future generations. Mr Busson recalls sadly that, by an unhappy twist of fate, the day the Local Collection room opened, was the day he attended my uncle's funeral.)

Van Gogh had no salary, but received board and lodging for teaching elementary French and German, arithmetic, and for giving dictation to twenty-four boys 'from the London markets and streets'. His pen and pencil sketch of the 'View from 6 Royal Road' shows a view which is unchanged in essentials. The house itself still has a bow front and balcony and white globe light, in an area on the West Cliff which has crescents and squares, which whether run down or not, are attractive.

It is on this Cliff that the Regency Royal Crescent stands, surely one of the most amiable Regency crescents anywhere.

The Regency Hotel is in the crescent, and is run by the managing director, Ian Josephs, on lines which again give one hope for the future of Ramsgate. Besides being a hotel, the Regency is a School of English, the third or fourth in size in the country and the only one in a hotel. Students have the advantage of the hovercraft service from the Continent, and in addition to classes, can have taped lessons in their own rooms, many of which look out on the lawns that front on to the sea. The bar is crowded with well-educated young people of many nationalities; Ian Josephs can be seen in shirtsleeves and waistcoat, playing chess there with a student. There are a swimming-pool, sauna, steak bar open until 2 a.m., and a friendly dining room with long tables and mainly student staff – 'This ees today's menu,' smiles a pretty French girl. 'I like Kent very much,' said an Italian living in Luxemburg (he had also been to Rye, and Padstow, by car).

Not surprisingly non-students also enjoy staying at the hotel; salesmen are allowed a half bottle of free whisky if they stay two nights, a whole bottle for three, to offset their dwindling expense accounts.

This is typical of Ian Josephs's originality. Before he took on the hotel, it had gone bankrupt three times since 1948. In 1957 he saw an advertisement by the Council, who had bought the hotel, offering a lease at £800 a year. He didn't know where Ramsgate was ... He had come down from Oxford with a law degree, been articled to a chartered accountant in London and had, with Michael Heseltine, who was an Oxford friend, run a bedsitter house in London in the good old bedsitter days, when they were able to put padlocks on doors if someone didn't pay his rent.

Ian Josephs took on the lease of the Regency, running it at first with free rooms for friends and others who would come down from London to spend money there. He opened one of the first discothèques in the country, and for some months the Regency had a fashionable success. When this waned, he remembered the students who has asked him where they could learn English, and opened the school.

What does he think of Ramsgate, of its future? 'The Council should spend a greater proportion of the revenue keeping the town clean, tidy and painted – less on prestige projects.' Could I quote him on this, I asked? 'Yes,' he said. Acts of vandalism, he said, go unrepaired. 'Repairs and gardening are what is needed,' he said, 'or in other words, paint and flowers.' He is a promoter of honesty. He has been a County Councillor, and found himself the 'Ombudsman for Kent'. He spoke strongly in favour of open council meetings (since I spoke to him, Thanet District Council have started an excellent newsletter; in addition most committee meetings are now open to the public). He has stood independently and later as a Liberal for Parliament, as an independent candidate in the 1970 election polling the largest number of votes for an independent candidate. He feels electoral reform is essential. Although he is not expanding his business in Ramsgate, but rather in France where he has a school, he feels optimistic about Ramsgate's future. The signs are, he said, that people are wanting to invest money in the town.

It is not hard to see that this part of Kent has much to offer foreign visitors. Ramsgate's restaurants make the effort to put out menus in three languages (no gourmet could despise the local soles and plaice). London is near, Canterbury nearer. Round about lies some of our most unspoilt countryside. Sophisticated pleasures are not necessary here, and you can walk down to Ramsgate harbour on a spring or early summer evening and see the sandbar in the outer basin exposed, with gulls wheeling over it; the last fisherman leaving his swabbed-down trawler; the sands deserted except for three boys fishing, one or two children; a long stretch of clean tide-marked shore, with curious wave patterns, coruscations in the sand; a smell of clean seaweed. In such a mood the town seems to have returned to its simpler days of a couple of centuries ago. There is no reason why it should not have a re-birth of prosperity too.

Given paint and flowers ...

*

One of the places visitors to Ramsgate will pass through, on the Canterbury road, is the 'Ville de Sarre', so-called on signs in the village, where once was a ferry across the Wantsum channel. The village is famous for its Crown Inn, which dates back to 1500, but became famous in the reign of Charles II when a Huguenot refugee was landlord, who had brought his secret recipe for cherry brandy from France. The cherry brandy of the house is still made for the inn to its own recipe, and there is nothing better after a long cold drive than a warming glassful of this or the 'Crown Invicta' Sloe Gin, which is sharper but just as good. We did not try bottled beers called 'Abbey Ale' and 'Bishop's Finger', but they sounded promising.

Dickens patronized the inn, and among mementoes is a play-bill of a comedy in which he and Wilkie Collins acted in 1851, 'to encourage Life Assurance and other Provident Habits among Authors and Artists ...'. Another pleasant memento is a frame of signed autographs of survivors of the Charge of the Light Brigade, with a dinner menu of ten courses, desserts and coffee, to celebrate the anniversary of their return. 'Huitres au citron, Consommé à la Infante, Crème de tomate à l'Américaine; Suprême de Turbot Valeska; Blanchaille; Poulet sauté Mascotte;

Tournedos Rossini, Pommes Parisiennes, Céléri au jus; Sorbet au Kirsch; Faisan rôti au Cresson, Salade; Croûte aux Fruits; Pouding Glacé, Gaufrettes vanillées; Dessert; Café.' And presumably Crown Invicta Cherry Brandy.

The inn is also famous for having been patronized by actors and actresses, and those playing in the theatres along the coast. Photographs of Tommy Handley, George Robey, Marie Lloyd adorn the bars. Today's patrons include Jack Warner. 'He was in here the other day, for Sunday lunch ... looking very fit.'

*

1842. *'This place is most beautiful just now ... the weather being past all descriptive powers. Heavens how crisp the water is – I bathed yesterday. Ballard too has got me some Port Wine which is quite remarkable – for a place like this, really astonishing ...'*[8] A letter from Dickens, from Broadstairs.

Broadstairs is one of those places which disarm you if you go there fearing it will be a quaint tourist trap. It is ridiculously attractive, everything appearing to be on a small scale, yet unprettified, still basically geared to a good breezy family holiday on the golden sands of the wide bay, and to the enthusiasm of Dickens *aficionados*. Mothers in unfashionable sundresses bare their pinking backs to fitful English sunshine, while children dig, scream, paddle and roll.

In Dickens's day, there was a cornfield between Fort House (now Bleak House) and the sea, and here, with a view to the horizon, he wrote *David Copperfield* (not *Bleak House*). The house had been the captain's house in the days when a fort stood to seaward of it. From here Dickens would walk to visit Miss Mary Pearson Strong, who lived in a little house at the north end of Victoria Parade. She, as one of his sons later confirmed, was the original of Betsey Trotwood, and was probably quite justified in her sorties against donkeys, as the garden, then a green, across the parade from the house, still belongs to the house. It is now the Dickens House Museum, with letters and postcards from the author (together with the minute envelopes of that time), first editions, his inkstands, candle screen, travelling desk; with upstairs, Victoriana such as bonnets, valentines, finest kid ankle boots, chatelaines and skirt grips. From the upstairs window,

Broadstairs might not have changed at all since then, with its small houses surrounding the bay, boats and brightly clothed people by the pier, children playing ball, a café with 'Jugs of Tea', a two-masted boat close inshore on the 'ocean winking in the sunlight like a drowsy lion' (*Our Watering-Place*, 1851), and the mewing of the gulls. He visited the town many times between 1837 and 1851, staying first in the High Street (a site now next to Woolworths), at the Albion Hotel, and elsewhere.

A letter to Professor Felton in 1843 describes his day:

... In a bay-window in a one-pair sits, from nine o'clock to one, a gentleman with rather long hair and no neckcloth, who writes and grins as if he thought he were very funny indeed. His name is Boz. At one he disappears, and presently emerges from a bathing-machine, and may be seen – a kind of salmon-coloured porpoise – splashing about in the ocean. After that he may be seen in another bay-window on the ground-floor eating a strong lunch; after that walking a dozen miles or so, or lying on his back in the sand reading a book ...

But by 1847 the town was becoming too popular for his liking. 'Vagrant music is getting to that height here, and is so impossible to be escaped from, that I fear Broadstairs and I must part company in time to come.'

A downstairs room in Dickens House is furnished exactly as Betsey Trotwood's parlour.

As I laid down my pen, a moment since, to think of it, the air from the sea came blowing in again, mixed with the perfume of the flowers; and I saw the old-fashioned furniture brightly rubbed and polished, my aunt's inviolable chair and table by the round green fan in the bow-window, the drugget-covered carpet, the cat, the kettle-holder, the two canaries, the old china, the punch-bowl full of dried rose leaves, the tall press guarding all sorts of bottles and pots, and, wonderfully out of keeping with the rest, my dusty self upon the sofa, taking note of everything.[9]

There is little vagrant music out of the high season in Broadstairs. In the spring there are preparations for the June Dickens Festival, which is, as Mr J. Poole of the Dickens Fellowship told me, 'quite a lark'. He was on duty at the museum when I visited it, an enthusiastic guide, and said of this onerous duty most aptly, looking out at Betsey Trotwood's green, 'Somebody's got to do the donkey work ...' He told me that about 18 thousand visitors a year visit the museum, half of them foreigners, the Germans and Japanese in particular being amazingly knowledgeable about Dickens.

The house itself was originally Tudor, but is mainly of a later date. There are many Georgian and Regency houses round the front of Viking Bay, which is a conservation area. In Dickens Walk are trellis-work balconies; narrow streets and cul-de-sacs wind back from the harbour; in Serene Place are cobbles and bay-fronted cake-shops; York Street has a pillared fruiterers, toy-like post-office and the ironmongers H. E. Harrington's curved corner front. The High Street leads steeply uphill, and here is Pierremont Hall where the Princess Victoria stayed, more trellis work in the glass conservatory bar of the Olde Crown, and a flower kiosk shaped like a coach lantern. Underlying all the pretty details is the sturdy core of Broadstairs which until 1792, when a pier was destroyed (the town was known to have a pier in Henry VIII's day), was busily engaged in the Greenland and Iceland fishing industry. There was also a famous boat-building yard – White's, later of Cowes, a family business traditionally linked with the Armada fight and having a close association with the Thanet smugglers, who appear to have been their best customers.[10] Close association with 'the gentlemen' was no bar to social standing in the island in the eighteenth century and before. Smuggling indeed brought its own kind of prosperity.

A flint arch that crosses Harbour Street, the York Gate, was built during the invasion scare of 1540, by George Culmer of Broadstairs, for the protection of his native town and the Kentish coast. Heavy doors once hung from it. Near by are the remains of the chapel of 'Our Lady of Bradstowe', a shrine that was so revered by sailors that they lowered their topsails as they went past.

*

'Mr Pickwick's here, for the thirteenth year, there he is, over there ...' He is unmistakable, with blue coat, and belly, top hat, small spectacles, faint smell of lavender water ... and an extremely cultured voice.

'Do you know how old I am, my dear ... seventy-six ...' He is John Rowe, from London, and the only Dickensian from London at the 1978 Dickens Festival, although there are two visitors from France in their costumes, and members of Dickens Fellowships from Bristol, Eastbourne, other parts of the country. They gather at Pierremont Hall, the first to come being a character from The Old Curiosity Shop in maroon with lace, bonnet and mittens. Later in the afternoon she trips on a short flight of steps and kindly crinolines rush to her aid; the walk, to the Pavilion on the Sands, with cameras clicking all the way, the whole week's festivities, are gruelling for the gallant Fellowship members who do much for their (and our) tourist trade – a Hungarian photographer and his wife ('Dickens is very well known in Hungary too') jostle with a Japanese photographer and many Europeans, as we all troop down the High Street.

'It gets the town together,' says a Peggotty-like figure. 'You put on clothes, and people talk to you ... Nobody knows us next week ...' she adds sadly.

Perhaps we English should have carnivals more often, in the manner of this sedate version of a Bacchanalia, when anything can happen. Little boys in floppy caps and tailcoats, little girls in shawls, women in immaculately embroidered bloomers (it is a windy day, a great day for bloomers), bewhiskered men, and Fagin and his crew skilfully picking pockets. It is strange how Dickensian the faces under their bonnets and tophats look – more knobbly suddenly, more measured and dignified. The rest of us in the crowd – not them – appear to be in fancy dress. Mrs Mac-Stinger in her tall oval hat is far more regal than the Mayor, who opens the ceremonies wittily, 'Broadstairs ... the town we hope you grow to love ...' 'Last week was Disability Week', said a man heaving a wheelchair over a step. 'Broadstairs being Dickensian, we have no ramps ...' But we are all happy in the sun, and there is a cup of tea for everyone in the pavilion. Brian Caplen from the *Isle of Thanet Gazette* is taking notes beside me. Joyce Smith, the festival organizer, who also runs a hat shop, in a pretty bonnet with roses over her ear, is no doubt dreaming up next year's festival. 'I came to stay many years ago, and gradually got into it, through the costume side ...' she says (she is curator of the Museum). 'And yes, it's for the town ...'

Outside the pavilion a row of grey donkeys crosses the sand; children roll over and over towards the sea, screaming; two men with monkeys on their shoulders tout photographs; a game of football is in progress. In the chalets above the beach couples sit with their plastic mugs of tea, with coats and chiffon headscarves, and a fag; the wind catches the little breakers and the sun beats back from the clean sand. It is holiday time, and the air is full of a cheerful, vulgar and unmistakably vagrant music.

Mr Pickwick and I are content. Although he says wistfully, 'They never star me ...'

'I'll see you here next year,' I say.

He smiles very sweetly. 'That's a challenge,' he says. 'Yes, you challenge me ...'

*

Inland from Broadstairs is St Peter's, which is older than Broadstairs, and which became a Member of the Cinque Port of Dover. St Peter's church dates in part from the eleventh century; the ceiling, which is wooden, and colourfully painted in the chancel,

The Cinque Ports Confederation, showing the Head Ports, Corporate and Non-corporate Members as listed in the Charter of Charles II in 1668

is reminiscent of an upturned boat. The tower was used as a signalling station in the Napoleonic era. Four men kept a look-out, and signalled from there to ships at the Nore. Since that time St Peter's has the rare privilege of flying the White Ensign.

Quite near, on Beacon Hill, Kitchen Hill and at Ossunden farther inland were sites of the beacons which can be traced throughout Thanet. These beacons consisted of a tall upright piece of timber, to the top of which a barrel of pitch would be drawn by pulley and chain and set alight. In the early nineteenth century, the remains of one of these beacons was dug up by a farmer between Stone and the North Foreland.

Fire used to be lit on top of the North Foreland lighthouse also in the old days, but a fire of coals in a brazier was replaced by large oil lamps with patent reflectors, then by more modern means. There has been a lighthouse here, at this extreme eastern point of Kent, since 1505, the present one having been enlarged and adapted from an octagon lighthouse of 1683. It was off the North Foreland that the great four-day battle between the English fleet under Monck and the Dutch under De Ruyter and De Witt took place in June 1666. The outnumbered Monck, tough, hard-headed and tobacco-chewing, bore down on the enemy in such straight formation that a French onlooker observed, 'They fight like a line of cavalry . . .'[11]

Near-by Kingsgate, once St Bartholomew's, was renamed when Charles II landed here with his brother, later James II. Henry Fox, first Lord Holland, had a magnificent house here, copied from Tully's Italian Villa, but only a small part of it remains.

When we visited Kingsgate and Joss Bay, the beaches looked clear and deserted, but notices, as elsewhere in England that year, warned of 'Temporary Oil Contamination'.

We drove inland, through the flat yet domed countryside, hedgeless fields of cabbages and mustard stretching to a hazy horizon. There are not over-many houses and the few church spires make landmarks in this open countryside, rich with cow-parsley, vetch and later, poppies. The warm chalky soil seems to lend its muted colour to everything; there is a great feeling of peacefulness now, in the island of beacons. St Nicholas at Wade is noted as a typical village of the area, but I found Acol, on the way to Manston, even prettier, more changeless.

The Royal Air Force Station at Manston is now the only active RAF station in Kent. It was one of the Battle of Britain fields. By the roadside stands a Spitfire Mark 16, with a notice saying 'Do Not Touch – I Am Old – Treat Me Gently'. Beside it are a Javelin MK9 and a Canberra PR3. The Spitfire looks tiny, almost a Dinky Toy. And in such a plane, towards ungentle treatment, went the young men 'alone and cold in the thin blue air, peering through the condensation into the glare of the sun, unable to see the man who killed them.'[12]

In his recent book on the Battle of Britain, *Fighter*, Len Deighton has given a powerful account of Britain's refusal to submit to Hitler's *Adlerangriff* (Eagle Attack) in 1940, which was to be the precursor to 'Sea Lion', the invasion of Britain. He dispels some myths, points out that the Germans still insist there was no such event as the Battle of Britain, that Hitler doubted whether invasion was 'technically feasible', and that Churchill did not gain the wholehearted support of the British public until after the Battle of Britain was won. 'No wonder then that he devoted so much of his time and energy, to say nothing of rhetoric, to convincing the British that they had won a mighty victory.'[13] *'Never in the field of human conflict was so much owed by so many to so few.'*[14]

And yet ... Both Deighton, and A. J. P. Taylor in his introduction to the book, also point out that it was in not being defeated, in continuing to exist, that the Royal Air Force made this a decisive moment.

The Battle of Britain was a fairly small affair ... The British on the other hand were invigorated. They believed that they had won a great victory or rather that the pilots of Fighter Command had won a great victory for them. And so they had ... Great Britain came nearer to defeat in the prolonged Battle of the Atlantic against the U-boats than she did in the Battle of Britain. But psychologically the Battle of Britain was the more decisive.[15]

It put the country back in the war, and meant that Britain was taken seriously as a combatant Great Power, particularly by the United States, who felt that with help, the British might win. Hitler called off Sea-Lion on 17 September and turned his thoughts to the invasion of Russia.

Manston airfield lies on the exposed jutting land of Thanet, with seemingly nothing between it and an invader. Because of the typical roll of the flat countryside, planes flying low would be on you before you saw them, and the German fighters came in off the sea at near ground level. Equally, German bomber pilots, who were shot if they returned with their bombs, would drop these, failing all else, on Manston, as they left the coast of England. Deighton's picture of Manston therefore ('... it was not everyone's finest hour'), with airmen who had 'been sitting in the air-raid shelters ever since the attack on 12 August', of terrified men who would not budge, and looting by local civilians, seemed to me to be open to challenge, as is his statement that the field is 'built on a cliff-top alongside the sea' (Manston lies inland from Ramsgate).

There are few men at Manston now who were there during the war. The raid on 12 August 1940 was devastating, leaving about a hundred craters on the field, two hangars damaged and work-shops destroyed. Radar stations at Dover, Rye and Dunkirk in Kent had previously been hit. But as the bombs fell, most of No. 65 Squadron, who were taking off in their Spitfires, managed to get off the ground, and after the raid Nos. 65 and 64 Squadrons managed to land their Spitfires. The station was serviceable again the next day.

Mr Jack Finnis, who was a civilian driver at the time, and who now lives in Ramsgate, told us that forty-five minutes after this raid planes were operating again. 'Morale was good among the Force.' Mr Finnis has a strong, open face, and of twenty-nine civilian drivers was one of fourteen to stick it out at Manston – his view clearly has the ring of truth. He told us that planes were still able to get off the ground because as the Germans swept across and back across the field, they 'left a path on the grass run-way between the craters where the lads could take off and land'. He also said that they normally arrived just as the all-clear had sounded. It is not surprising then that men who had been ordered underground to shelters, and then up again, endlessly, got stubborn, if not 'petrified' with fear as Deighton has it. Courage is not quantifiable, as a present-day RAF officer pointed out – those who were afraid may have been the most brave, and Manston as a field hung on, denying the Germans a propaganda victory. There were raids all through August, culminating in a raid on the 24th when seven men were killed, the field covered with bombs and unexploded bombs, buildings and planes on fire and communications cut. After the raid it was decided to evacuate all those not involved in Station Defence or servicing aircraft.

Mr Jack Petley, who still works for the Department of the Environment at Manston, arrived there in 1941, and also said, 'From what I've seen of the Force, I think that's a bit wrong myself ... they were only too willing to have a go.' He spent much of his time repairing craters, which had to be continually topped up, and keeping the grass down – areas were camouflaged and cinder tracks laid down to look like roads, lights set for dummy airfields. Mr Petley had heard nothing of civilian looting. Surely rumours would still have been rife in 1941 if much had occurred?

*

Manston, Saturday 23 August 1940. Post Office engineers worked next to an unexploded bomb sorting through hundreds of wires to reconnect the operations room and the fighters to Group Headquarters.[16]

Manston, August. During the long, grim summer days RAF 600 Squadron continued to fly their twin-engined bombers.

September 3rd, in the sea off the North Foreland, Richard Hillary was shot down, and rescued, disfigured by burns, by the Margate life-boat.

I was falling. Falling slowly through a dark pit. I was dead. My body, headless, circled in front of me. I saw it with my mind, my mind that was the redness in front of the eye, the dull scream in the ear, the grinning of the mouth, the skin crawling on the skull ... The sickly smell of death was in my nostrils and a confused roar of sound ... I looked down at my hands, and not seeing them, realized that I had gone blind.[17]

'Never in the field of human conflict was so much owed by so many to so few ...'

*

But the Battle of Britain was only part of the war. A records book at the Station is kept open, showing casualties and direct hits scored on trains, barges and other enemy targets at places such as Dixmude and Dunkirk, by planes from Manston. In 1942,

Lieutenant-Commander Eugene Esmonde was awarded a posthumous VC for his valiant unsuccessful attack on the German battle cruisers *Scharnhorst* and *Gneisenau*. Manston was also used as a refuelling and briefing base by squadrons from other fields.

The history of the airfield goes back to before the RAF was formed. It came into existence in 1916, when the landing ground at Westgate was proving inadequate. An Air Mechanic, Henry Wood, spent many nights at Manston in a large packing case equipped with two bunks, a telephone and six bowls of oily rag which were lit as an emergency landing system. Today, apart from the RAF station, land is leased to Invicta International Airlines, who carry freight. An Air Kent passenger service to Brussels and Rotterdam has been started. In an area of unemployment, the field provides a good source of employment. RAF Manston is a Master Diversion Airfield, which means planes can land twenty-four hours a day, seven days a week, and is one of only two fields in the world with equipment for laying runway foaming. There is also a Search and Rescue helicopter unit, linked with Coast Guards by telephone. In the summer months, the cry will ring throughout the station: 'It's the lilo season again ...' The crew are on fifteen minutes readiness and usually leave in five minutes. (If they take longer than fifteen minutes, 'They're out.') Then there is the Air Experience Flight, which has many volunteer reservist officers, and No. 617 Gliding School, entirely manned by reservists and civilian volunteers. Every weekend up to seventy or eighty Air Training Corps cadets visit Manston, probably more than any other field. Finally, there is the Central Training Establishment of the Air Force Department Fire Service, which is civilian and autonomous, and the only training establishment of its kind, training firemen in aircraft crash-fire duties.

The role of the armed services is still to protect, as we were told by an officer at Manston. And the same protection is offered, whether it is in sending a helicopter to inspect an oil slick, to rescue a sick man on board ship, boys sucked into mudflats, or an errant yachtsman. Every air traveller may have cause to be thankful for training given at Manston. And certainly those who set out to sea on a lilo.

3 Margate; Westgate; Birchington; Reculver; Whitstable; Faversham

'Margate, which is Bartholomew Fair by the seaside.'

Thomas Gray[1]

'...the oyster beds at Whitstable... flower beds on the shore.'

A. O. COLLARD

The labels on the funny hats say 'KISS ME SLOWLY'. When I was a child they had the more modest 'KISS ME', but the dirty postcards haven't changed. 'It's rising again!' (looking at the barometer); 'My Goodness, Mr Hornbeam, you're up early' (at nudist's hotel); the popping eyes and breasts. The candy floss is the same, the roundabouts on the sands, the smell of vinegar, the 'fashion dolls' in nylon crinolines, the cups of tea ('How About a Nice Cup of Tea like Mum Makes'), the boarding houses and cafés called 'Harbour Lights', the dizzy slides at Dreamland funfair, the whelks and rock.

'It's blooming hard work, making rock,' we were told by a man with his own stall, the rock arranged in its multi-coloured palisades. He had worked in a rock factory once. Now, he said, 'seasons are unpredictable'. In 1978 and '79 the economic climate, for the unemployed in particular, was just beginning to make itself felt in Margate – and rock was a casualty. He told us how seaside patterns had changed. 'Trade starts at five o'clock in the afternoon. They're up all night, and there's none of that morning bathing and morning teas on the sands.' The centres of entertainment had shifted, but Dreamland stands where once was the famous Hall by the Sea – a ballroom, and before that the menagerie of 'Lord' George Sanger, whose grave we later visited in Margate cemetery, part of a fitting monument to the whole Sanger family, ornate with angels and a life-size horse.

Dreamland hasn't changed. We wandered past the seafish stalls (whelks from Whitstable and cockles from Southend), to the amusement park which in my early childhood had seemed such a legendary place. It looks smaller now; out of season shrouded under its dustsheets, with a few brave flags flying, almost a survivor. But in the short summer season the scenic railway runs to shrieks of delight, the cowboy hats are twirled, coconuts tumble, 'kiddies' kopters' and 'super hurricane jets' whirl, a small boy sits entranced in a driving machine and children clutch hands as they fly down the astroglide. There is an attraction about even this, the gaudiest of gaudy funfairs, that can dispel sophistication.

John is a crack shot at the rifle stands – unless the sights are really too bent for anyone to hit the target. I considered the fortune teller's tent, but the queue was already long. 'And you don't know how much she'd charge, do you,' a woman said suspiciously. 'She might say £2, mightn't she ...'

'Here, have this. Pure gold – Sotheby's,' said a boy at the darts stand, handing me a bracelet. He had worked at the funfair since he was nine and works in the market in the winter. It was a poor season, so far, he said, croakily. 'I'm losing my voice ...' and he called past us to the thinning crowd.

We went back to our hotel up in Fort Crescent, Cliftonville, which is 'superior', and took off our shoes sitting among the lace doilies, crochet doilies, plastic doily, pink-and-white striped satin curtains and potted plant; and looked out through the lace 'nets' across our little white-painted balcony to one of the fireball sunsets, among the most beautiful in England, often painted here by Turner. (He would be lodged in the house of Sophia Caroline Booth between 1827 and 1846, when she moved to London to keep house for him in Cheyne Walk.[2])

*

Fishermen in England used to build their huts facing away from the sea. And it was not in Kent, but at Scarborough, that sea-water 'cures' began, when Dr Wittie promoted them there in his book in 1660. Other learned treatises followed: sea-water could cure everything from cancer to ruptures, from asthma to madness. Dr Richard Russell, who moved from Lewes to Brighthelmstone in 1753, added glandular disease to the list, and the properties of sea-water as a dentifrice. But it was in Margate that the Quaker, Benjamin Beale, invented the machine that robbed bathing of its original innocence, when nymphs could be seen cavorting naked in the waves and men dived in gamely from rowing boats. Beale with his horse-drawn huts gave Margate a head start over other resorts, starting a fashion that lasted for nearly a century and a half. At Brighton, gentlemen were still shivering and hesitating on the brink, 'their persons ... wholly exposed', which practice remained 'a stain on the *gentility* of the Brighthelmstonians', but at Margate the bathing machines lowered their hoods, which were like folding versions of a prairie wagon, to encapsulate the bather in a salty privacy. I have not been able to find a description of what it was like, swimming about in one of these circumscribed – and gloomy? – canvas snail-shells, but prints and drawings show people happily splashing beyond their confines once safely in the water, although there are also grimly vivid *Punch* cartoons of giantesses dressed as bathing women, saying to crying infants, 'Come along in, my little lad,' as they manhandle them into the waves.

Sea bathing was a serious business, and had to be performed in the early morning while the pores of the skin were still 'shut'. (Sea-water was also drunk, particularly by cripples.) For the rest of the day there were all the other pastimes of the more elegant spas – card games, libraries, dancing, rotundas and the theatre. In Margate, Cecil Square, built in 1769, provided an 'elegant assembly room' (the largest in Europe), rooms for tea and cards, dining parlours and a 'lofty piazza'. The little Theatre Royal in Hawley Square was modelled on Covent Garden, and the town had three libraries, one of which was decorated with corinthian columns, chandeliers and a dome. In 1792 the Sea-Bathing Infirmary was founded, an imposing building of pillared brick, sponsored by George III, which still stands. However, Margate was always one of the more frivolous spas, it is clear, renowned for young and comely bathing attendants or women. Prudes, in 1780, labelled Margate as 'devoted to gaiety and dissipation', and by the end of the century, it had already lost its social lead to Ramsgate and Broadstairs; by 1842, a journalist could write, 'the Shambles of Whitechapel seek the shingle of Margate'.[3]

*

We set out to find the Theatre Royal. 'The theatre? You mean the Old Theatre,' a pensioner said. 'We call it the Old Theatre. Everything changes ... and not always for the best I'm afraid to say ...' He hobbled along beside us through Cecil Square, where an attractive Baptist Church of 1899 still stands, whereas the Hippodrome Theatre has been replaced by a library – 'It was a bingo before that.' 'The Centre' looms in red brick and white concrete.

'I've been here thirty-five years,' our companion said. 'For my health ... nice breezes here –' We turned off into narrow streets. 'They're all like boxes now, aren't they. Look how narrow the streets are. They used to be all carriages, didn't they ...'

He left us before we reached the Theatre Royal. It appeared now to be the 'New Royal Bingo Club' but was closed. The signs were tattered, and the paint peeling. The small building's elegance (which can be seen in a print of 1804 at the Ellen Terry museum near Tenterden) was clouded by decay. In the foyer, above mops and heaps of clothing, hung a delicate central lantern, the only reminder that here Mrs Siddons held audiences spellbound, and here the ghost of Sarah Thorne, who managed the theatre between 1867 and 1899, is said to wander.

One man influential in starting the theatre was 'King' Cobb, of the Cobb Brewery family who did much to improve Margate, obtaining a patent for the market, building their fine brewery, promoting charities. 'King' Cobb was also a banker and was Chief Magistrate and Deputy Warden of the Cinque Ports for over thirty years. His son was a great supporter of the anti-slavery movement, and when Margate became a chartered borough, the family continued to play an important role.

The market place is still attractive, and the old Town Hall has a small green cupola. There are these lovely scattered relics in Margate, such as the Taj-Mahal-like Baptist Chapel in New Street, some Georgian houses, and in the streets running down to the sea, curved eighteenth-century window architraves above more recent, and more ugly, shopfronts. One can trace the outlines of the old spa, but now, as in Hawley Square, where an imposing Wesleyan Chapel is labelled 'Townbrooke Limited – Manufacturers of Ladies Jersey Outerwear', all panache seems to have vanished. Hawley Square on a cold Sunday evening was desolate, seedy, a place of one solitary dog and chiropodists' name-plates, litter and dying flowers.

Margate is conscious of the changing scene. With the rest of Thanet, it is lucky to have as Chief Executive of Thanet District Council, Ian Gill, who is also the Registrar of the Cinque Ports and Clerk of Dover Castle. Earlier he was Town Clerk at Dover, and before that in the Midlands, where at Lincoln he was involved in clearance of buildings in the city centre. He freely admits that this entailed pulling down old buildings of merit, and that to him, as for others at that date, 'social need was upper-most'. One of the first things he did on being appointed Chief Executive was to go round conservation areas. Now one project that has come to fruition, for instance, is the restoration of North-down House, which is to be a combined community and arts centre. While prosperity and an end to unemployment are clearly his prime objectives, he speaks optimistically and with complete lack of Town Hall humbug about the variety the area has to offer, preservation of the quality of life for local residents (he would like to see each ward have a special council allocation for whatever they considered vital in their area), and obviously has the ability to orchestrate all the clashing elements in a council into a progressive whole. That the Liberal Conference was to be held in Margate in 1979 was a great bonus, he felt, as it would give the town more television coverage than it usually achieved.

A headline in the *East Kent Times* recently proclaimed 'Margate Must Have a New Image to Survive'. It was 'finished as a family resort', the article ran, and must become 'a paradise for mature visitors'. At present it is also a paradise for conferences. Our hotel was opposite the Winter Gardens, where there is 'Variety at Eight' in the Queens Hall – the following week Thanet District Council was presenting Freddie (Parrot Face) Davies and assorted artistes. This week was the conference of the Manchester Unity of Odd Fellows. The Odd Fellows strolled the streets, at eight, in evening dress and carnations, and the wind along the front worried at satin hems and chains of office.

The water in our guest house/hotel was boiling, the landlady accommodating – 'No restrictions, here's a key,' she ogled, bare-footed and long-skirted, as we carried past her our very married

suitcase. In the dining-room the traditional breakfast was traditionally vast.

Gentlemen of the road shovelled it down. 'Two hundred to do
when I get back ... What I'm doing's illegal of course ... have to
chase things up when I get home ... The simple answer is, of
course ...' He speared a sausage.

Beyond the ferns a lady Odd Fellow raised a pink fingernail
from her teacup.

'Blackpool last year ... Freedom of the town ... coffee morn-
ings ... Lord Mayor's ball ... The cabaret was wonderful. There
was a man throwing knives; a lady in the audience went up and
she burst into tears afterwards ... it was wonderful ... Well, you
put your trust in Him above, don't you. More tea, dear?'

So in the evening we ate out, at Fenners Restaurant, which
is run by Italians – warm, so welcoming they opened the restaurant for us on the second night although it was closed and where
we ate *en famille* and watched television, and the proprietor
sighed, 'That's nice', as Jane Russell peaked beyond the omelettes,
and good Italian wine filled the glasses.

That is the seaside town. There is also the sea, and the men of
the sea, whom Camden called 'a sort of amphibious creatures,
who get their living both by sea and land, as having to do with
both elements ... According to the seasons of the year, they knit
nets, catch cod, herrings, and mackarel ... and carry in the
corn ... As shipwrecks are frequent here ... they are very active
in recovering lost goods ...' They fished in the North Sea, but
when this brought low yields, turned to 'foying', which was the
supplying of ships with provisions and helping them in distress.
(This latter could turn into *paultring* which was pilfering from
those they had gone to help.) Margate itself was built on streams
and ponds (hence mere-gate), but inland was what Cobbett
called 'a garden indeed ... a country of corn', and the corn was
shipped from the harbour. The cargoes were carried in one-masted
sloops called hoys, which on the return voyage brought supplies
and, later, passengers to the resorts. On Saturday evenings the
'Husbands' Boat' brought the father of the family to join his
brood. Charles Lamb gives an account of a journey to Margate
in 'The Old Margate Hoy', and of a poor boy with scrofula who
smiled patiently and hoped for a cure – 'and when we asked him

whether he had any friends where he was going, he replied "he *had* no friends." [4]

Like others of the coastal towns, Margate had a fort, and was (and still is) a Member of the Cinque Port of Dover. In the sixteenth century the historian Lewis writes of there being a watch-house there, and arms and ordnance. A gun would be fired and a flag raised to warn merchantmen going round the North Foreland into the Downs that enemy privateers were about, and to tell the people of Bradstow (Broadstairs) of danger. The Fort is now the Winter Gardens, and the famous caves, where smugglers probably hid their booty (which were earlier probably Saxon caves, and later, places of worship, given painted murals by their eighteenth-century rediscoverer) are now thronged by tourists, who shudder at the medieval dungeons or torture chambers where the tide would wash over live prisoners.

But the men of the sea live on, and the defenders of the shore. Margate suffered from air attacks in both World Wars, and in 1916 and '17 was shelled from the sea. If England had been invaded in the Second World War, Thanet would have been evacuated (as it was the seaside towns were ghost towns), but 3,000 Home Guard members, firemen, Civil Defence workers and others would have remained. The Margate life-boat was in the forefront at Dunkirk, and the town has many mementoes of earlier acts of bravery, such as the statue of a lifeboatman to commemorate the men of the surf-boat *Friend to All Nations*, which sank in December 1897, nine of the crew of thirteen being drowned. In Margate cemetery, many graves have stone anchors with chains winding round the gravestones; below the worn inscriptions, unknown sailors lie at peace.

*

The sea has always been both friend and enemy to Margate. The harbour pier, which had long existed in one form or another, was washed away in a great storm in 1808, and replaced by the present stone pier. The jetty, which was always called jetty, although it could be thought another pier, was battered many times before the dramatic storm of January 1978, when its iron girders were thrown like matchsticks on to the beach and the life-boat, which was traditionally housed in a little pavilion on the jetty, had to be rescued by helicopter. During this storm, giant waves swept over the harbour and into shops across the street. Four hundred and fifty smashed deckchairs floated like flotsam on the sea, and what remained of the jetty was twisted into tortured shapes. At Ramsgate, concrete blocks were torn from the harbour and tossed about like toy bricks; at Sandwich marina yachts were lifted into the air and thrown on to the bank.

The Margate jetty was built in 1855 on the site of the wooden 'Jarvis's Landing Place', which was used as a landing stage for passengers from the Pier and Harbour Company steamboats (Dr Jarvis was chairman of the company). It was also a fashionable strolling place, and in 1856 a thousand people were given a dinner there to celebrate the end of the Russian war. In 1877 a fierce gale knocked part of it away; in 1897 there was another violent storm, and in the drastic floods which swept Thanet in January 1953, and which reached inland to Margate Town Hall and moated it, the jetty was again attacked, although the harbour fared worse and the lighthouse was toppled into the sea.

After the 1978 storm, there were rumours that an Arab had made a bid for the jetty, in order to repair it. What price Margate then? But it was finally decided to demolish it. However the old jetty refused to go, and after more than a dozen attempts to blow it up, some of its tenacious girders still clung to the seabed, and in 1979 were jutting out of the water. Sitting staring at part of the structure on the sands, a bulbous-nosed holiday-maker in a tweed tartan cap could have walked out of those seaside post-cards. Towards the water, picking their way through the salty pools and braving a cold paddle, a group of women in loose dresses and old-fashioned straw hats held hands and shrieked at crabs. Margate is still the same.

The previous year, it had braved another modern hazard. The three beaches were polluted with oil from the Greek tanker *Eleni V* wrecked off Great Yarmouth. There were notices all along the coast warning of oil on the beaches, and the smell by Margate harbour of rotting seaweed, oil and other detritus would have deterred even the hardiest and most scrofula-ridden of Dr Wittie's dawn bathers. The sea is our bastion in more ways than one, and we persist in ignoring and polluting it. To Victorian poets it was the mistress, the wild fickle element; now it is our whore.

*

Beneath the candy floss, Margate has other treasures tucked away. One is a perfectly preserved sixteenth-century house, the Tudor House, which was once refaced but has been restored to its original underlying structure – a particularly clear architectural example because it is in the main bare of furniture; beams, fireplaces and cupboards are unvarnished and uncluttered. It does house, however, a collection of Roman oil lamps found at Margate and a bronze fibula from the floor of the Roman pottery site at Tivoli here; with other items such as a smuggler's oil lamp, and a piece of the sail of HMS *Victory*. The *Victory*, carrying the body of Nelson, anchored off Margate in December 1805.

Another find is such that if, as the novelist Marie Corelli pointed out, it 'existed anywhere but at Margate, it would certainly be acknowledged as one of the wonders of the world'. In 1835, the son of the owner of some land on the brow of Dane Hill dug his spade into what he thought was a disused well. It turned out to be a serpentine passage, cut in the chalk, leading to a rectangular chamber. Another entrance was then fully uncovered (the boy's sisters had previously been playing in it), so that a whole complex was revealed: a passage leading to a rotunda, round a pillar, and on beneath a dome to the serpentine way into the end chamber. The walls of all except the first passage were entirely covered with millions of minute shells, in intricate symbols and designs.

The discovery was unfortunately named the 'Grotto', and visitors paid to see it. Gas lighting soon spoiled the colours of the shells, the background colour being the gold of yellow periwinkles, which with the pink and blue of other shells, must have been jewel-like. As it is, the grotto is superb enough, a beautiful piece of intricate craftsmanship, and when one has seen it, it becomes impossible to feel that it was built for other than a religious purpose – the amount of work is too vast, surely involving more slave-hours than the building of a small pyramid, and the whole design too intricate, to be a secular 'folly'. Many people – 'and most of them haven't been to see the Grotto', said the girl at the entrance sharply – dismiss it as an eighteenth-century shell grotto. Why then, was it kept secret? I have a Thanet guide of 1775 and it mentions every folly and burial mound in the district, but not this. Who could afford to build it? About 150 years ago the Duke of Newcastle built a grotto very inferior to this near Weybridge, with two types of shell (here there are twenty-eight different varieties), which cost £60,000.

One theory that has been put forward is that the grotto was built by Phoenicians, and there is much to support the idea.[5] Traders from the Phoenician settlement of Carthage are known to have reached Britain in about 450 BC, and may well have carried tin along the Channel to Thanet and then across to France and overland through France. The Wantsum channel would have provided a safe harbour for their ships – they travelled in fleets – and from Thanet they could have taken other goods in exchange for glass beads (which have been found in British burial sites and of which the Phoenicians were the first makers) and typical Phoenician wares. The grotto could have been a shrine to their goddess Tanit (Bede refers to Thanet as Tanat), the moon and fertility goddess. Many of the shell symbols, such as the palmettes and lotus flower designs, are typically Phoenician, and there was originally a small figurine bearing a cup over the pillar which could have been the goddess. In the rectangular chamber are a recessed arched altar and a circular pediment for cult objects; nowhere is there a cross or any Christian motif.

It is interesting that the 1775 Guide remarks on 'that species of whelk which formed one of the ingredients of the ancient purple', being found on rocks at low tide. The Phoenicians were the makers of the famous purple die, manufacturing it from whelks of the *Purpuridae* family, and their name may even be derived from the Greek word for purple. Perhaps in Thanet they found another source for their purple cloth, a luxury article, or left their secret with the native inhabitants (the Britons who were certainly civilized in this area by 200 BC, importing brass, pottery and ivory and having a gold coinage).

Until further research and excavation is carried out, much is conjecture. Perhaps the English shy away from something so strange. The nineteenth-century naturalist Frank Buckland pointed out that the shells must have been stuck on while still alive to remain in so good a state of preservation. Very un-English. The Phoenicians of Carthage, of course, went in for human sacrifice ... Human sacrifices in Thanet?

*

But times change, and strange things happen, even in England. From Margate we went on to Westgate, where John was once at school, a place which he remembers with great affection. The buildings are still there, and the playing field across the road, but it is no longer a school. Westgate still has pretty iron canopies over shop-fronts, and much red brick and white woodwork, but something has changed. No longer do the trains disgorge polite hordes of boys and girls, regimented in their different uniforms, on to the Victorian platforms.

A huge figure lurched towards me in a pub, brandishing his plastic shopping bag. Later I saw him loitering in a cinema entrance, apparently unheeded by a few girls – a friendly giant?

The son of a taxi-driver of the pre-war days explained it to us bluntly. The many schools have gone, 'even the ones along the front', and in their place are 'private nursing homes' ('and nut houses' he said), where the elderly can end their days in the good bracing air where once little boys learned to be 'leaders of men', and those whose minds have clouded can wander the streets as freely as Billy Bunter out on a jape.

In the evening the sun went down over a milky sea. A few shrimpers were wading out beyond the sand and seaweed, in white evening light. It was a scene as in Turner's most haunting painting, 'The Evening Star', in which a shrimper walks home over the yellow-grey sand, and a single mast, a single star, are reflected in the water.

There are endless beaches here, and at Birchington and Minnis Bay, where children can play among the chalky rocks and rock-pools, and wade for miles in shallow water. We were taken to Minnis Bay as children to recover from whooping-cough, and it is to me a place of shrimping and sand, watery discoveries, hot crackling seaweed and cold winds blowing over a small cliff-top park where we sheltered from the most biting of the healthy breezes.

Inland Birchington is a jumble of old and new, a cluster of old village, new houses, with a church and an unusual Methodist chapel with a green painted tower. Dante Gabriel Rossetti died here, and is buried beneath a cross in the churchyard carved by his friend Ford Madox Brown. 'Honoured ... among painters as a painter and among poets as a poet ... born in London of parentage mainly Italian ... died Birchington 9 April 1882', on Easter Day.

Nearby is Quex Park, which now contains the Powell-Cotton Big Game Museum. An early Crispe, Sir Henry, of Quex Park, was kidnapped during the Civil War, and held to ransom in Flanders by friends of Charles II for £3,000 – in style more reminiscent of today. When he finally got home he was known as Bonjour Crispe, because that was the only Continental word he had learnt, being an Englishman, and he used it from then on whenever he spoke to villagers.

From Minnis Bay we walked as children along the perfectly flat stretch of coastline to Reculver. It was a pilgrimage of a sort, seeming, in memory, to take all day, lightened by hard-boiled eggs and the intense excitement of seeing the twin towers of Reculver (locals call them 'the Reculvers') loom out of a haze of heat and distance.

The Roman Regulbium (Reculver) guarded the northern end of the Wantsum channel, as Richborough did the southern end. Regulbium was probably the only specifically military post south of the Humber and east of the Severn after the initial Roman landings, which gives an indication of the peaceful nature of the civilization they encountered until the coming of the Anglo-Saxons and Jutes. Roman villas spread over the rich and fertile south-east.

Some of the Roman walls of the fort at Reculver remain, others have been eaten away by the sea, which has encroached farther and farther inland. (It was a Member of the Cinque Ports but dropped out in the fourteenth century as the port had been swept away by the sea. In Leland's day, Reculver was a quarter of a mile from the shore.) King Egbert of Kent built a monastery church and a palace here. In the early nineteenth century the church was demolished, but Trinity House saved and restored the twin towers, recognizing their value as a landmark to shipping.

A sea-wall and groynes keep the sea at bay, but it laps round the foot of the mound the towers stand on and looks as though it will not be kept out for ever.

On a calm day the waves slap peacefully down on the shingle and out at sea a small trawler hauls in orange nets. Behind the towers are caravans and tea stalls and wire netting, but there are few people about unless it is high summer and the King Ethelbert pub remains firmly and discouragingly shut until 6.30 pm. Your thoughts can unwind, as you walk between the breakwaters, or spin pebbles, or listen to the tide drawing out. One or two anglers; a young couple in jeans leaping from rock to rock with their weeks-old baby, in search of shellfish; the hazy salt-ringed sun. The plain and unretouched face of the English seaside. But here again are ugly patches of oil, like black treacle fallen from a spoon. One feels the wire-netting and caravans encroaching from one side, the polluted sea ready to close down on the beaches on the other. What I knew as a child – and how many million others – seems threatened, by something more final than Romans or Vikings or Boney himself, and that time will not necessarily undo.

*

Whitstable lifts the heart. Lying farther along the flat coastline beyond Herne Bay, it is one of those towns having a peculiar nature of their own, springing from the trade carried out there, which make them, to me, the best English towns. Pottery at Stoke, beer at Burton ... these towns have an entity, and an identity of which their inhabitants are proud, and which makes the places themselves self-sufficient, full-blooded, virile. Unlike the museum towns, the towns where the past is past but carefully preserved, their reason for existence is still there, throbbing, pounding, grinding or steaming away, and the community is linked not by artificial links, but by the task of wresting a good living out of their bit of the map, and keeping a healthy give-and-take – and barter, bribe, invent, cajole, celebrate – going.

At Whitstable it is oysters – an industry having an unbroken history of two thousand years. An industry with ups and downs, so that the traditional ways have had to be adapted.

And the harbour, which is a working harbour, with stone and

seadredged ballast on the quays, a sizeable fleet of fishing boats and a good import and export trade. It is important because it is near the mouth of the Swale, which runs into the Thames estuary, and also provides a link with the River Medway. In its present form, the harbour dates from 1832, and since it had traditionally been the port for Canterbury, was developed to supply the coal for that city. In 1830 the first passenger steam railway in the world was built linking Canterbury to Whitstable. The fare was 9d each way. The engine of the first journey, the *Invicta*, can be seen in Canterbury, a star attraction of the celebrations in 1980 to mark the 150th anniversary of the opening of the line.

Today the Harbour Authority is Canterbury City Council. Cargo exports and imports have increased; imports include gravel, steel, wood and grain, while exports include agricultural equipment, cereals, aggregates and fertilizer. At one end of the harbour the fishing boats, some of them from Ramsgate and neighbouring ports, rock and bump in the tidal water while fishermen sit in them mending their nets. Ross have an inland wholesale unit on the quayside, with refrigerating rooms in which one can easily imagine becoming frozen to the fish fingers. The firm takes in fish from thirty-two local sources among others, including spare-time fishermen (on the larger trawlers, fish is frozen on board). The catch will depend upon whether it is a good season, and on the fish quotas. (Where stock has been over-fished a quota is fixed for that species; vessels are only licensed to take out that amount of fish fixed by quota for their district; each vessel is licensed for a certain amount of fish.) The herring season, for instance, is a short period for two to three weeks in March; there is a small quota for the Blackwater area, only. There is an equivalent quota for sole in the North Sea, their season, as for other prime fish such as lemon sole and sea bass, being the summer. (The time for cod and whiting is September and October; January and February are slacker periods, when the weather is unfavourable anyway).

At the harbour and elsewhere, there are boatyards. Whitstable is almost as famous for yachts as for oysters. Anderson Rigden and Perkin are large yacht and boat builders and marine engineers – 'They'll build you anything' – and Ziegal are famous for fibreglass yachts and the catamarans they export. Beyond the sea wall boats are moored in the estuary. Along the wall timber boatsheds are painted black with pitch. There are upturned boats, shingle and tide wrack; narrow alleyways down which men are hammering wood in sheds; the old oyster stores; a black hulk beside a black house; and far out in the estuary, red-sailed sailing barges gliding like galleons towards Faversham and the Isle of Sheppey. (The formation of the Kentish Sail Association in 1972, and the Swale Smack and Sailing Barge Matches now held annually, have attracted traditional craft to these waters, where Thames barges have sailed for over two hundred years).

In Island Wall, into which other streets called 'wall' run, a row of modern council flats for the elderly – the Saltings – have their upper storeys gabled and painted black like boathouses; the most ingenious bit of modern architecture, and one which has won two awards, one from the Environment Department, and one from the Civic Trust. Boats pervade Whitstable. The town and the tide are one, and remind me of Peggotty's Yarmouth in *David Copperfield*, and the house in an upturned boat. During floods, perhaps, the inhabitants might sigh with David:

... a mound or two might have improved it; and ... if the land had been a little more separated from the sea, and the town and the tide had not been quite so much mixed up, like toast and water, it would have been nicer.[6]

Sea defences are a major problem in Whitstable. 'Mend the Sea Wall *Now*' slogans were in windows after the 1978 floods, but a man in a boatshed told me that the groynes which hold the shingle in place were the vital factor and had been damaged (and were wrongly designed compared to old ones anyway). Newspapers have stressed the fact that the Department of the Environment has not got funds to spend on sea defences, or for beach material which costs over £7 a cubic metre. But the Canterbury City Council has taken its case against the Department of the Environment to the High Court, in their determination to ensure that Whitstable is adequately protected. Beaches are being eroded, and a radio report quoted the south-east as sinking at a rate of one foot every hundred years, with tides getting higher. Flood damage is compensated for, but at places such as Davington, near Faversham, where land has been contaminated by salt and sheep drowned, farmers are naturally bitter that sea walls are not high enough.

This is a burden that all these towns along our shifting shoreline have to carry. A new flood warning system has been initiated at Herne Bay and Whitstable, and inhabitants have long been aware of the threat. If the Thames higher up floods London before the barrier there is completed, it will not be because the inhabitants of Herne Bay and Whitstable have not raised their voices.

*

'Whitstable's a funny place – you discover it ...' Terry Pryor told me. I stopped to talk to him outside his house because he was standing by his bicycle, and people who bicycle have the time and mind for places and people; we went back to visit him again because he is a painter, with an artist's ability to see the world clearly.

His house is on the landward side of the High Street, snugly podded in one of the intersecting rows whose main feature is their backs and the twittens that run between them. These backs are a maze of sheds, alleys, greenhouses, gates, with shrimping nets drying on the sheds, budgies chirping from doors, roses and lilac bursting the walls at the seams – one yard so overgrown with giant hydrangeas and vines that its lace-curtained house was drowning in a froth of summer. This is a territory that warms the heart, as homely and spicy as whelk stalls or weatherworn clothes or Christmas, and as alive as a dozen beehives.

Typically, Whitstable people have had nicknames such as Hook-'em-on Ramsey, Rub-a-Dub Rigden, Lappy Horne, Jack the Dasher Wyles, and Whitstable words range from nipcheese (mean) and puckersnatched (cold) to cluther bucket (buzz off) and pill garlic (a poor specimen of a man).

Whitstable residents value the shape of their town, and recently a plan for radical alterations to the town centre roads was turned down. Terry Pryor bought his house very cheaply some years ago, and used it at first as a weekend cottage. Inside the rooms gleam with beautifully carved and polished cupboards and surrounds and bookcases which he has made from secondhand wardrobes sawn to shape. One cost 4s 9d in the old days. 'I like to keep things *going*,' Terry said. And he told us you could live very cheaply in Whitstable. 'You look over the wall and say, do you want that pile of wood ... and exchange.'

87

Mrs Pryor welcomed us like friends of long standing. 'You must see Hernhill and Chilham, we'll take you there ...'

Upstairs are Terry's studio and study, which is equally full of paints and books. He generously gave us sketches of Whitstable, and showed us his vibrantly coloured land- and seascapes, and abstract paintings, some built up over sand on rabbit-skin size – 'Wedgwood Benn has one in his office.'

'There's a wonderful light here ... a Nordic light,' he said. 'It changes over the sea. Sometimes the sea is the colour of lemon juice ... There are the beautiful tones of the black boatsheds against the walls, and marvellous textures ... and the seaweed and roses. Whitstable smells of decomposed seaweed when the sea's out and clean seaweed when it's in. Marvellous, the seaweed and roses ...'

In June, England is not just Wimbledon and strawberries, but Whitstable and roses, and seaweed ... And when there is an 'r' in the month, oysters.

*

In about AD 80, Julius Agricola first exported oysters from the North Kent coast to Rome. Today, there is only one man dredging oysters regularly from the sea at Whitstable, and the Royal Native Oyster Stores, with the royal arms on its brick front, are no longer in use as such. So the yawls – the sailing-smacks which were used by the dredgers and later converted to motor – no longer carry the triangular wrought-iron dredges, although one or two take part, with the red-sailed charter sailing barges from Faversham creek, in the Smack and Sailing Barge matches. At Whitstable, other oyster sheds stand empty, like huge barns without a harvest.

In 1793, the Company of Dredgers who had had exclusive right under licence from the Lord of the Manor, from time immemorial, over the portion of the Manor of Whitstable covered by the sea, became the owners and were incorporated by an act of Parliament under the title of 'The Company of Free Fishers and Dredgers of Whitstable'.[7] The Whitstable Oyster Fishery Company, their successors, who were entitled to call their oysters Royal Whitstable Natives, owned beds of several thousand acres (and, I was told, the territory cannot by law be leased, so that when after a bad year across the Channel in 1953, Dutchmen tried to lease the rights, they could not do so). The stores were part of the freehold. Here the oysters were cleaned and graded, being kept in pits over which the tide flowed, changing the water, and later being sorted into tubs. The boats might not be able to get off for a week or two, so a reserve had to be kept.

The decline of the trade has several causes, not least being natural hazards. (The jingle about an 'r' in the month was in fact brought in to protect the oyster, which used to be eaten all the year round.) Their main enemy was freezing weather, when the sea froze over. Bad years, when millions were killed, were 1895, 1929, 1947 and 1963. They were also hit by disease in the 1920s. Since 1963 the beds have declined.

Brian Hadler, who lives in Whitstable, and is also a member of the life-boat crew, has done major research on the Whitstable industry and its social history, and is working on a book. He generously helped me with information, and in his article 'The Rise and Fall of the Whitstable Oyster',[8] tells of the role of the Freemen of the Company, who had a seven-year apprenticeship. (His grandfather and his grandfather's brothers were Freemen.) In 1838 there were 190 men with fifty boats, by 1847, 250 men with 150 boats. Because of large falls of spat (spawn) in the 1850s, by the 1860s, Whitstable's prime era, over £100,000 worth of oysters were sold on the London market in one year. (In 1912, over nineteen million oysters were still being landed at Whitstable.) If no spat fell, stocks became depleted and oysters would have to be bought from Essex or France, but would be relaid and fattened on the unique local algae to become the distinctive Natives. By 1881 there were 500 Freemen, and from then on, only the eldest sons of Freemen were allowed entry. Some of the others became Flatsmen, who scratched a living on the Kentish flats. (In 1900 there were 600 Flatsmen, by 1914, 200.) But they used to say, Bill Coleman, whose father was a Flatsman, told us, that 'a Flatsman would never starve', because he could probably get enough oysters in two or three days to keep going for a fortnight, and in his dredge he would also catch mussels, crabs and fish, so that all he needed was the money for his tea, sugar, bread and a bit of rent. Freemen were not allowed to work at night, so during those hours, Flatsmen, who during the day had to work over free territory off Herne Bay, could do a bit of poaching.

The Seasalter and Ham was another oyster company, and Seasalter Shellfish is their successor (based at Whitstable, not at Seasalter, which is just along the coast and named after its one-time salt-pans). To reach Seasalter Shellfish you dodge under cranes on the quay, and come to a wire fence. 'Rather secret,' a man beaching a rowing-boat told me, grinning. I went into a caged area, and heard the sound of water being filtered through tanks, outside the buildings. Inside, there was no sign of anyone; bright lights, notices and mysterious equipment. I was weighing up a descriptive alternative between Dracula and James Bond, when a door down a passage opened and a sparkling blonde in jeans, barefooted in sandals, came across the puddles of salt water. A James Bond set up, clearly.

'I can show you round. No, not a scientist ... just experienced. It's a very pleasant place to work,' Sarah Lane smiled. She is in charge of the growing of the algae, which is an oyster's staple diet. Four main kinds of algae are grown in bulk, starting off from cultures in test tubes, having been isolated from natural cultures taken from the sea at Whitstable. John Cashman, who studied microbiology at East Anglia and who runs Seasalter, believes in getting the best local diet for his oysters. (It is certain algae carried down by freshwater streams and the unique mixture of fresh and salt water at Whitstable which have made its oysters thrive above all others.) The algae are then grown in tall plastic drums, which are kept warm and under bright light. I was shown one type, a green 'motile' species, Tetraselmis, swimming about under a microscope.

In another room are adult oysters (Whitstable Natives and Japanese oysters) and clams, in tubs of pasteurized water. When a release of fertilized eggs is obtained, it is transferred to other tubs for the larvae to grow. Strangely, oysters can sometimes change sex; an oyster which has grown eggs can stop producing eggs and produce male sperm instead. The millions of minute larvae look at first like specks of sugar, and then like small bits of grit, which you can pick up on a finger like rough sand. Looking closer, you can see a small black dot with its shell forming round it. A Native takes seven years to become adult, a Japanese oyster two, but these young growth are sold when they are about 1.5 mm in size, and Seasalter need to sell two or three million a month to be economic.

The oysters are sold worldwide, particularly to places such as the Channel Islands, where there is no pollution in the sea, and also to many beds and fisheries in this country.

None of the people working at Seasalter seemed keen on eating oysters, however. 'It puts you right off,' said Sarah, eyeing the clams with their 'lifesticks', their prong-like syphons like white arms which suck in air and then expel it. But the adult oysters in their tubs, with their rough and barnacled shells, look cool and rare.

*

And the man who still dredges oysters? Bill Coleman, whose boat the *Gamecock* rides at anchor out in the bay. He is a shipwright, specializing in traditional craft. After the storms of early 1978, repairs to damaged boats took all his time for four months. But he has been dredging oysters in the winter months in his spare time for fifteen years. The *Gamecock* was built in Whitstable in 1908, and is a traditional smack. She was a wreck in the harbour when he bought her. Next year he plans to treat the sails, tanning them to preserve them, and they will then be the dark red which looks so magnificent on a grey sea.

Bill Coleman sells oysters for breeding to Seasalter Shellfish, and also sells to local pubs. The season starts in September and goes on until February, but whereas the ground or 'soil' is soft in the autumn, making a good home for the oysters who have finished laying their spat there, after Christmas with the easterly winds, the ground becomes too hard for the oysters to be reached, and only the 'waifs and strays' are caught.

We arranged to go dredging with him, and he was genuinely anxious to tell us all he could about the subject, showed us books, and was concerned for the skills to be told to a wider public. But the weather continually frustrated us, although he was unworried. 'I'm used to it,' he said, as he telephoned to tell us that fog had descended over Whitstable, or that a gale was pounding the coast, just as we were packing up our gumboots. We were impatient, but the discipline imposed by the climate on those who depend on it – fishermen, farmers – becomes transmuted into something mellower and more difficult to define, a philosophy of seeing what the day will bring, of knowing that there will be another day.

On one of these occasions we had got as far as Herne Bay, and the day did bring us luck, because we stayed overnight with Mr and Mrs Crome. In the hall of their comfortable house was a print of a 'Mr Crome' – engraver and landscape painter. The face had curiously triangular black eyebrows. Near it was a photograph of the present Mr Crome's father, with the same dark triangular eyebrows. We hesitated to ask, but were glad we did. John Crome the painter, Mrs Crome told us, had a 'black sheep son', Michael, who went on the stage and then to Ireland and finished up in a garret in Hornsey, starting the London branch of the family. Would the painter's talent re-emerge? Mrs Crome told us that her daughter paints and her son, creative in his own line, is going to be a chef. 'It's bound to come out some time, isn't it?' she said.

Herne Bay is not as attractive as Whitstable, seeming as flat and long as the coastline, with windswept streets, and restaurants which tend to be closed 'for a well deserved break', when it is not the holiday season. (However, inland at Herne is a church whose tower Ruskin called one of the few perfect things in the world.) We were glad when we finally reached Whitstable, on an October day of autumn mist and promise, and saw the *Gamecock* riding towards us as we stood on the harbour arm, her solidly graceful build becoming sharper as she moved out of the fog across the pale water. Painted white, she was like a ghost ship, a boat emerging from the past, but the sun caught on the small metal gamecock on the mast which Bill Coleman's nephew had made for him in his school metalwork class, and he himself greeted us with the business-like lack of fuss of a sailor at work, alert and concerned with the possibilities of the day.

Whitstable is now the only place on the English coast where boats lie at anchor in the open sea. At one time there would have been over 700 boats there; now there are about 150, but the *Gamecock* is the only working oyster smack. 'What these boats had to put up with (in the old days),' Bill Coleman told us. 'Out at sea all winter ... you'd never credit it.' He showed us where to stow our gear, and the tea and condensed milk we had brought for the galley – a neat area with a gas stove and an old coal-burning stove which he usually lights on a day's work to dry out the boat. There are two bunks, and he is converting the cabin to make it more comfortable for himself and his wife on summer weekend cruises up the Swale creeks, and to make more room for the crew to sleep in during racing events, when the boat is under sail (he was using the motor when we went out – there was no wind anyway).

Because of the anchorage, you go out on the high tide, and won't be able to get back until the next high tide. (Spring tides are better than neap tides, as there won't be a couple of hours slack.) When the area to be dredged is reached, the boat is allowed to drift down sideways across the tide, so that the dredges aren't pulled along too fast – or if under motor, the same speed is used. A boat under power can enable three times the number of oysters to be dredged. Whitstable is now the last place in the open sea where dredging is done, so to preserve the precious stock of Whitstable oysters, which is now also depleted by large fishing boats, Bill Coleman suggested to the authorities that they should ban all dredging under power (as is the case in the Fowey estuary), and allow hand gear only. They would not agree, so he decided that, 'to hell with it', as he said, he would use power too. 'They're killing the fishing ... It was a living for them, in the old days. It's all grab today.' And he also had sharp words for the way oil pollution is treated. 'Spraying does more damage. It pushes the oil down (to kill marine life). They'd do better to let it come ashore.'

As we went along, he told us about the trade (he first went out with his father when he was fourteen), and about local history, on which subject he is very knowledgeable. 'That ripple is the Reach – if you come up too far, you go ashore on that. That over there is called Whitstable Street. It stretches out to sea. They say it's an old Roman road, but it's certainly moved.' A buoy marks the underwater hazard – 'Whitstable Street'. It is strange to realize that the seabed can be as varied and familiar as roads or fields, or a garden, to which oyster beds have often been compared (in the summer they had to be weeded and cleaned). *'It is literally true to say that the oyster beds at Whitstable are as carefully prepared and maintained though always under water, as if they were flower beds on the shore,'* A. O. Collard wrote at the beginning of the century.[9] The dredger's harvest is like a farmer's, to be nurtured and culled with care, and protected from vermin and predators, and is naturally protected from frost by the sea and the shale.

The peaked black weatherboarding of the Whitstable boatsheds had long since disappeared in the mist behind us. We passed two boats out fishing and some whelk pots. We 'ran down' for about thirty-five minutes and then turned east. When we were about two-and-a-half miles off Herne Bay, Bill Coleman started dredging, and we worked the ground 'from the Mill and the Pier in the Stream' to 'the Claypits', over the 'Confetti Beds', on the flats, named after a rich fall of spat. First one dredge is put out, to 'cut the cream off the milk', or test the soil lightly to see what is there. The dredges are double-sided rectangular nets or bags of chain-links looped together with wire or unravelled ship's rope, which fold together to draw up the catch, and have an iron frame to cut into the ground at the front and to protect the lower sides of the net. Under sail, a crew of three may work two hand dredges each, or vice versa; the two large dredges used when we went out were lowered on pulleys from a derrick. The tiller was fixed with a peg, according to a compass on the deck. 'I lost the other peg the other day.' We didn't offer to help. 'I took these people out the other day ... said they knew all about steering a boat ... all over the place ... got in the way ...'

The first dredge brought up shale and a few shells. The next one a little farther on spilled open on to the desk with a sea harvest – jellyfish, crabs, starfish, mussel shells, small sea-urchins ('we call them burrs'), oyster shells – and oysters. Starfish arms were sticking out of the wire-netting, small crabs scuttled frantically over the deck. Bill Coleman's hands worked with the speed of lightning sorting out the oysters and whelks to throw in his baskets. He cut his hand on an urchin; but never wears gloves. Large oysters can be sold for breeding; four-year-olds are about the best size to eat and their age can be told by the rings on their shells, some of which are covered with weed or tiny pink shells ('We call them quats – they squirt liquid into your eyes and make them smart'). An old oyster can live to fifty or sixty years.

Whelks went in one basket. The £2.50 they would fetch pays for a day's fuel. A basket full of the right-sized oysters will fetch £20. One hundred and fifty to 200 oysters is reckoned a day's catch (the big trawlers will take out 800), and although we did well that day, it was what would in general have been called a 'sheep's head day', when the lack of wind would have meant just enough oysters to buy a sheep's head.

The sea and sky were blue all round us. The sun was white. A migrating starling settled in the rigging for a rest and accompanied us. 'They have to look out the gulls don't eat them.' The water lapped gently against the hull; the engine throbbed quietly. Between hawls I made mugs of tea in the cabin. A dredge came up with starfish bulging like oats in a bag; they feed on butterfish and oysters. Hermit crabs peered from their shells. 'We call them farmers.' There was sponge-weed and pipeweed – the scourge of Whitstable – sea anemones, large horse mussels – which aren't eaten and which have a minute 'pea' crab inside their shells – Spanish crabs, more oysters.

'Are you enjoying it?' Bill Coleman asked us anxiously, and kindly, when he could draw breath between the two dredges and the tiller. 'It's a lovely time of year. They say the weather alters, but I can go back twenty years and pick out days, the weather will have been the same on the same day in the years before.'

Now the sea and sky were white as milk; the sun melting on the water in a golden path. One gull floated on the surface like a toy in a bath; the space around us was filled with silence.

We were going over a different area. Where there were small, two-year-old oysters, because here there was plenty of 'soil' so that the brood hadn't got washed away. These small oysters are very pretty, with pink-tinged shells. Then finally an area over what is called 'Puddington Rock' or the 'Pudding Pans' – rock with puddock holes in it which crumbles away when dry and which was used by the Romans, Bill Coleman told us, to make cement. Roman Samian ware has been found in this area (we only found a modern green lager bottle), but no one knows whether a spit of land once ran out here, where pots were made, or whether they came from a ship which was sunk here. Divers have found no trace of one.

The dredges were hauled in for the last time (they are very heavy to heave on board, with a skilled movement, as John found when he caught hold of one to help). As we turned for home the boat rocked gently, then was almost motionless again. The flat sea was now oily as petrol or white condensed milk, indistinguishable from the colourless sky. Another single gull floated with the boat towards the sun, which burnt pinkly with a single cloud beneath it shaped like a man's profile, or snow-capped mountain.

For a while the boat began to rock more violently, seemed to make no progress. Images of hidden sucking sandbanks came into my mind. I looked at Bill Coleman's face. He was peering into the distance, seemed to be frowning. Had we come farther than he thought? Would we stay rocking here in the mist while a storm got up? It seemed unlikely anyone would find us.

Then slowly we moved forward again. I realized that Bill's exceptionally keen blue eyes could see farther than we could, and that he certainly knew where we were. Later he could see, although we could not, Herne Bay pier on the haze of skyline.

We didn't talk much. Nothing was needed except the space which at sea encroaches on you and sets you free – a new dimension, not known on land. I had never understood before why someone might want to spend all his days sailing. Now, with one hand on the tough furled canvas, I did understand. It was a rare day, an unmarred day of golden white light, poised between summer and winter.

'You don't often get a day like this,' Bill Coleman said. And then, 'It's associated with this weather, and you get all the migrating birds.' It also used to be called 'spratting weather', in October and November, when birds feed on the sprats, so you could tell where certain fish were and drop a net, and as the tide went away it washed the sprats into it – this was called 'stowboating'.

'Fifteen buoys were taken away last year. All the ships have some sort of radar now, so they know where they are. They talk about deep-sea fishing, but an estuary chap needs to be far cleverer. You can tell by the colour of the water ...' (He also had a certain amount of scorn for the Essex men who dredge in creeks, rather than in the sea.)

'It'll never come back. You've got to have about ten million oysters this year, of all different grades, to start next year's oysters off – no one can afford to lay that number. It takes about fifty million oysters to start a fishery. The French oysters are in as bad a way as ours.'

The red sun was going down now. Black rings of gulls on the water; thin zebra stripes of black crossing the sun, and two geese streaming westwards towards the horizon. Then the sea indistinguishable from sky and the land looming darkly, sprinkled with lights. A strange crying and croaking, like a million frogs, from the shore – curlews. 'They have to get their dinner when the tide's

Alleyway by the Stour at Sandwich

Pegwell Bay, Kent

Richborough Castle, with power station in distance

Dickens House, Broadstairs

The Custom House and the
Queen's Head, Ramsgate

World War II Spitfire, RAF Manston

Faversham Creek

Bill Coleman oyster dredging on *Gamecock* off Whitstable

running, before the mud is covered.' (Bill Coleman knows his birds, and another great passion, besides oysters, is wildfowling, shooting with punt guns up the Swale river. 'I have three great passions . . .' he laughed.)

We had come back a little early, and had to wait for the tide, a short distance from *Gamecock*'s mooring anchor. He told us more about the shipbuilding trade, and that there were only seven firms building wooden boats in England, two in southern England, one of which is Anderson Rigden and Perkin at Whitstable, who will build a wooden boat for you. 'But wooden boats are coming back,' he said, although most are still fibreglass. He also told us of the grey seals which can be seen on uncovered sand out from Whitstable (as on the Goodwins). Mentioning the recent outcry over the Orkneys seal cull, he said, 'You can't have a garden without weeding it. Man was put on this planet to hunt everything that grows – he's the only one that does it.'

The tide rose, and we could slip over to the drum to which he moored the boat. Then he rowed us ashore, a task made harder because *Gamecock* now has to be moored 500 metres out because of the zealous council's 'wave machine' to detect dangerously high tides. 'Our surveyor also put a light on the end of Herne Bay pier. It had to have its battery changed by helicopter once a week –' his voice of incredulous scorn. 'Now they've got batteries which can be changed every three months.'

We landed, and pulled the dinghy up the shingle, and went with him to the Pearson's Arms pub opposite the Royal Native Oyster Stores for a drink, a warming rum and orange. It is an exceptionally good pub, and serves fresh seafood. (Oysters were at that date priced at £2 for half a dozen.)

Outside, in the night, the *Gamecock*'s small riding light shone through the darkness far beyond the harbour mouth. Larger boats use it to tell where the harbour mouth is, despite their radar. It is like a small friendly beacon, marking the way to Whitstable.

*

On another day we drove along the flat marshy coastline beyond the modern suburbs (Tankerton is the modern 'beach' suburb in the other direction), to the reedy, low-lying area bordered with bungalows, chalets and caravans, that is Seasalter. We stopped at

Ye Olde Sportsman pub and had some Bishop's Finger Ale which is brewed by Shepherd Neame in Faversham and which is powerful enough to take one's mind off suburbs.

'Two Bishop's Fingers, please,' has a strange ring to it. The conversation in the pub could perhaps be put down to its potency – it was as crude as the oil from a tanker, and came from two neatly hatted matrons perched on bar-stools. 'Well, they do say the morning's the best time ...' and they dissolved in gales of laughter to make a gull blush.

And so on to Faversham, which is a town like Leominster in Herefordshire which basks in tatters of past grandeur of unimaginable size, although here there is still much activity going on. Faversham lies on the old Watling Street, the Dover Road which is the access-way to Europe, and Faversham Creek comes right into the heart of the town. Many Saxon and Roman remains have been found (the Roman settlement was Durolevum), and an important Saxon collection is in the British Museum. In Roman times, the area between Faversham and Rochester was thick with potteries. Faversham was the 'Fair Town' of the Saxons and in a charter of the Saxon king Coenwulf was called 'the King's little town of Fafresham'. In the early Middle Ages it became a Limb of the Cinque Port of Dover. King Stephen, grandson of William the Conqueror, chose it as his burial place and founded a great abbey here, the abbey church being nearly four hundred feet long. Excavations in 1965 showed that it was larger than Westminster Abbey in Edward the Confessor's day or Canterbury Cathedral at the time of Lanfranc. The town still has two breweries, Whitbreads and its own Shepherd Neame; the carefully preserved wide Abbey Street with fine houses, one, number five, with windows which span two floors through which a gallery and chandeliers can be seen; a market place with a curiously attractive sixteenth-century Guildhall (Shakespeare played with Lord Leicester's company in Faversham market place); many other notable buildings, and the Chart Gunpowder Mills dating to the late eighteenth century (Elizabeth I patronized the opening of the original mills; the trade had an eventful history, and in 1847 a bad explosion killed twenty people and was heard as far away as Maidstone).

Faversham is also a town of mills, of seeds and chemicals, joinery works and timber, fruit canning works. The port, on the creek, is a busy one, although when the tide is out, it has only a thin stream of water between mudflats. Coasters from the Continent bring bulk fertilizer for Agrigano; grain is brought in the Crescent Shipping motor barges for Pauls and Whites Foods Ltd animal food mills down on the creek. From the Upper Brents, or Front Brents which run along the far side of the creek, you see steam rise from the brewery chimneys in satisfying juxtaposition to the fine filigree lantern tower and steeple of the Parish Church; the smell of beer drifts on the air with the smell of elderflower bushes; cranes clank; mills whine; gulls peck in the coffee-coloured mud banks; workmen hurry home to lunch past upturned rowing boats; ragwort and wild roses blow in the wind from the sea.

In Abbey Street, beyond and opposite alleys with names such as Smack Alley, is a house near the ruins of the abbey, number 80, in which the Mayor, Thomas Arden, was murdered at the instigation of his wife in 1550, by her lover and two accomplices. It is a gruesome story, retold in Holinshed's *Chronicles* and in the Faversham Wardmote Book with phrases such as 'strake him with a taylor's great pressing Iron upon the scull to the braine', followed by throat-cutting. The wife was burned to death at Canterbury, her lover hanged at Smithfield, another accomplice hounded to Flushing and burnt there, and only the fourth, called 'Loosebagg', escaped. The play *Arden of Faversham*, published in 1592, has immortalized the dramatic story, being the first tragedy to be about people who were not princes or great rulers.

The country round Faversham is a mixture of wide, airy views of the flats round the creek, of the sky-filled estuary, with its misty outlines of barges, of island shapes looming and changing like water, and of rich, fruit filled hollows. Apple trees and gooseberry bushes thrive in neat rows, and near Graveney are cherry orchards, full of gypsy-like vans with cherry-pickers at the ready. This is one of Kent's famed fruit areas, and in this and other ways, Faversham has kept the best of many possible worlds.

Beyond Faversham, on the Medway estuary, was the most northeasterly of the Limbs of the Cinque Ports (except for Brightlingsea in Essex). Grange was a Non-Corporate Member of Hastings, but was not equal in importance to the modern Chatham which has superseded it. It was in the sixteenth century that the Medway became vital to the Navy, and the peninsula now covered by dock-yards was found to be an ideal place to refit ships. Chatham, which would need a book in itself to describe, did not take over the role of Cinque Port. The manor and hamlet of Grange merged into Gillingham, which applied for membership of the Ports in 1937, but was rejected.

Brightlingsea, the only one of the ports away from the southeast coast, was a Non-Corporate Member of Sandwich, and the Mayor Deputy of Brightlingsea, whose job it is to pay ship money to the Head Port, has a ceremonial chain which is made of crossed silver fishes and silver oyster shells, with a medallion containing one of the largest opals in the world. No doubt the town once challenged Whitstable in dredging oysters from the gardens of the shore.

who thought there should be more sea-police and who was secretly in debt, the Wife of Bath with her flowing mantle concealing wide hips and past lovers, the honest ploughman not ashamed to cart dung.

They are still there, and more, because there are larger contingents from abroad. There are wives of Bath in plenty, matrons from Australia and Canada, American women in black with thongs, bedraggled Vikings, an Irish hospital sister on holiday, with a wide brow, thin lips and lace petticoat; a young man with pale face, furled umbrella and books in a plastic bag, ornate Arabs, leerers in tweed blazers with wide striped ties, elegant Scandinavian single women, dwarves, a Spanish peasant with bullfighter curls on the nape of the neck leading his small son by the hand; women with blanket-cloth skirts to the floor, French children in kerchiefs, men with sticks; priests, teachers, oriental monks, men in wheelchairs. There are enough cameras to build a cathedral, enough ice-creams being licked inside and out with a crunch of cornets to waken the dead. The pilgrims arrive by car, coach and train. A Japanese in the train asks me desperately: 'Do you know where is Tintern Abbey where Becket was murdered? . . . This tour says one and threequarter hours – I have two hours then I must go to Paris . . . And where was Churchill living before he died?'

Buses, coaches, lorries and motorbikes thunder through the Westgate – through which came countless kings, including Henry II in penitence to be scourged for the murder of Becket, and Henry V in triumph from Agincourt – past Joe Coral and the Golden Gate Chinese Restaurant, the Pak-Koh I Noor Restaurant and 'Chop Suey Bar', the obtrusive sign saying 'Gentlemen' and the Falstaff Hotel, established 1403. Up St Peter's Street and the High Street the crowds throng in cars and on foot, with blue swollen legs in plastic shoes more uncomfortable than pilgrim's sandals, under the beams of genuine Tudor houses, past gilt and flint and schoolgirl screams from The Weavers where boats glide on the river, and the best of British wares in the shops and tawdry trinkets. With flowing robes and short shorts and bared bosoms and occasionally beautiful faces, and rucksacks, and larger rucksacks, they teem with a surge of expectation and a susurration of camera shutters through the sixteenth-century Christchurch Gate with its coloured coats of arms and a niche for the absent statue of Christ (lassoed by Cromwell's soldiers). Up to three million people visit the Cathedral in a year. Not one will be disappointed.

*

Sited on the River Stour, Canterbury is a natural place for a settlement, and probably was founded as such in the Stone Age. The first known large settlement was in about 300 BC – remains of a palisade and ditch of this date have been discovered in Castle Street. When Belgic tribes came from the Continent, they fortified a camp at Bigbury, a little to the north. It was this camp which Julius Caesar stormed in 54 BC. By the time of the Claudian invasion, the Belgae had settled in Canterbury. The Romans replanned the city, and made it a key centre for the administration of Kent – Durovernum, the city of the marsh. Here Watling Street, which ran from Richborough, and the roads from Dover and Lympne (Lemanis), met, before going on to London, and for four hundred years the legions marched through this junction. The city walls have Roman foundations, from the third century, when defence was becoming vital; there was a Roman theatre, the largest so far known in Britain, public baths, barracks, villas. Recently pieces of coloured Italian marble and other rich fragments have been found, indicating most probably a temple courtyard.

In Butchery Lane is a fine example of a Roman mosaic floor, which would have belonged to a town house. This is in the part of the city which was badly bombed in 1942, and where redevelopment has made excavation possible. Excavations are in fact a striking part of the scene in Canterbury today; sun-bronzed backs bend tirelessly and carefully over the sun-baked earth, as pit after pit, layer after layer is uncovered. It is a race against time, a rescue operation; each site has to be negotiated with the redevelopers before building begins, and the work done before the past is buried again. As I write, there is eighteen months left before the Marlowe carpark site, for instance, is redeveloped. The Canterbury Archaeological Trust is a recently created unit, now a registered charity, and appointed its first professional archaeologist in 1975. Because it is recent it receives a fraction of the funds from the Department of the Environment that other urban areas are granted; an appeal for £200,000 has been launched and urgently needs support. Apart from the Roman finds, this is after all archaeologically the richest area of Anglo-Saxon England, with Canterbury its chief city. Superb Anglo-Saxon jewellery has been found; an engraved pocket sundial was found in the cloister gardens; in the Cathedral crypt other treasures have been on display, such as a silver and brown glass pendant found in the grave of a Saxon girl of six, on the back of which is a cross which only shows in a certain light. This is typical of the cunning artistry of that age, a sophistication brought home by a bone comb found on the Watling Street/Rose Lane excavation site – well shaped with large even teeth on one side and small teeth on the other. These finds open one's eyes, sometimes with a sense of shock. A find from Rosemary Lane – a 1976–7 excavation – is a first-century Roman bowl of dark-red Samian ware with a relief of pornographic designs. A man blowing two pipes has a giant's phallus which rises towards a woman presenting her naked back to him, head becking over shoulder, in the stance of a cancan dancer at the final line-up. The design is repeated, with a slickness that artistically has something of the Soho poster about it – somewhat disillusioning if one had a mental image of stern legionaries forever marching or taking salubrious baths in the hot room of the bath house.

For Tim Tatton-Brown, who is Director of Archaeology at Canterbury, it is the discovery of the layout and structure of buildings that is of prime interest. Understanding of the Anglo-Saxon pattern in the sixth and seventh centuries is newly coming to light, revealing a great Anglo-Saxon town here with huts built inside the ruins of the Roman town. From about AD 650 kings and archbishops were producing coinage in one of England's earliest mints. England's first penny was minted here in 780. (Earlier Iron-Age coins have also been found, including a unique coin of Cunobelin, Shakespeare's Cymbeline, who was recognized by the Romans to be the King of Britain or leading chieftain. The coin has a boat on one side, with anchor, mast and sails – the first boat ever to have been found on a pre-Roman coin.)

Tim Tatton-Brown has been an archaeologist since he left school, and has worked in areas as varied as the City of London, Italy and Turkey. His unit headquarters is a ramshackle building on a peppercorn rent. Here the tons of pottery found each week have to be sorted, shelved, or sent to experts on a particular period. Here careful drawings are made. Workers are a mixture of paid and voluntary, with grants under the Job Creation Scheme for school leavers. Archaeology is one of the few professions remaining where a prior course or degree is not essential. 'People with degrees are often useless until they have worked on excavations,' I was told. I asked what were the essential skills. 'The ability to work neatly ... to do physical work ... to understand soil levels,' Tim Tatton-Brown replied, and he pointed out that women have been involved in archaeology for a long time, not necessarily, as I suggested, because they might be neater, but because they can be 'just as good with a pick and shovel as men'. Archaeology is not all jewellery and finds.

It may take a site supervisor about four years to reach his position. One who had trained as an engineer had found that career not very challenging, 'just a routine job'. The rewards of archaeology are outside work and the interest involved, 'enjoyment rather than money'. The enjoyment and interest spread out to the thousands who now take an interest in local history, as well as archaeology, and every piece of knowledge of these past civilizations could still help us shape or protect our own.

*

The Saxon name for Canterbury was *Cantwarabyrig* – the stronghold of the people of Kent. There had been a number of Christian churches there in Roman times, and when St Augustine came with his mission, he rebuilt some of them, including St Martin's Church where Queen Bertha had worshipped before his arrival, and where he is said to have christened King Ethelbert, and a church on the site of the Cathedral, which was dedicated to Christ, so that it remains the Cathedral Church of Christ to this day. Some of his monks lived with him near the Cathedral, while others lived in the monastery outside the city walls which later became St Augustine's Abbey.

From this time, the history of Canterbury, by then one of the half-dozen most important towns in the country, is highlighted by the lives of great men in both the spiritual and temporal worlds. Archbishop Theodore of Tarsus, a Greek from Rome, who collected masters about him to instruct all who wished to learn, founded a school at Canterbury which was later refounded to become the King's School (in the reign of Henry VIII). Bede writes of his era: 'Nor were there ever happier times since the English came into Britain.'² St Dunstan, the saint and statesman who was also an artist and craftsman; St Alphege, who was carried off by Danish raiders in 1011 and who refused to allow his tenants to ransom him, so that he was pelted to death with beef bones during an orgy; Lanfranc who at the age of seventy rebuilt the Cathedral, which had been destroyed by fire in 1067, taking only seven years to get the work done; his disciple the saint and scholar Anselm; the great warrior archbishop and saint Becket; the architects William of Sens and William the Englishman, and later, Henry Yevele; the Black Prince.

The Archbishop of Canterbury has, from the time of St Dunstan, crowned the King or Queen of England. These two powers in the land have been interrelated, and in the early days have struggled for supremacy, archbishops opposing the secular powers of the monarch and upholding the role of the Church, a fight which led to the murder of Thomas à Becket. It was also a fight of internationalism versus nationalism, in the days when an archbishop referred to Rome, a central theme of English and European history in the Middle Ages. After many centuries, one can see an echo of this theme today, the question of the identities of a particular Church, a particular monarchy, against the background of a growing tendency to merge and unify. It is also perhaps not surprising, although Christchurch Priory was the greatest landlord in southern England in the Middle Ages, that the great heroes of Canterbury have been champions of the people: Anselm who protected his tenants; Becket who in exile found French peasants lining the route as he rode because he had defied two kings to uphold the Church which was their only ally against oppression, and who, on his return to England in 1170, was greeted by the fishermen and poor of Sandwich who ran into the sea to draw his boat ashore; the Black Prince who although he loved finery and could be cruel, rekindled the patriotism of his countrymen by his conduct at Crécy and Poitiers, and who said to his ordinary foot soldiers: 'Your courage and loyalty have been well proved to me. In many times you have shown that you are not degenerate Englishmen; but flesh of their flesh and bone of their bone ...'³ His arms for peace were the three ostrich feathers which still form part of the arms of the Prince of Wales, and one of his mottoes was *'Ich dien'*, I serve.

As a counterpoint to this championship by the Church, and linked with it, is the quality of independence and freedom nurtured by the people of Kent. 'The yeomanrie, or common people ... is no where more free, and jolly, then in this shyre ...,' wrote Lambarde in 1570.[4] 'The forward in all battels belongeth to them ... there were never any bondmen ... in Kent.' And he traces this freedom back to the fact that Kent was never vanquished by William the Conqueror, but 'yeelded itself by composition'. After overthrowing Harold and taking London, William marched on Dover, but the people of Kent elected the Archbishop of Canterbury and the Abbot of St Augustine's as their captains, bore branches over their heads as they marched towards the Conqueror and then burst forth, offering him peace and obedience if he would safeguard their liberties, or if not, deadly war. He granted them, and them alone, in all England, their ancient privileges; they did not have to submit to tenant rights and by their custom of Gavelkind, every man was a freeholder with 'some part of his own to live upon'. In return,

No where else in all this realme, is the common people more willingly governed. To be short, they be most commonly civil, just, and bountiful, so that the estate of the old ... yeomen of England, either yet liveth in Kent, or else it is quite dead and departed out of the realme for altogether.

In later times, if a king or archbishop misused his power, men from Kent, like Wat Tyler in 1381, or Jack Cade seventy years later, were swift to rebel and redress the balance. In 1461 the City of Canterbury became a county in its own right, separate from the county of Kent. Even earlier, it had a democratic assembly unknown even in London.[5]

Combined with the privileges of the Cinque Ports, controlling as they did the main entries to England and those who crossed the Channel, this gave the region every claim to independence, which has shown itself through the years as an honourable liberty, which if misused sometimes led to intransigence, high-handedness and piracy. For the privileges of the Barons of the Cinque Ports were real privileges in early times, and when the Barons bore the canopy above the monarch's head at his coronation, this symbolized their power, as did their presence in full ceremonial dress at the enthronement of an archbishop, a privilege still carried on today. After the coronation of a king, the Barons laid their silver staves and the canopy in Canterbury Cathedral and acknowledged the spiritual lordship of the Church. The archbishop often had to intervene in quarrels between the ports, although legally they had their own courts.

Canterbury had its own port in Fordwich, which was later made a Limb of the Cinque Port of Sandwich. It was a busy port in the Middle Ages, importing materials for the Abbots of St Augustine's, and it was here that the Caen stone for the building of the Cathedral was unloaded.

*

'It is the bounden duty of every English-speaking man and woman to visit Canterbury at least twice in their lives.' Archbishop Frederick Temple.

'Every time I come here I find something new and even more beautiful which had escaped my notice before ... To release our souls, albeit briefly from their material imprisonment ... That is the wonder and majesty of Canterbury. That is the genius of our forefathers who in many ways understood more about life than we do now ... It means a great deal to me.'[6] Prince Charles.

*

'It's lovely inside ... go on.' Intrepid tourist, to companion.

Battle through the groups outside the door, past Buddhist monks striding through the doorway alongside party outings, school children and pilgrims. The voices, the crowds, intrude, unless it is evening, or early morning, but the voices of the past are louder, the voice of Canterbury makes itself heard.

For all its beauty of stone, it is perhaps the glass in the Cathedral, and its monuments, which make it truly unearthly. It has the oldest glass in England, some of the most important in Western Europe. Having survived Henry VIII and Cromwell and two World Wars, some pieces are now corroded to less than a quarter of their original thickness by modern atmospheric pollution. The Friends of Canterbury Cathedral have launched the Cathedral in Crisis appeal for £3,500,000.

'St Augustine Founded It.
Becket died for it.
Chaucer wrote about it.
Cromwell shot at it.
Hitler bombed it.
Time is destroying it.
Will you give to save it?'

'It's like the Forth Bridge' – Mrs Pritchard, Friend of Canterbury Cathedral.

One of the oldest action pictures in glass in the world, *Adam*, 1178, has just been returned, restored, after five years. Adam is delving, with a sheepskin and hooves tied round his waist, instead of a finicky figleaf. He is sturdy and alive. The panel was originally in the clerestory of the choir, then in the West Window of the nave. (Now in a special exhibition. 'We're not allowed to put him up because the glass is so fragile.') In the great West Window are other surviving figures from this unique series of genealogical windows, tracing Christ's ancestry, and along both sides of the Perpendicular nave, designed by Henry Yevele at the end of the fourteenth century, is a high burst of colour, a blaze of blue and green. The impact is staggering. William of Sens, who rebuilt the choir after a fire in 1174, until he fell fifty feet from collapsing scaffolding and was severely injured, probably brought with him glaziers from France, to work on the earliest surviving glass. Another example is the beautiful rose window in the north-east transept, filled with blue and pink light.

William retained in his design the Romanesque chapels of St Anselm and St Andrew, and the towers of these chapels with their lovely cap spires. William the Englishman completed his work, building the Trinity Chapel and Corona, to house the shrine of Becket, and a relic of a piece of his skull in a silver reliquary. This rebuilding of the eastern end of the Cathedral was the first example in England of the transition to the Gothic style. It took place during the great cathedral boom of the Middle Ages. Between 1050 and 1350, eighty cathedrals, 500 large churches and thousands of other churches were built in Europe. Strasbourg Cathedral alone was the height of a forty-storey skyscraper.

*

*'In New York it was difficult to get to the twelfth floor of some
of those skyscrapers ...'*

'Where's Doris?'

'Still down in the crypt ...'

'I said to my Marylin ...'

'Hullo there ...'

The floor where Becket's shrine used to stand is worn by the
knees of pilgrims. The shrine itself was plated with gold and
set with precious stones, given by kings, princes and pilgrims. The
most famous stone was Louis VII's great ruby, the *Régale* of
France.

Round the Trinity Chapel, still, are the famous thirteenth-
century Miracle Windows, which show the life of Saint Thomas
à Becket, and miracles performed by his intercession. In dramatic
and homely scenes, monks ride their horses and rise from their
sickbeds; pilgrims kneel; the saint appears in a dream to Louis
VII of France. The colours are strong greens and blues and
browns: the faces and figures full of character and gesticulation.
Round the ambulatory press the equally diverse, homespun and
characterful faces of today's pilgrims, eager or lethargic.

'... is Doris still in the crypt?'

'It's all a load of rubbish ... Wasn't he decanonized?' (chewing
gum).

'It's all in the lap of the gods anyway, isn't it ...'

*

In the Martyrdom, where Becket was murdered, is another magnificent window, the so-called Royal Window, given by Edward
IV, and showing his family. A plain plaque now commemorates
the spot where Becket was struck down. The four knights, ridding
Henry II of his 'low-born' priest took some time to kill him;
although he offered no resistance, he was a strong, very tall man
(one record even says six feet eleven inches), and as a trained
warrior found it so hard not to fight back that he raised his arms
in prayer and to exclude the sight of the swords.

*'For the name of Jesus and the safety of the Church I am ready
to face death.'*

His story, triumphant on a spiritual level, is equally powerfully
tragic on the human level. Born of a leading City merchant in

London (he was not in fact 'low-born'), Thomas had the opportunity to learn the knightly skills of hawking and riding, and loved finery. When his own career prospered and he became Chancellor to Henry II, who was younger than himself, hot-headed, energetic, questing, but lonely, the two became firm friends. When disagreement came, it flared with all the bitterness and pain of a clash between two people who loved each other. Thomas, who set about doing everything he did well, and who wore, in secret, a hair shirt under his fine archbishop's robes, found himself bound in conscience to uphold the power of the Church – the right of the Church courts to try any offence by clerks, and of churchmen to appeal to the Pope. If he had weakened, the temporal power of kings could have become overridingly despotic.

Both men refused to compromise, but tried for reconciliation. The Pope, the King of France, half Europe tried at different times to reconcile them. At one point Thomas was moved to kneel and greet Henry as his old friend, and Henry held Becket's stirrup for his spiritual overlord to mount his horse, but the truce was short lived. When Thomas finally returned to Canterbury, he was aware that Henry had not given him the 'Kiss of Peace', which would bind him in honour not to harm Thomas. Becket had tried to win this sign by every means, including trickery, but Henry would not give him false reassurance. Both men must have known that on this level they could not deceive each other – Henry might kill him, but could not finally betray him. No other end became possible, and Becket knew that it was the end.

When the murderers came, he did his utmost not to desecrate the Cathedral by being killed inside it, and to prevent others being hurt. To achieve the latter he finally had to enter the Cathedral.

Great was he in truth always and in all places; great in the palace, great at the altar, great both at court and in the Church; great when going forth on his pilgrimage, great when returning, and singularly great at his journey's end.

Herbert of Bosham, Becket's chaplain.[7]

*

'While she was up there, this midwife came in ...'

'Es ist nicht gleich ...' German eyeing postcard.

'She's been struck off, hasn't she now ...'

'Go on,' woman slapping husband's rump on Martyrdom steps, as they canter up to the Choir.

The Black Prince's tomb almost commands silence. It is magnificent, as befits one who was the flower of chivalry of his age, who lived in superb style with a court in France even copied by the French, and married the woman who was the beauty of an era, and according to Froissart, *'en son temps la plus belle de tout la roiaulme d'Engleterre et la plus amoureuse'*[8] – the Fair Maid of Kent.

Edward the Black Prince first visited Canterbury when he was three, and was given an alabaster cup by the monks. Throughout his life the place was important to him; he often visited it and made triumphal pilgrimages there, as when he returned with the captive King of France after Poitiers, leading his prisoner first to the shrine of Becket at Canterbury. He gave many gifts to the Cathedral.

The military hero of his people, the Prince's renown was based on true courage and knightly valour – a national hero who caught the imagination, and who when he died lay in state in Westminster Hall for four months while crowds from all over England walked past his embalmed body, as in another era they were to walk past the coffin of another who had led the nation to victory – Winston Churchill.

The Prince was the first to be made a Knight of the Order of the Garter, and it was probably Joan, the Fair Maid of Kent, who, before their marriage, dropped a garter while dancing, and caused the Prince's father, who is supposed to have seduced or raped her on other occasions, to say *'Honi soit qui mal y pense'*, as he picked it up. In spite of her beauty, with long auburn hair which she may have tinted red and a perfect figure, her low cut gowns, jewels and furs, Joan, Duchess of Kent, was not unvirtuous, and the Prince loved her unalterably. It seems to me that his executors erred, although they thought to do him well by placing his tomb in the Trinity Chapel in place of honour (they carried out his wish for a beautiful gilt effigy, in armour, surmounting it with a tester and his funeral achievements), in not placing his tomb, as he desired in his Will, in the Chapel of Our Lady Undercroft in the crypt. He had given beautiful filigree stone screens to this small chapel. With its black ceiling painted with golden stars it is the most elegant and unusual part of the building, and would seem to fit him perfectly. In the Black Prince's Chantry next to it, one of the carved stone heads is said to be that of Joan of Kent. Here he would have been close to her image, for she, who had been married twice before, chose to be buried in another church, beside her first husband.

... and say to them that they send no more to me for any adventure that falleth, as long as my son is alive: and also say to them that they suffer him this day to win his spurs: for if God be pleased, I will this journey be his and the honour thereof ... Edward III, of his son the Black Prince, at Crécy.[9]

'Ich dien.'

*

'Lovely, isn't it ...'
'The Archbishop's robe at the Coronation ...'
'All Japanese silk mind you ...'
'And hers was heavy ... It was a cold day, but she had that great crown on ... mind you she's quite small, tiny ... not as though she's buxom ...'
'I declare before you all that my whole life, whether it be short or long, shall be devoted to your service ...'[10]

*

Other treasures of the crypt, which is also the traditional place where the French congregation have their chapel since the days of Huguenot refugees, are carved capitals, and from Reculver, pillars and fragments of a stone cross – 'one of the fayrest, and the most auncyent crosse that ever I saw,' wrote Leland. It was probably seventh century, the only known example of such a cross in southern England. Although a Celtic cross, the carving is Mediterranean in style, with draped figures, and pillars. 'Figure sculpture, foliage scrolls, interlace: where else are all three found together in seventh-century Europe? The answer is nowhere ...' writes John Newman in the *Buildings of England*.[11] And he goes on, 'Where else in sixth-century or seventh-century art are there drapery folds as delicately carved as these are ... Where can one find poses so lively and convincing?' By their existence, they prove that other pieces of art of equal quality must have been made at this period.

But one can't enumerate all the fine works in the Cathedral. Striking ones are the alabaster monument of Henry IV and Joan of Navarre; that to Sir John Boys, who was a Recorder of Canterbury and Judge of the Claims Court of the Cinque Ports – reclining in ruff and robes, with a handsome Elizabethan face, ruddy cheeks and beard; the triple-decker monument to the Hales family, showing at the top Sir James Hales being buried at sea after the ineffectual counterattack following the Armada in 1588; the handsome Renaissance monument to Dr Nicholas Wotton, the dean who was more often absent on skilled diplomatic missions for four successive monarchs than in Canterbury, but who kneels here at prayer at his desk for all eternity, a slight, bearded figure, with close-cropped curls and fine-boned head – 'His mind,' so runs the epitaph, 'devoted to Bookes ... beautifully stored with knowledge of the Roman, Italian, French and Dutch languages. After he had been Dean twenty-five years and 293 days he piously resigned his soul to God'; in the nave, the monument, with horses, to the officers and men of the Sixteenth Queen's Lancers who died during the campaign on the Sutlej in 1845–6. Canterbury is no stranger to wars. In Cromwell's day the nave had been treated like a barracks with 3,000 arms and 300 horses kept there. Warriors have their own chapel in St Michael's Chapel, which is the memorial chapel of the famous Royal East Kent Regiment, the Buffs, now incorporated in The Queen's Regiment. Every day at 11 am a page is turned in the book commemorating those who fell in the two World Wars.

How most of the cathedral escaped is a miracle of the war years. A third of the city just by it was razed to the ground, in the 'Baedeker' raids in May and June 1942. Fire fighters patrolled the roofs each night, and services carried on. In the summer of 1944 there were three services in the nave for the men of the Allied Forces who were about to invade Europe. On 8 May 1945, VE Day, a crowd of more than a thousand people poured into the cathedral spontaneously for an impromptu service of thanksgiving. Archbishop William Temple, probably the most brilliant archbishop since Anselm, a convinced socialist, and much loved, had led his people through the war years, and although he was ill in 1944, prepared his clergy for the changes they would have to face after the war. Archbishop Geoffrey Fisher, his successor, modernized the Church's canon law, and as part of the growing ecumenical movement, visited Pope John in Rome, the first time the primate of England had visited the head of the Church of Rome since 1397.

'*From this cradle of the Nation's spiritual enlightenment, the Word goes forth ... live in mutual love; live in peace ...*' – Archbishop William Temple.

At six in the evening a bell tolls in the distance. The beautiful singing of the choir at evensong echoes an amen. '*Come Holy Spirit ...*'

Prayers are said, briefly, several times a day from Easter until October, so that all but the brashest of tourists stop in their tracks. '*Our Father, which art in heaven ...*'

Music is part of the Cathedral, woven into its fabric as is the stained glass. Church music was brought to England by St Augustine. 'It was his patron, Pope Gregory the Great, who codified plainsong. It is interesting that hymns were sung in church by the end of the eighteenth century, but were not a regular part of worship in the Church of England until the nineteenth century.) Canterbury has always inspired music and the arts: T. S. Eliot, Dorothy Sayers and Christopher Fry wrote plays specially for the Cathedral, and John Masefield wrote a mystery play *The Coming of Christ*, which was the first mystery to be performed in a cathedral since the Reformation; in 1914 Elgar conducted *The Apostles* there; in 1927 Holst conducted *The Planets*; the choir school, which was part of the ancient foundation of the Cathedral, and which sang through the Blitz, still fills the whole building with a piercing joy.

Evening is the best time to see the Cathedral. The crowds ebb away. The last ice-cream is licked. Light burns like fire in the modern glass of the Hungarian artist Bossanyi; Becket's 'ghost', a coal stain on a pillar in the crypt, looms blackly; the little chapels are deserted and light flickers on stone and fluted ceilings and the pale cheek of a statue, catches the frail but lasting colour on the painted ceiling of Saint Gabriel's chapel, and the gold suns and stars in that of Our Lady Undercroft; the voices of the past join in prayer, and for a long moment the prayer is answered.

'*My God, I love Thee Thyself above all else and Thee I desire as my last end ... If Thou give not Thyself to me, Thou givest nothing; if I find not Thee, I find nothing ...*' Prayer, in St Anselm's Chapel, of Archbishop Bradwardine of Canterbury, who died from the Black Death in 1349.

*

How does Canterbury feature in the modern world? Is it an anachronism? pure pageantry? The more one explores it (and by Canterbury here I mean the Metropolitan City of the English Church – the see of the Primate of All England), the more clearly one sees that this is not the case. Its influence spreads far beyond the old city walls and the cliffs of our offshore island.

In 1978 the Lambeth Conference, which was first summoned by the Archbishop of Canterbury in 1867 and meets every ten years, was held at Canterbury at the University of Kent. Over four hundred Anglican bishops from all over the world attended, from places as diverse as Japan and Papua New Guinea, for prayer and debate, and there were also observers from, for example, the Orthodox Church in the Soviet Union. Canterbury was laced with cohorts of imposing figures flashing purple bibs, with crosses swinging in businesslike fashion on their chests.

At the station I talked to Justin Ndandali, Bishop of Butare, Rwanda, whose eyes were singularly beautiful above the purple silk. He was surrounded by luggage; it was his first visit to Canterbury. In his country, he told me, the Church was growing daily. In a year ten to fifteen thousand people, adults and children, would be baptized, and no one 'drops out' of the Church. Services are traditional, but also make use of what he termed 'neo-African tunes'. The Anglican Church has far more vitality in Africa than it has in England, and yet a core is still here, a centrepoint to refer to.

I made my way to the University of Kent, which has more of the air of a campus than most universities over here, and a view down over the city, a spectacular view of the Cathedral. There seemed to be an unusual number of busy students for vacation time, walking between the modern blocks of the colleges and the Library. However, the paths were strewn with striding bishops like leaves in autumn, and an outfitters by the Gulbenkian Theatre had a window of copes, silver crooks and regalia – also suitings such as a foreign bishop might be tempted to buy. One or two girls with hair in black velvet bows, wearing white shirts, who could have been students or deaconesses breasted the greensward purposefully. (The ordination of women was under debate that year; the bishops finally came out – more or less – in favour.)

Bruce Rosier, Bishop of Willochra, South Australia, had kindly agreed to meet me. He seemed young, as many bishops are, and practical. He had, he said, a feeling of coming back 'to that place to which our roots go down to', although he added that another age-old centre of the English Church would be a place such as Iona. The Christian Church under Augustine had united England, he pointed out, but had not had that role to play in Australia. Also, now, there were strong settlements there from the Free Churches and Roman Catholic Ireland. A 'missionary role' was needed in at least half the country, the other half being firmly associated with their church. The Lambeth Conference provided an opportunity above all to talk to bishops from other countries, from India, the West Indies, Africa, and to be 're-freshed in our faith'. Canterbury was the centre of family links in the Church. 'It makes us realize we need to work together ... that we can do it and that there is great benefit in doing so ...' He regretted he hadn't had time to walk along the Pilgrim's Way. 'In any place where there has been a long tradition of prayer, I am very much aware of that ...'

I wanted to meet a bishop from Rhodesia, to see how our cosy world struck a man sitting on a time bomb. The system for making appointments was complicated, consisting of notes left at a desk. A man at the desk suggested I leave a message for Robert Mercer, Bishop of Matabeleland, who is also a monk of the Community of the Resurrection. 'You'll know him by his black robe, with that grey apron thing over it ...' Eventually, he allowed that I might try at the porter's lodge of the college where Bishop Mercer was staying. The porter was much more sporting. 'Go on, go and knock on his door ... it's number – up the stairs, turn left, then along ...'

'Would that be very suitable, do you think?' I demurred.

'Why not?' He shooed me along the corridor. I got lost. Bishops' names were affixed to doors, but not the one I was looking for. A post-prandial silence reigned.

I found the door I wanted and knocked. No one was there. I was relieved and disappointed. Along the corridor, a chain was pulled. I looked away, then turned back in time to see a grey apron flicking round a corner.

'Bishop Mercer ...' I cried, running like Alice after the White Rabbit. 'Can you spare a minute?'

'We have so little time,' he said, half turning, still on the trot. 'No time to go to the loo ... I must get to the bank ... Can I carry your bag?' The last indicated that I needn't go away, I felt.

He looked like an attractive, grey-haired, olive-skinned Shakespearian actor playing a monk – but the eyes had the authentic great depth of kindness and humour and understanding. His voice was quick and light, with an almost Welsh lilt (he was born in Rhodesia; spent three years in Yorkshire and three in South Wales).

'This (the Conference) is an elaborate and expensive waste of time ...' he said, as we ran over the campus grass towards Barclays. 'But the city is marvellous ... the singing ... the modern Hungarian glass. We keep having these flipping meetings instead of looking at the glass. I skip the evening meetings; I say "Blow this thing", and go and look at the medieval glass. I must cash a cheque,' he repeated in his light, lilting voice, 'so that I have enough money to *get away from here*. Then I'll be all right ... You may have to lend me your pen to sign my cheque ...'

I noticed later that it was already signed, but I am sure this consummate charm works well with Rhodesian matrons who, he said, are better than people over here at 'going to church' (he put the phrase in quotes), and at 'spending money and time'.

He said he also went to 'locals' in the evenings during the Conference. He was amazed at the young in 'their locals'. 'So *traditional* in spite of their long hair and boots ... playing darts ... probably their fathers and grandfathers played darts there.' He had also been watching cricket, at the famous St Lawrence ground – the Conference had coincided with Canterbury Cricket Week. 'You can change because you are secure in your roots. We are not good at evolution – we go in for revolution – we are violent ...'

I asked how it was, for him, out there.

'One doesn't think too much about it . . .' He still spoke lightly. His eyes smiled. And yet he would of course be going back. He had enough money, and enough courage, to 'get away from here'. I felt the least I could do was leave him to cash his cheque in peace.

*

One always hopes for pyrotechnics in an interview. In Kent one rarely meets with them. Kentish people are not serfs, they have kept their independence. They are not showy either, and have a reserve which is always polite, but which gives nothing away. In my travels in the Black Country I found people uncommunicative, but there their sheer vitality and aggressiveness would make them burst out with a stream of colourful information and dramatic story-telling. Not in Kent. How can they help you? they will ask, courteously, and with a mixture of dignity and humility. They do not see themselves as spectacular, but what they are they will keep privately to themselves, with a stubborn and stoical reticence. Of their business ventures they are proud, but not so proud that they will tell you the secrets of the trade. They are perhaps the kind of Englishmen that foreigners used to find both infuriating and yet worthy of respect – the reserved but honest chips off the old block.

One should not generalize. But strains of lineage inevitably run through history, and history itself concertinas at times to give a startlingly vivid image that links past with present. Maids of Kent, for instance, are still fair. Girls in the region have soft, fair hair and pale skin, with ivory-coloured not ruddy cheeks. They seem as though bred of the chalky soil. Recently in a train I sat opposite three different groups. In one was a round-cheeked little girl in a sunhat, in another a pale-haired boy, in a third a fine-boned, sun-weathered grandmother, with austere, immaculate white shirt and unsensuous mouth. With her silver-ringed hands, she could have been an abbess from a medieval priory, and the children, so palely pretty, must have been replicas of those who made Pope Gregory exclaim – not Angles, but angels.

I met with the same dignified, courteous and crisp reserve, tempered with humour, talking to Canon Derek Ingram Hill, who has written an illuminating contemporary book on Canterbury Cathedral, *Christ's Glorious Church*[12], and, as he is a specialist on the stained glass, also *The Stained Glass of Canterbury Cathedral*[13] ('Go and look at Adam ...' were his parting words to me). As a Canon in Residence he lives in the Green Court, his house having a view through an archway of the Cathedral, and particularly of its finely sloping roofs and small capped towers, of Bell Harry Tower and the rose window, that is he says, one of the most famous views you could find. Offset, he added, by the irritation of having tourists picnicking hard up against his private garden and lounging where they have no right to be. He deserves his privacy, because it is he who trains all the Cathedral guides personally, to give an excellent service to the fifteen thousand visitors a day who throng into the nave. (Two million visitors a year is the annual figure; a few years ago when British tourism peaked, it reached about three million.) Foreign guides haranguing their diverse flocks in stentorian tones are not allowed. 'I suddenly emerge from behind a pillar and say "Stop!"' he says, the light of battle in his eyes. When I met him he had also just asked a hirsute man to cover his chest with a shirt. 'All that hair ...' Canon Hill waved a hand vaguely. He has a very English appearance, with white hair cut as schoolmasters used to have their hair cut. He looks down while talking, and then looks up with a witty, jolly smile.

It would be most sad if the Cathedral ever became just a museum, he said. The hope was that some of the spirituality of the place would 'rub off on them'. For that reason, prayers are said daily, using at these services the unvarnished Common Prayer book. 'People don't go to church very often, but everyone goes to cathedrals.'

How did he see the role of the Cathedral? How did an archbishop stand as a power in the land? (Dr Donald Coggan was not afraid to speak out on subjects such as strikes, or even tyranny, as his sermon in East Berlin in May 1979 showed. He was equally an archbishop who was approachable, and on one occasion wielded a brush and handcart at the start of an anti-litter campaign.)

The monarchy and the Church are almost interrelated, Canon Hill pointed out. The new archbishop, Dr Robert Runcie, will have been the first to be nominated by a Crown Appointments

Commission, the Prime Minister then passing her recommendations to the Queen, and the nomination then put forward for election by the Dean and Chapter of Canterbury – a body consisting of honorary canons, with the Dean and four residentiary canons responsible for day-to-day affairs. An archbishop from abroad has the right to be elected, but problems would arise, as the Primate is in line of succession to the Queen. Which of the two establishments, Crown or Archbishopric, could best survive without the other seems open to conjecture, but one cannot see Canterbury ever being without an archbishop, or redundant.

Canterbury Cathedral, Canon Hill said, 'should be the church of the English people'. He stressed English. It should be thought of as the historic church of the land, reaching out into personal and domestic life. The Church of England was, he said 'almost the last church left in the world that has an automatically received place in the life of the nation.' His first ministry was in Dover, in the old days when the church really was the centre of the community. Now, modern trends make this difficult. 'You could always find someone in, then. If you call at a home nowadays when a favourite television programme is on, you won't get in ... and many women are out at work ...' I felt he would like to emerge from behind his pillar and say 'Stop!' to television, but there were, he said, 'some signs that the gross materialism of the post-war period is wearing a bit thin ... People come to me and ask whether perhaps there isn't another side of life that ought to be considered ...'

I asked him what he thought, not of ecumenicalism, which is so clearly valuable, but of a trend, which even the Lambeth Conference had discussed not unfavourably, of welcoming other faiths, such as Buddhism, trying to find common ground.

'I am not prepared to compromise ... there is only one ultimate faith.'

Becket would have approved. If I had hoped for fireworks, I was shown the unalterable, determined Englishness of a faith which will preserve its own integrity, its own quiet wish to serve, which will not be swayed by alien flamboyance, and which is held in safety within the old walls of the city of Canterbury, in this most English of English cathedral cities.

*

There is much to Canterbury besides the Cathedral, as residents and some tourists will tell you. The industrial revolution largely passed it by, but it is a flourishing market town and shopping centre, with varied modern industries. The buildings that replaced bomb damage are low and unobtrusive; in the shops, tweeds, china and glass are better than I have seen in any other provincial city. Restaurants meet the tourist challenge, and by the Cathedral is an ice-cream parlour which is the perfect antidote to too much tomb watching. Information is freely available. Besides wandering through quiet backstreets (the completion of the by-pass in late 1980 or early 1981 will relieve traffic problems), visitors can quickly find the way to St Augustine's Abbey, the Norman Castle and the Dane John mound; to St Peter's Church, one of the oldest; St Dunstan's, in the Roper vault of which lie the remains of the martyred Sir Thomas More, whose head was brought to Canterbury by his daughter Meg (Margaret) after his execution in 1535; the Westgate, which was a one-time prison; the Pilgrim's Hospital, cool and ancient with its trestle tables, with upstairs nine flats for people such as Mr Evans, an ex-verger, who told me there were 'no money qualifications, only age'; and to that island between two arms of the Stour, where the arches of the Grey Friars straddle the reedy river, and a market garden is perfectly in keeping with the spirit of the first Franciscans who came to England, who were given hospitality here by the Poor Priests' Hospice and allowed to build their chapel. Today, Anglican Franciscans once more hold services in the chapel. St Francis lived among people, and his friars, although loving solitude and prayer, are not monks. They own no property, and in Germany are called 'barefeet'. St Francis stipulated that they were to wear poor clothes (habits), which they could patch with sacking and other bits, with God's blessing.

Canterbury is a town renowned for cloth, and weaving. There was also a flourishing silk-weaving industry, introduced by French protestant refugees. In Defoe's day there was 'at Canterbury the greatest plantation of hops in the whole island.'[14] In 1979, the new Canterbury Brewery, making local brews, was opened by three brothers, on a traditional site. Another traditional industry is tanning, which has existed in Canterbury since the twelfth century. One of the largest export industries in East Kent operates from St Mildred's Tannery in Stour Street, manufacturing high quality leather for upholstery in cars and furniture and for parliament buildings. The tannery, started by the Williamson family in 1791 and run by descendants of the founders, also makes leather for, among other things, industrial gloving, and during the Second World War made specialized RAF pilots' suiting.

Canterbury is also the city of cricket – and of cricketers such as the inimitable Frank Woolley, the great all-round cricketer, whose ashes were scattered in 1979 on his beloved St Lawrence ground. It is the city of the King's School, perhaps the oldest school in the country, numbering among ex-pupils Christopher Marlowe and Somerset Maugham. (Another school, the Simon Langton, produced the differently dynamic man of our age, Sir Freddie Laker. A boyhood friend has claimed that a school trip in 1937 fired Freddie Laker's enthusiasm for travel; when asked by the careers master at school what he wanted to be, he answered, 'a millionaire'.) It is the city where Richard Harris Barham of the *Ingoldsby Legends* was born, and where Joseph Conrad is buried – 'Sleep after toyle, port after stormie seas,/Ease after warre, death after life does greatly please.'[15] It has the oldest library in the English-speaking world in the Cathedral Library, housing magnificent Bibles and books of hours, items such as a bestiary of *c.* 1250, showing a phoenix, and a mermaid, a copy of a fourth-century codex given by the Tsar to the Cathedral in 1861, and Erasmus's edition of the Greek New Testament. ('An author,' Erasmus wrote, 'should handle with deliberate care the subject which he has selected, should keep his work long by him and retouch it many times before it sees the light. These things it has never been my good fortune to be able to do.' A thought which many contemporary authors might echo.)

Besides looking at the past, Canterbury looks outwards. It was a starting place for the great European march to mark the thirtieth anniversary of the Council of Europe. The University of Kent runs part-time degree courses in modern European languages. (Also in Kent, South-East Arts have allotted bursaries for projects relating to contemporary European literature.) Old and new run side by side. In the town museum (there is also to be another museum, the Museum of Canterbury) are paintings by Canterbury's own painter Thomas Sidney Cooper RA (1803–1902), showing peaceful landscapes with sheep and cows, together with present-day studies in line of Canterbury Pilgrims by Elisabeth Frink. There are mementoes of Major Mick Mannock VC, the legendary air ace who was almost blind in one eye but had seventy-three confirmed victories before being shot down (still a record today), and in the Regimental Museum, trophies of the Buffs, first mustered by Queen Elizabeth I in 1572 (their descendants in The Queen's Regiment now back in Canterbury, reforging their links with the past). Among prints, uniforms and swords in the museum, is one most moving testament, written by Captain Joseph Fenwick, The Buffs, in his own blood, when lying wounded at Chamusca in November 1810 during the Peninsular War – one of the most thrilling campaigns in the regiment's history. 'I am shot through the body and arms,' he wrote to his commanding officer, 'for God's sake send me a surgeon English if possible – if I don't recover God bless you all ...' He died on 10 December.

*

Then people long to go on pilgrimages ...

Everyone will look for a different shrine in Canterbury. To me, the place which is most palpably holy is St Martin's Church. Outside the city walls, past the ruins of St Augustine's, where grey and white doves fly above the old stones, past the spiked modern chapel of Christchurch Teachers' Training College, with its thin pencil spire, up a hill to the oldest church in use in England. It is very small, often empty, with at most three or four tourists. It was here, in a building dating from Roman times, that Queen Bertha and her chaplain Bishop Luidhard prayed in the sixth century. It was here, most probably, in the plain circular font with Saxon carving – graceful, uncluttered interlace – that her husband King Ethelbert was later baptized. The west wall shows traces of the original Roman windows, and incorporates the red Roman tiles which were used when the church was restored; it is a staggering, conglomerate piece of architecture.

Behind the church the hill continues upwards. You walk past grass-grown graves. There is a heady smell of honeysuckle and syringa; white butterflies petal the air. (The guardian of the church key protects the tortoiseshell butterflies among the nettles by transferring them – 'I just beat the Council to it.' He also moves newly hatched hawk-moths to safer hedges.) Birds sing; a spade chunks into garden earth; a bell tolls from a distance; a lazy aeroplane flies overhead. Seen between yew trees, the Cathedral appears frail, rounded, feminine, and on the hill ringing the city on the other side are the white buildings of the University. This is the view that Dean Stanley described as 'one of the great panoramas of the world'.

From the rear the little church of St Martin's is warm and homely, infinitely consoling; two tiled roofs huddling behind a tower which is barely higher, and which is accompanied by a domestic brick-and-tile chimney beside the nave. The hillside, with its conical cypress and warm grasses, its view of a city surrounded by hills, is Italianate. A pink-streaked evening sky echoes the lines of red Roman tiles in the stone and flint. The colours deepen. Birds fly across the wide bowl of clear air. You don't want to leave.

Walking to the gate after my first visit, I felt renewed in a way which it would be inapposite to call strange, and which stayed with me for a long time. A happy-faced tramp was sitting under the Lych Gate. He had the large yellow teeth peculiar to tramps, and agreed with me about the church. 'They were built a long time ago these places ... that's why they've got atmosphere ... it's got an atmosphere about it. Nowadays people don't believe. They believe with their heads not their heart ... they walk round the churchyard choosing their plot ...' He had, he said, been to the Social Security to 'look for work', but with 'no luck'. He was thinking 'where next to go'. He had a small bundle or old grip with him; I wasn't sure if there was dismay under the cheerfulness.

I asked him if the trickle of water from a bank of the glebe field was the spring which never dries up, and which may have originally, long before the Romans, have caused this site to be called holy. He wasn't sure either. 'If it smells, it's someone's washing-up water ...' The teeth bared uproariously. I wished him luck, and turned back to wave, feeling inadequate.

It wasn't until I had left Canterbury that I read the story of St Martin, to whom the church is dedicated. Originally a soldier, born in Hungary in AD 320, Martin was always holy, and often cleaned his batman's boots. One cold winter's day, when he had already given away all his clothes, he cut his cloak in half and gave half to a beggar. That night he had a vision of Christ, who was dressed in the piece of cloak he had given away. Sulpicius Severus, in his life of St Martin, wrote that he 'recognized that a being on whom others showed no pity, was in that respect left to him ...'[16]

On another evening, when I had had bad news, I visited St Martin's again. The door was as always open, but prayers were being said, by a nun and young priest or lay reader. It was the tenth anniversary of the Soviet-led invasion of Czechoslovakia, and the prayers were for that country now, putting into perspective the placid problems of existence in England.

Canterbury is not a museum. It thrusts you back into reality with a strength which stretches far outside the city. I put my hand in the trickle of water that time, thoughtfully.

*

Canterbury was once much closer to the sea, or rather, linked to the sea by the Stour estuary or inlet, which came inland as far as Sturry. When this silted up to become marshland, it still left the wide river, with its ford at Fordwich – a flourishing port, with a safe anchorage and busy quayside. Here the stone for the building of the Cathedral was unloaded; here the Abbots of St Augustine's, who owned the land, could import wine, oil and other monkish necessities, which led to constant strife, since they had been granted income from tolls by Edward the Confessor, and Fordwich, as a Corporate Member of the Cinque Port of Sandwich, probably from early in 1066, had the Cinque Ports' immunity from all tolls and customs duties. Fordwich was in fact an important member of the Ports, and it was not until after the decline of its maritime activities that it became a Noncorporate Member. Fordwich still pays ship money to its Head Port: the Mayor Deputy of Fordwich hands over 17p (the sum has not been affected by inflation) to the Mayor of Sandwich, in a ceremony at Sandwich Guildhall.

In the Town Hall at Fordwich are photographs of barges at the quay here as late as 1893. (The death knell of the port, after a slow decline of shipping from the fifteenth century, was ushered in with the opening of the Canterbury and Whitstable railway in 1830.) The Stour today here looks clean and fast flowing, with small houseboats, and willows reflecting in the water. The coat of arms of the town is a trout, with a lion. The great angler, Izaac Walton, wrote:

There is also in Kent, near to Canterbury, a Trout called there a Fordidge trout, a trout that bears the name of the town where it is usually caught, that is accounted the rarest of fish; many of them near the bigness of a Salmon.... and none of these have been known to be caught with an angle, unless it were one that was caught by Sir George Hastings, an excellent angler, and now with God . . .[17]

This special breed of trout is no longer found there, but one can eat trout at the Fordwich Arms, a pub which stands where an old one stood, providing food by the waterside – home-made pâté and toast or prawns with salad. The calm is barely diminished by businessmen, not pilgrims. 'Don't we all ...' 'Need I repeat all we told the chairman ...' 'Last night, I said to him, you chase that up ... he didn't say anything –' 'Mine, I think –' The faces above red, gold-crested ties and nylon shirts bend over the Fordidge fare.

Beside the pub is the Town Hall, the oldest and smallest town hall in England, with beams and herringbone brickwork which I see has the appropriate name 'brick-nogging'. On the first floor is the court room, with an Elizabethan table, press-gang drums showing the Cinque Ports arms, and the ducking stool that was used to submerge scolds. To one side of the building is the crane house, for the town's crane in the days of barges, and below the court room is a storeroom, and the old town jail, lined with split logs, with logs to sit on and a privy hole, all looking deceptively comfortable.

There are many other old buildings in the town, in weathered brick, or beamed: Monk's Hall and Monk's Cottage, once the home of the port bailiff, near the site of the storehouse belonging to Canterbury Cathedral, granted to that church by the Abbey of St Augustine in return for a red rose, to be given every year at Midsummer. Watergate House, the Manor House, Tancrey on its island, and the earliest house, part of Give Ale Cottage, with its roof sloping almost to the ground and covered with flowering stonecrop. The bridge was a horse-and-cart bridge, and is not suitable for modern traffic. 'We fought the juggernauts.' I was told, 'and won.' A list of the number thundering along the old street was taken to Canterbury. In the old days there was a toll for every waggon, two pence, and for every cart, one penny. There is only one farm in the neighbourhood now, but there used to be several, now amalgamated, with produce as varied as hops, apples, beef, mutton and corn. Between Fordwich and Sturry is the Sturry Plant of the Robert Brett Group, a firm founded in 1904 by a farmer's son, Robert Brett, who came to Canterbury in the 1880s to work for 3d an hour. From gravel which had been lying below the marshes for millions of years, the Brett Sand and Gravel Quarry produced annually about 150,000 tons of aggregate – for concrete, tarmacadam and asphalt. When this quarry was exhausted, one to replace it was opened up at Thanington.

Fordwich Church is, *The Buildings of England* joyfully states, 'unrestored'. It flies the Cinque Ports lion and ship arms on its weathervane, and has their arms above the mayor's box pew. The beams have a distinct list, perhaps caused by the disastrous floods and tidal waves of the 1200s on the south-east coast.

The Fordwich Stone is a heavy shrine-like stone, with interlacing columns and a fish-scale tiled roof, that may have stood over a tomb. As such, it is even possible that it marked at one point the tomb of St Augustine – it is popularly known as St Augustine's Tomb. Even more ancient, of unknown age, is the rough wooden chair, hewn out of one trunk in one piece, found embedded in the plaster of the wall, which could have come from a Viking ship, or from some raider's wreck. But this area is rich in objects of immeasurable age. Traces of pre-Roman Belgic huts have been found on an upland site, with handaxes which have been accepted as one of the earliest traces of man in Britain. The church has a Saxon arch in the tower, a wooden shingled spire. Inside is a model of a Carrick of 1470 commemorating the men who fell in the 1914–18 war. The sea is never far away in this part of Kent.

Up the road is Sturry, where the Roman Canterbury road met the road to Reculver. Set back from the noisy modern main road is the peaceful church of St Nicholas, where long stones cover graves with decorative headstones, the finely chiselled writing topped by smiling sun-like faces. Other old buildings keep their mellowness, as does 'Friendly Hall' on the Fordwich road. The most memorable building is the 160-foot long barn of Milner Court, now the Junior King's School, which was the barn when

Canterbury Cathedral

Monument to
Dr Nicholas Wotton,
Dean for twenty-five
years, in Canterbury
Cathedral

The Royal Military Canal, with lock-keeper's cottage, at a
junction with the River Rother

Walmer Castle from the gardens

Statue of Charles Stewart Rolls, looking out over Dover Harbour

Dover Castle: outer towers and curtains from the Constable's Gate, past the Treasurer's Tower to Godsfoe and Crevecoeur Towers

Twin towers at Reculver

St Augustine's Abbey had their grange here. Sturry Court, as the hall which then existed was called, was the pleasant retreat where abbots could spend the summer, surrounded by farm buildings, brewhouse, bakehouse and two mills. It is still surrounded by magnificent trees – willows, sycamores, and – from the days of the monks? – almond trees. As my guidebook says, 'monks were clever with drains'[18] and they also knew a thing or two about living.

5   Deal; Walmer

'Deal is a most villainous place ... full of filthy-looking people.'
William Cobbett[1]

A villainous place to Cobbett. Now one of the most invigorating
– a blustery, windswept, near-perfect town, with its own forthright,
salty attraction. Walking from the High Street, across the long
and famous Middle Street with its double-fronted bays and fretted
woodwork, its Flemish brick, strike down one of the short streets
that lead to the sea – Market Street, Brewer Street, Farrier Street,
Gold Street, Silver Street; the names spell out their ancient purpose – and the sea bursts upon you with a suddenness and force
that surely cannot be matched anywhere – between the small
houses with their thick walls, bread ovens and corners cut away
for carts, blazing its square of blue or stormy green or turbulent
ochre, across which may move the dark red sails of a yacht, the
grey of a dredger, the distant shapes of ships in the Downs. Doors
slam in the wind, and into the square of blue at the end of the
street moves the rounded navy-blue belly of a seaman's sweater,
its retired owner walking along that endless stretch of shingle to
cast a weather eye on the view from Sandown Castle. In Deal you
are on the sea, of the sea, engulfed by it, seastruck. There's nothing
like it on earth ...

*

The character and purpose of Deal were shaped by the Downs –
the stretch of water between the shore and the Goodwin sands –
that for two thousand years was one of the busiest maritime scenes
in the world. Until the coming of steam, when a harbour arm
became vital, the Downs provided a safe anchorage, except in

unusual storms, for sailing ships, and it was common for 400 or 500 vessels to be anchored there – as many as 800 are recorded. It must have been a magnificent sight.

Mr Hickman, who was born in 1889 and is the oldest boatman on the old beach at Deal, remembers seeing ships of the Union Castle line taking troops to South Africa from here, during the Boer War. He was then a schoolboy and, later, at fifteen, earned £1 a week coasting in sailing ships off Whitstable. But he thinks modern hovercraft are marvellous, '... only forty minutes!', and his cheerful, healthy face, with a profile reminiscent of Wellington's, lights up at the thought of them. Another memory is seeing the ship which Crippen boarded, anchored off Deal; and the sight of the stretch of Goodwin sands, as the tide covers them – 'once the water's on it, it's all alive.'

The anchorage in the Downs was often compulsory, because the wind which brought a vessel up-Channel and round the South Foreland prevented her from getting round the North Foreland and into the North Sea or to London, and vice versa. While in the Downs, the ships would replenish their stores, carts no doubt bustling down Brewer Street and Market Street and the whole town becoming one giant supplier, the local mills grinding away, ale flowing, and the Deal 'Sharks' as they were called, using all this activity as a cover for their own private brand of business. Rich merchants' houses are evident, and the butchers and greengrocers of Deal still have windows laden with decorative rows of produce, as a legacy from the days of their prime.

Deal was once the premier harbour town of south-east England, having taken over from Sandwich when that town became silted up, so that although Deal and Walmer were Non-Corporate Members of the Cinque Port of Sandwich in medieval times and even in the seventeenth century, they had gradually outstripped their Head Port in importance. Deal is today a Corporate Member, although now overtaken in its turn by the ports of Dover, Folkstone and Ramsgate. From the early eighteenth century the Lord Warden of the Cinque Ports has had his official residence at Walmer Castle; indeed the eighteenth century has indelibly left its stamp on the towns, and there is little of the grandiose seafront architecture of Victorian days. Deal has escaped being a 'resort'. (It has also escaped redevelopment. In the 1950s there was a proposal – which barely seems credible now – to pull down the entire seafront. The Deal Society was formed, and defeated the plan. As Mr Michael Hosking of The Golden Hind bookshop pointed out to me, a 'secondary distributor road' is now in abeyance, and industry should ideally be kept to the outskirts of Dover and Sandwich, leaving Deal as a suitable centre for small conferences.)

One thing the town is today is an angling town. On arrival you are likely to hear in any pub:

'Been out today, Charlie?' (or Bert, or Bob ...)

Hoarse laugh in answer. It's blowing a gale.

'They were pestering me, though. Last lot I took out, I said you'll have to stay out for six hours if you go now ... in minutes three of them were down, then the other three ... sick ... I'd warned them I could get them off but not back this tide ... they think boats are like cars, you can just park them. Stubborn bastards, you always get one who wants to stay out, anyway ... Then the whole lot are sick.'

But in the main, sea-anglers take their sport seriously, and Deal is the leading English centre for angling within easy reach of London, being able to offer beach, boat, pier and river. Fishing from the beach is free; boats are licensed by the Council, and the boatmen are skilled and friendly (their association is the Deal and Walmer Inshore Fisherman's Association); there is a small charge for fishing on the pier (all day 30p, all night 50p), and there are all-night sessions on Saturdays, a prize each month from the Council for the heaviest fish; in the River Stour nearby there is freshwater fishing – where it is fast running from Minster to Sandwich there are bream, roach, perch, sea-trout and grey mullet; fishing is free between Sluice and Richborough road; day tickets are available for fishing in Reed Pond, Sandwich (roach, rudd, bream, tench, perch and carp). There are two angling societies at Deal – the Deal and Walmer Angling Association and the Deal Angling Club. The Deal Open Beach Fishing Festival is held in October. In 1978 Courage Ltd sponsored the event, providing the prizes and in 1979, P. and O. Ferries Ltd.

Why is this sport such a national favourite? Why do fathers spend happy hours on the pier showing a small son or daughter what it's all about, men sit on the beach day-long hoping for a full bag, that glazed, fishy look come into the eye of an expert at the mention of angling? It can be called a cruel sport, but rarely is classed as such. In essence, it is perhaps one of the purest, least adulterated forms of hunting, since it has a very basic original purpose, as basic to man, more ancient, than his need for bread or beer (or, perhaps, grouse). It is still possible to be thankful to take what the sea provides first-hand.

'I sometimes eat fish twice a day. My wife fillets it and we keep it in the deep freeze.'

I was talking to Harry Denne, who came back to Deal two years ago, after twenty years in Cornwall, and now works as a pier attendant. He and his wife gave up their house in Cornwall and were living in a 'furnished place' for the time being. 'That's how badly we wanted to come home to Deal ...' (He was born in North Deal.) 'The sea ... the quietness ... and we have a lot of friends.' He digs his own bait in Sandwich Bay – 'yellowtails', big lug-worm (£1 per twenty in the shops, with ordinary lugworm 60p to £1). He gets a couple of hours fishing in the evenings, and plenty at weekends, and last year caught 132 codling and cod, average weight 2–2$\frac{1}{2}$ lb., largest 10$\frac{1}{2}$ lb. (Small cod or codling are known as 'Tommy Cod'; at three years old they are classed as cod, weighing about 3$\frac{1}{2}$lb.) In summer he might also catch pouting, flatfish, bass and mackerel. Crabs can be caught off the pier, and lobster on the rocks off Kingsdown.

'It's the relaxation ... and –' his eyes gleamed, 'the possibility of catching that extra large one ...'

He knows most people down on the foreshore, is part of a friendly, self-sufficient society. 'If you can't help, don't hinder, I say ...' It is to him that I am indebted for an introduction to Wimpy Fishlock, who knows more about Deal than almost anyone, or many another townsman his town. 'I didn't buy any coal last winter,' Harry Denne said. 'There's plenty of coal and driftwood on the beach.' The sea, the all-provider. If you are a man of the shore, and know your lug-worms.

*

The provider – and the taker. No wonder Victorian poets, after a previous dearth of literature about the sea, saw it as a cruel destroyer.

Rung to his restless everlasting sleep
By the heavy death-bells of the deep ...[2]

The Goodwin sands, four miles out from Deal, stretching about ten miles parallel to the coast, are the most treacherous shallows in the English Channel. '... not unlike a great lobster, with his back to the east, and with his claws, legs and feelers extended westwards towards Deal and the shipping in the Downs'[3], or as Shakespeare wrote, 'a very dangerous flat, and fatal, where the carcasses of many a tall ship lie buried, as they say.'[4] In five centuries they are reported to have engulfed fifty thousand lives and one hundred million pounds' worth of shipping.[5] In Deal Maritime Museum there are maps showing sites of all the wrecks that have been recorded between the Forelands and round the Goodwins – the pinpoints lie as thick as flies on a flypaper. Only one wreck, that of the *North Eastern Victory*, is clearly visible, but when there is a spring tide and a gale to shift the sand in patches, hulks of other wrecks can be seen sticking up from the sand, and part of the *South Goodwin* lightship, wrecked in 1954, still on her side, becomes visible. 'I've been out there when you can count twenty or thirty,' Wimpy Fishlock told me.

The Goodwins are by legend the island of Lomea, Earl Godwin's territory. Godwin, one of whose sons was King Harold, by marrying his daughter to Edward the Confessor, achieved such power for himself and his family that he became extremely unpopular with his countrymen, 'treading under foote the nobilitie by great disdaine, and oppressing the common people by insatiable rauine, extortion and tyrannie.'[6] His memory was blackened by legend, and his land at the Goodwins said to have been swallowed by the sea. (More prosaically, the name could come from the old British word *Gwdyn*, meaning soft and spongy, an apt description.) Certainly they seem to have had more solidity in the past. Borings carried out in the last century revealed blue clay resting on chalk at various levels so that there could have been an island, like Sheppey, consisting of clay that was carried away by a storm such as that mentioned in the Anglo-Saxon chronicle for 1099.[7] Caesar may have passed the Goodwins, travelling southwestward with the current, and then rowing hard in a northwesterly direction.[8]

Nor are the Downs always calm. Caesar fell prey to storms

during both his landings, in 55 and 54 BC, many of his ships being destroyed. His landing place is held to be Deal. Then there was the Great Storm of 1287, and the other storms of the thirteenth century which ravaged the Cinque Ports coastline. In 1703 there was such a terrifying storm that people thought the Day of Judgement had come. 'This terrible blast began,' wrote Defoe, 'at which time England may be said to have received the greatest loss that ever happen'd to the royal navy at any one time ...' Four out of twelve ships in the Downs were lost, with out of the total crews of 1,361 men on these four, all lost except seventy-one men. And this despite the brave Deal boatmen.

The boatmen and pilots *were* Deal. In the early nineteenth-century Deal pilots wore tall chimney-pot hats, and they are immortalized in brick and stone at the old parish church of St Leonard in Upper Deal, which has a Pilots' Gallery of 1658 over the West Door, and a cupola on the tower which was kept in repair by Trinity House as a landmark for shipping. This is on the highest bit of land around, in the old village, which spread downwards to the shore during the seventeenth-century, replacing the fishermens' huts with a seventeenth-century New Town grid of alleyways bisected by Middle Street. Both the shoreline and the upper village are sturdily planted with late eighteenth- and early nineteenth-century cottages, and some earlier ones with typical seventeenth-century brickwork. The road upwards is lined with almost tropically abundant gardens, thick with palms, pampas grass, jasmine and nut trees; old houses are buried in creeper and roses, modern ones bask behind laurels and lavender. In summer and autumn it can seem like a sun-baked zone, another climate. (Deal has been called the healthiest place in the land.) Past fig-trees and walled orchards is Pilots' Avenue, roofed with chestnuts and limes. The church, on its knoll, is a mixture of styles, dating from the twelfth century but with a 1684 tower, and what the curate who showed me round called a 'disastrous extension' of 1819, although his objection was mainly that two aisles face different ways, and without the central point of the old three-tier pulpit necessitate a strange assortment of altars. Despite the functional difficulties involved, the church is full of space and light, with its contrasting woodwork and dark painted coats of arms, one of which shows two midshipmen signalling with flags.

There is a card in each pew to welcome newcomers, offering coffee after the 10 am service.

A memorial states that 'Here in this Ile lyeth the bodde of Thomas Boys esquier ... which Thomas was in his youth a gentleman at armes at Calles and attended upon the person of Kinge Henry VIII at the seige of Bullen ... mayor of the towne of Calles ...' Other memorials chart the course of English naval history – Sir John Harvey, Admiral of the Blue Squadron ... made Captain 'during the long and eventful war in which this country was involved in the French Revolution ...' Henry Wise Harvey, Lieutenant in the RN ... Captain Henry Harvey RN ... Third son of the late Admiral Sir Edward Harvey GCB who died of yellow fever off Nassau ... Robert Willimot, midshipman in the Indian Navy, who died on board the HCS *Atalanta* in the Red Sea 14 July 1843, aged 17 ... Henry Simpson Harvey, Midshipman, Aged 18 years ... mortally wounded in a skirmish with the Chinese in the River Yang-Tse-Kiang ... Commander ... Aged 27 ... At Macao ... Aged 24 ... The youthful ages are sadly prominent.

In the churchyard are other stories chiselled in stone, and especially moving because of their brevity. 'Memento's ... Catherine, wife of Geo. Ludewig, died the 5th of December 1782 ... is interred here ... Their children Eliz., Catherine, John and Charles, died infants and are buried near ... George was killed in Battle on board His Majesty's Ship Serapis, the 23rd September 1779 aged 18 years ... William, died the 11th of March 1780 aged 17 years, and is Buried here. Also the above Geo. Ludewig died the 18th August 1792 aged 69 years ...' 'Memento – Richard Williams Esq, Commander RN, Beloved by his connexions, Estimed by all who knew him, died of strong paralysis 12th January 1835 Aged 19 years ...' 'Here Lieth Presilloway, Wife of William Garner, Deal Blacksmith who departed the 24th Day January 1695 Aged 40 years who had 7 children and now alive William Presillow Eliza (new line) Beth Mary Jo (new line) Nah and Thomas.' 'In Memory of Mr Willm Pocock late Lieutenant of Deal Castle who died $\underset{y}{e}$ 28 of Novem. 1749. Aged 80 years ...' And the Deal Pilots. 'Here Lyeth $\underset{y}{e}$ Body of John Blewitt Pylot he dyed November 1731 Aged 44 years.' 'In Memory of John Adams Pilot 1800 Aged 37 years.' 'In Memory of Mr John Doorn

Walker, Pilot.' On the head stones carved faces smile above clouds, or waves. The pilots watch over Deal, look out over the sea.

*

There is no tame 'beach' at Deal. Gritty yellow shingle rises in steep tiers and finally becomes part of the land. It has engulfed what remains of Sandown Castle, is held back by a few firs at Walmer, and at Deal carries the angling boats right into the town, except where a new low wall or promenade has recently been built, much to the horror of boatmen and shopkeepers along this 'north end' of the shore. 'We tried to stop them,' an old sailor told me. But it is this north end of the shore which is particularly vulnerable to storms and which was inundated by shingle and floodwater in the worst flooding for twenty-five years in 1978, with damage estimated at over £1,250,000.

Where the wall ends, by Sandown Castle, there is a magnificent view across the Royal Cinque Ports Golf links to Richborough with its power station, hazy in the distance, and over to the white cliffs of Pegwell and Ramsgate, lit by shafts of sun beyond a sea that is grey or lime green, with shadows of brown and gold on which gulls float. It is whipped into constant movement by the wind, and out towards the horizon is another line of white breakers, half seen and all the more deadly, as they surge over the Goodwins.

The shore seems open to invasion, to invite attack. Even after the building of Henry VIII's castles Celia Fiennes noted: 'the Downs seemes to be so open a place and the shoar so easye for landing I should think it no difficulty to land a good army of men in a little tyme ...'[9]

This is what was always feared, and occasionally nearly happened. Henry VIII built his three castles at Deal, Walmer and Sandown as part of his defences against the threat of invasion by François I of France and the Holy Roman Emperor Charles V, whom the Pope was trying to enlist against Henry, who had defied him by divorcing Catherine of Aragon and establishing himself as head of the Church of England. The castles were new in design, shaped like a Tudor rose, probably inspired by forts in northern Europe, especially Germany, where massive rounded tower-like forts had been in use since the fifteenth century. They were low in profile to resist bombardment, since gunfire had become a new factor in naval warfare, and were in fact glorified gun-platforms, referred to as the King's three new 'Blockhouses or Bulwarks'. But the design is intricate, and in Deal Castle, the largest, it is easy to become lost in the curving maze of the 'rounds' or continuous gallery within the bastions. Deal Castle is gloomy today, redolent of gunpowder and cold stone, still protected by its huge studded door and thirty-two-pounder guns; but it is well presented to the public with exhibition material, and some outstanding items in showcases – first-century BC Iron-Age bronze 'spoons' from Upper Deal, a very dandified toilet set of the first century AD with tweezers, ear pick and nail cleaner, sixth-century glass paste and amber beads and a superb Anglo-Saxon brooch from Eastry House, set with garnets and surmounted by a gold medallion.

The three castles were completed in only two years. During the building the workmen went on strike, demanding an increase from 5d to 6d a day.[10] Their leaders were imprisoned.[11] Fortunately the invasion did not arrive, and the castles were not besieged until the Civil War. They acted as a deterrent, however, and during the Napoleonic wars Cinque Ports' volunteers built earthen fortifications in addition. The castles had safeguarded the Downs during the Spanish Armada, and the main body of the fleet was based off the shore; it was from the Downs that the fireships were sent out, which demoralized the Spanish. It was from here, too, that Blake set out to fight de Witt nearly a hundred years later, as he was approaching the Thames with a large Dutch fleet. During the last war, the towns had their share of bombardment, and the Governor's Lodgings at Deal Castle were destroyed by a bomb in 1941. Kent earned the name 'Bomb Alley', and a map of flying-bomb sites in the country is pinpointed as densely as that of the wrecks round the Goodwins. But as de Ruyter, whose victims were brought ashore to be buried at Sandwich during the seventeenth-century Dutch Wars, said: 'You may burn English ships, kill English sailors, but you cannot conquer the English!'[12]

Another martial note is sounded in Deal by the Royal Marines. The Royal Marines Depot was established there in 1861, but there had been a detachment at the Naval Hospital since 1812, and a platoon of the Duke of York and Albany's Maritime Regiment was stationed at Deal in 1665 – a year after the regiment was formed – to co-ordinate the defence of the area against a possible Dutch attack. The Duke of York and Albany's Maritime Regiment of Foot or 'The Admiral's Regiment' was the original name for the force, formed by James Duke of York, brother of Charles II and Lord High Admiral, because by the time of the Restoration the proportion of soldiers to seamen had dropped alarmingly. In those days ships were run by sailors who did not fight, with military detachments on board to carry arms – then as warships evolved, the Navy took over both jobs.

Marines were called 'Bootnecks' by the sailors, because of their leather collars. The title 'Royal' was conferred on them by George III, Earl St Vincent having recommended that they should be called 'Royal Marines' in consideration of their loyalty against the French, and during the mutinies of Spithead and the Nore. He said:

In obtaining for them the distinction of 'Royal' I but inefficiently did my duty. I never knew an appeal made to them for honour, courage or loyalty, that they did not more than realize my highest expectations. If ever the hour of real danger should come to England, they will be found the country's sheet anchor.

His words have been proved true in two World Wars, notably in the Zeebrugge attack on St George's Day 1918, for which two of the 4th Battalion Royal Marines, who had trained at Deal, were awarded vcs; and at Dieppe on 19 August 1942, in the beachhead commando assault. Today the 41 Commando Royal Marines is based at Deal, although they are often overseas, and have recently been in Malta, Northern Ireland (seven awards for gallantry while there have been made to them) and Canada. The barracks are now an operational base rather than a training centre; although during the Second World War the Depot trained various units, including the Royal Marines Seige Regiment who manned cross-Channel guns, and 40 Commando, the first Royal Marine Commando which formed at Deal in 1943.

The Royal Marines School of Music, the only naval school of music today, has its quarters in the old Hospital Building, which is the oldest of several buildings, with fine Georgian windows. There is an air of space about all the barracks buildings, which are surrounded by grass and well proportioned, and which as

Lieutenant Noakes, Senior Instructor Officer, who showed me round, pointed out, one would never find in a modern barracks. They were mostly built in the peaceful time – the Pax Britannica – between Trafalgar and Jutland, when Britain was thinking of empire rather than wars. Lieutenant Noakes also showed me the Historical Room exhibits, pointed out the converted stable blocks and the paddock beyond the old operating theatre quarters which, it is said, used to be a graveyard for corpses taken straight up the beach, in at the gates and summarily buried there.

The town has always been closely linked with the Marines, and many ex-Marines have retired there. One woman I spoke to, however, whose late husband had been a Marine, felt it was not the same now, 'since the commandos have taken over ...' They are, perhaps, one link farther away from the sea, Deal's true territory.

The town was granted a new coat of arms in 1966, the shield bearing the three demi-lions passant and the three demi-hulls of the Cinque Ports, surmounted by a silver oar. The oar is carried before the Mayor of Deal on ceremonial occasions to signify sovereignty over the seas directly offshore, and when he visits Royal Navy ships in local waters he is automatically given the rank of Admiral. The arms are also on the Town Hall, which is a graceful building with a curved corner and white-painted colonnade, and on the gate of St George's Church, built in 1715. Nelson used to worship there, and there is a tablet to his memory placed there by William IV – a king honouring a sailor. In the churchyard is the grave of Captain Parker, Nelson's 'dear, good little Parker', who died after an unsuccessful raid on Boulogne. As the coffin was lowered into the earth, Nelson leant against a tree and wept. Mr Hickman (the oldest boatman) assured us that it was at the Royal Hotel, Deal, that 'Lord Nelson used to spend weekends with Lady Hamilton'.

Farther towards the sea is Carter House, the home of Elizabeth Carter, the eighteenth-century bluestocking and friend of Dr Johnson. Near by is the Time Ball Tower, which was used for signalling messages from the Downs during the Napoleonic Wars. (It is now the Information Bureau.) On top is the time-ball, which formerly enabled ships' captains to adjust their chronometers, as the ball rose to the top of the mast at 1 pm.

*

'He doesn't live by the clock – he lives by the tides,' I was told, by way of introduction to Wimpy (Frank) Fishlock. And they all said, 'You'll know him, when you see him ... in his wellies ...'

A story circulates that a historian was giving a lecture on Deal's past, down on the foreshore, and broke off his learned talk to ask, 'Who's that scruffy bugger?'

Incensed, Wimpy (for it was he, and he doesn't deny the story), put on his best clothes that night, to attend a further talk by the lecturer. He challenged the speaker, by pointing out several bits of information, and finally said, 'That's not the Deal I know.' 'You seem to know more about the place than I do,' the lecturer replied, piqued. 'What's your name?' Wimpy told him, '... and I'm the scruffy sod you saw down on the foreshore.'

Scruffy or not, Wimpy is curiously light on his feet and waves his hand (of which he lost two fingers and a thumb by a mine during the war, piloting) in a graceful swaying movement towards exhibits in Deal's Maritime Museum, explaining their history. His English is impeccable (except for accenting castle as cassell); his rugged tanned face with momentously bushy eyebrows and two white front teeth which light up his smile is intelligent, with that assured light in the eye that one sees in Oxford dons. His mind moves quickly, and when he tells a story it does not ramble on like that of many an old inhabitant relating anecdotes. His worn sea-clothes hang about his burly figure, again in the style of a don's neglected gown. On his black beret is a Kent badge.

I tracked him down, via his home and a bait shop. He was in the little museum (which is run by the Deal and Walmer history society) after hours, as he has a key. He was poring over a large old leather-bound book. 'Just checking something ...' he smiled. 'Ah, here we are –'

It was G. F. Raymond's *History of England,* of 1790, dedicated to George Augustus Frederick, Prince of Wales.

'1100. *An inundation of the sea overflowed the lands of Godwin Earl of Kent, which, to this day, are called Godwin sands.*'

He had been putting some German students right. 'They speak very good English.'

Then he took me round the exhibits. He has found over a thousand coins, many in Sandwich Bay where he digs bait (he also has a stall in Sandwich market), and a large number of them are on display. Roman coins, Cromwellian shillings, trade tokens, Elizabethan coins. 'We discovered the remains of an Elizabethan jetty running out to sea, at the top of Farrier Street – these Elizabethan coins were on the last bit of it.'

There are also Tudor tiles with a cabbalistic sign, Stone-Age bone tools found along the foreshore, stone Celtic crosses which were sewn into shrouds as weights for burial at sea, a sailmaker's brad, stone cannon shot, Napoleonic howitzer shells, Trinity House flags (he found three of them, which left only the Master's flag oustanding – Trinity House sent him one); also strange stone circles in different sizes ('We think it may be Polynesian money.)' Of all these things, as Wimpy says, he 'found the biggest half of it.' Two fine exhibits which were given are two sternboards of 1858 and 1878, carved with bears and mermaids. Will Honey, whom we met at the museum on another occasion, told us that they had belonged to cutters of John Willis, the great cutter owner, among whose ships were the *Cutty Sark*, the *Black Adder*, the *White Adder* and the *Lauderdale*, the sternboards of the last two being the ones here.

Wimpy Fishlock was the only person I spoke to in Deal who could explain why the corners of some houses were cut away, especially in narrow streets by the sea. This was to allow heavily laden carts to pass, to victual the ships. 'But my grandad reckoned they were to make it better for him to roll round the corners when he was drunk!'

A large hull in the museum is that of the *Saxon King*, a Deal galley. The galleys went to the aid of ships in distress, in competition with the life-boat. They would help the captain put his kedge-anchor in deeper water, if he had run aground, so that he could winch himself off. First salvage right went to whoever came to the aid of a ship. Deal pilots were renowned, and Wimpy told me that they had been known in the past to go to Australia and back, piloting a boat. Will Honey confirmed this, and explained that these North Sea or Deal Pilots were not certificated Trinity House pilots, but unofficial pilots. The Deal boatmen or 'hovellers' would go to sea for ten or fifteen years, then buy a boat and start pilotage work. He had seen a Chancery record of the reign of Henry VIII mentioning Deal men acting illegally, recovering an anchor and wreckage, with the note 'This must be stopped'. Another record of 1910 showed them still at work, and the same remonstrance – 'we must put a stop to this'. There were also official Cinque Ports pilots, who in 1853 merged with Trinity House.

Galleys were in use at Deal until the Second World War; after the war they were used as pleasure boats. Did the race for salvage lead to wrecking? I asked Wimpy. (A painting in the museum by W. H. Franklin, a photographer, shows people on the beach salvaging from wrecks on the shore in 1870.) 'It was unnecessary for any wrecking to be done ... You've only got to get a slight wind and you can have a really strong swell out there (on the Goodwins) ... in twenty minutes it can be a raging inferno ...'

But he told me how the law was turned to advantage by the Deal sharks and their successors. The escapades were daring. Strangely, two ships called SS *Mahratta* were wrecked here, one just before the 1914 war, one just before the last war. They lie practically on top of each other, and their cargoes were almost identical – wine, tea and bales of cotton. Wimpy's father, who worked as a guide on HMS *Victory* ('You can actually sign on to serve under Nelson still, on the *Victory*') had also been a Marine. He was on leave from the barracks when the second *Mahratta* sank, and found barrels of wine which had been washed ashore. 'My Uncle Jack went to look for him, and the barrels, and found a customs bloke breaking one open. My mother said, "Go down and find your father and tell him he's due back at the barracks." So I went, and found them drunk as newts, riding their bicycles. "Mother says you've got to come home. If you don't, she'll fetch the policeman." "He's just over the shingle bank there ..." "Well, she'll fetch the customs man, then –" "He's over there too ..." So she sent Uncle Sam, and he didn't come home either ...'

The wreck of the first *Mahratta* led to greater drama still. Wimpy's mother told him how her grandad found some silver plate from the ship, and hid it in his soot shed (he was a chimney sweep). As customs men searched for it, the inhabitants along the foreshore thought they were after missing chests of tea, and quickly tipped their loot down the Deal manholes. More resourcefully, one Granny Smith's family opened her feather mattress, where she lay ill in bed, and filled it with tea. As the hunt grew hotter, 'Mother's Grandad went out with seven bags of soot over the silver hidden in his soot cart. In Middle Street, he met the customs bloke. When challenged, Grandad banged the sacks, soot flew, and he then undid one bag, enveloping the customs man. "That's number one bloody bag ..." "All right, Grandad, go along then ..." Meanwhile, from the top end of long Middle Street, could be heard a hollering from the other end. What had happened? "What do you think's bloody happened?"' Granny Smith on her tea mattress, had been taken short ...

And for days afterwards, the Deal drains, as the tea poured down the manholes became swollen, were clogged.

I became a little confused as to whose grandad or father the stories concerned, and the two wrecks. I hope I have retold the events correctly, and that Wimpy will forgive me if I have not. So legend is handed down, and time concertinas. But in a world where two ships with identical names can have an identical fate, what is time? There are more things in heaven and earth – and in the sea ...

But Wimpy is realistic about the past, does not romanticize it. 'One of the things I regret is people talking of "the good old days". I don't see a queue for six pennyworth of stale bread or outside the soup kitchens now, or on a Friday for bread at the Town Hall. We've got it far better today. If you didn't vote Conservative you didn't get a bread ticket ... or asked to the tea parties ... My mother used to ask for help from the church. We had bread and jam or bread and water for weeks on end. She used to send us down to Lipton's for cracked eggs. I've gone out and cracked the buggers to make sure there were some.' He could not see that inflation was so bad, in his trade of bait-digging anyway. However, he added that it had been friendlier on the whole, in the past. 'You all mucked in together ... hop-picking, pea-picking ...'

The boatmen of the foreshore were divided into districts. There were the North Enders, from the coastguard station to Silver Street, the South Enders, from Silver Street to the Castle, and the Walmer Enders. On Saturday nights the North Enders would congregate in the Boatman's Rooms or the Rose and Crown to share out their takings. The South Enders would do the same, and neither group would tell the other what they had made. 'But if some bugger was in trouble in that water – they'd come and get you out ...'

Now the wall has been built along the north end, no boats can be beached there, and some shops there have closed down. 'That bit of the shore is dying ...'

By now Wimpy and I were outside the back of the museum, where are bits of hulk and chain and other finds, such as relics from probably the oldest ship found in Kent during excavations at Sandwich. He showed me an iron-heavy 'lower wood' for launching a life-boat. To get clear of the shelving shingle beach, the life-boat must be sent down over these heavy horizontally laid planks, which prevent it nosing into the stones. (Angling boats use the same method, with lighter planks, and are winched back by heavy chains. Deal boats have rounded keels, so that they run smoothly – you can tell a Deal boat by this.) The coxswain watches the sea and sees it breaking, and knows when the next wave is going to be a 'smooth'. He calls to let go, and the boat goes down at about 60 mph. Men hold the 'woods' in line with a rope. If they let go, a vital hour can be lost as the boat hits the wood askew and finishes up across the beach. 'I've seen it happen. You've got to have a lot of nerve, to hold that rope ...'

He gestures with his hand and makes a shuffling sideways shoulder movement with his heavy shoulders, like a dance step. We walk towards the station. I give Wimpy our address and he laughs. 'To tell you the truth I've only ever been to London and Southampton in my life ...'

And he walks away, with a warm smile, lovingly holding the large and priceless leather-bound *History of England* in his arms, with his light-footed Wellington gait.

*

It is difficult to set foot on the Goodwin sands today. Victorian pleasure boats used to make the trip, and the Reverend Thomas Stanley Treanor in his book *Heroes of the Goodwin Sands* wrote dramatically of 'the ominous grating thump of our boat's keel against the Goodwins, while the stumps of lost vessels grinned close by ...' George Goldsmith Carter has written of running breathlessly across them, followed by the racing tide sluicing over bright sand as soggy and unstable as a bottomless bed of wet cement ... while the sand melts and runs like hot wax, pools merge together and gullies crumble, broaden and widen while you flee for your life from the roaring surf ... something to remember for a lifetime.[13]

Since an accident in the West of England some years ago, boatmen have been reluctant to take parties out where there might be danger. The celebrated cricket match played on the Goodwins by the Royal Marines does not take place every year, and then only briefly. But there are still men who know the territory, and probably none who are more closely linked to it than the crews of the lightvessels who have made it a very different area to what it was in the eighteenth century, when there were no lightships there and ships were lost almost daily. As one of a lightvessel crew said to me, 'We're like a forgotten army out there...'

It is a cheerful army. The General Lighthouse Authority for England, Wales, the Channel Islands and Gibraltar is Trinity House, responsible for providing lighthouses, lightvessels, buoys and beacons. Trinity House is also the principal Pilotage Authority, and at Walmer the charitable side of the Corporation maintains homes for former officers of the Merchant Services and their dependants.

The history of Trinity House is long and distinguished. An association or guild of shipmen and mariners with benevolent objects, it may have been founded in the thirteenth century. In 1514 there is a record of Trinity House being at Deptford Strand, and the guild was at that date granted a charter by Henry VIII, giving it the duties of the defence and pilotage of the Thames – duties later extended far beyond these limits. By the seventeenth century the headquarters had moved to Water Lane, London, where in 1666 they were destroyed by the Great Fire. As a spokesman for Trinity House recently put it: '... our records go back to the Fire of London but due to poor damage control we lost a lot at that time!' The present headquarters is the fine building on Tower Hill, originally designed by Samuel Wyatt, which had to be rebuilt in 1953 because it had been partially destroyed by enemy action in 1940. In the present building there is a painting of Wyatt presenting the plans to a large band of his seafaring patrons. There are also models of lighthouse lights, of early ships such as the Stuart Royal Yacht (made in the days when shipwrights used models instead of plans), and in the Court Room, portraits including those of Elizabeth I, George V, Edward VII and Elizabeth II. (The present Master of Trinity House is the Duke of Edinburgh. The Deputy Master is Chairman of the Board; there are about three hundred Younger Brethren, from among whom the Elder Brethren or Board members are appointed.)

About half the marine pilots in the United Kingdom are licensed by Trinity House. But all pilots are self-employed, with their own area committees to decide on manning levels. Their takings are pooled and then divided out, with a percentage going to Trinity House, which sets the examinations by which they must qualify. The two-way traffic separation in the Channel is maintained by Trinity House with the French Lighthouse Authority, and Trinity House hope that a new uniform system of buoyage they have initiated will be accepted throughout northwest Europe in the 1980s. Among all the other services it offers, it is easy to forget that Trinity House has always been ready to send ships to serve in time of trouble, whether it was the thirty ships offered at the time of the Armada, or the six vessels which laid and serviced buoys to mark the lanes for the assault forces of the D-Day Normandy landings in the Second World War, and the manned lightvessels *Kansas* and *Juno* which were established in the area to indicate the mineswept pathway. (Such vessels can be relied upon for unfailing accuracy. A Field Research Station is run at Dungeness, testing among other things reliability of navigational aids.) During the war lights were extinguished and decoy buoys set, and in the 1914–18 war, lightvessels were supplied with rifles and mine sinking ammunition.

In the nineteenth century, lightships had crews of eleven, who spent two months on a ship and one month ashore where, however, their labours were 'anything but trifling' since they had to inspect buoys and bring out provisions. A lamplighter was paid £2 17s 1d a month; a seaman £2 9s 1d, with rations of beef 'such as it is',[14] bread, potatoes and split peas. Stories still circulate of the old crews catching starlings for pies, and of rationed water. Recreation seems to have included making work-boxes, writing

147

desks and shoes for the family. Today there is television, colour if you are lucky. The crews' quarters look very comfortable, with sparkling woodwork and brass, showers, and a galley where they cook the food they have bought themselves with a food allowance and which looks better equipped than many kitchens.

'What about exercise?' John and I asked. We were talking to the masters and crews of the *North* and *South Goodwin* light-vessels while they waited at Manston to be flown by Trinity House helicopter to relieve the existing crews. (John went out to the *South Goodwin* lightvessel with two of the crew of five, piloted with practised expertise by Captain Geoff Bond who, with his co-pilot, had to find the lightvessel in thick mist which enveloped the helicopter once out at sea, and then to land on the small landing-platform at the stern of the vessel.)

Frank Allen, one of the *South Goodwin* crew, told us that he did isometric exercises in the eight-pace-long lookout. A constant watch has to be kept, to see that the timing of the light is right – the *South Goodwin* gives a group flash of two every thirty seconds. If anything goes wrong with the engines, the light will be affected, and all the lighting machinery has to be kept well oiled. If a ship is seen going too near the sands, a morse message is sent; PS, 'You should not pass too close to me' and then U, 'You are running into danger', followed by rockets as an extreme danger warning. Recently a German ship forged ahead ignoring all warnings – the worried lightvessel men learnt later that the captain had known a channel through the sands.

Crews now do twenty-eight days on duty, twenty-eight days ashore. Frank Allen started work as a cabin boy in Sheerness dockyard, followed by work as a seaman in the Merchant Service. He then married and worked in the building trade for sixteen years, but when he suggested working for Trinity House his wife encouraged him. He now sees more of his wife and children, he says, and can book holidays ahead. But of crews' wives he said, 'I think they're the heroes', because they have to face worries alone, and post may be delayed. Frank writes copious letters home. Passing yachts may take letters from a dip net, and in addition the Deal and Walmer Angling Club 'bring goodies out' (and the life-boat pays a Christmas visit). A yachtsman once posted Frank's letter home in France. 'My wife was under the impression that once aboard a lightvessel I was there to stay ...' He does quite a bit of fishing, and likes the responsibility of the job, and the companionship 'if you've got a good crew – you only need one bad apple.'

The Master of his crew, Mr George Kozak, sees that it is a good one. He runs a dry ship, and for exercise gets his men to do extra scrubbing-down chores. He has been twenty-seven years with the service, and was in the Free Polish Navy during the war. 'Once one's set his feet on water, it drags you back ...' He, too, liked 'achieving something ... doing some good to help somebody else.' He has been on the *South Goodwin* light since 1969, and his deceptively slight figure clearly conceals a courage that has seen worse dangers than the Goodwins can provide. His father was a doctor, and as an officer in the Polish Army was taken to Northern Siberia by the Russians. His mother and sisters were taken to Middle Siberia. At thirteen he was taken to Southern Siberia on a five-year sentence for being a Boy Scout. With five other boys he escaped and walked about two thousand miles to the Caspian Sea, where they managed to get on a boat to Persia. He then put his age up from 15 to 17 and joined the Polish Navy. He was not able to trace his family until 1961, but they were alive, and in the end, safe.

'We are like traffic lights at the *South Goodwin*,' he said. 'Like Piccadilly Circus ...' and he urged us to see the radar screen at Dover Coastguard, where the traffic shows up like a snowstorm, ships setting their course from the light, and hovercraft snaking in between. (The lightvessels themselves, are anchored with exceptionally heavy cable, and in a storm more cable is veered out so that the weight tethers the vessel.)

In fog, or at other vessels such as the *North Goodwin*, it can be lonelier. Nothing all round but the grey mist and sea. A forgotten army. And at regular intervals the regular vibrating moan of the compressed-air fog signal. After a long period of fog, I was told at the London headquarters, mens' conversations have regular gaps in them, spaced to coincide with the deafening signal...

There are honorary Elder Brethren of Trinity House, selected by invitation. Ted Heath and Harold Wilson have been awarded this honour. Churchill was an Elder Brother, as was that other distinguished Lord Warden of the Cinque Ports, Wellington.

*

At Walmer is the official residence of the Lord Warden. The shingle at Walmer – which is more spread out, less urban than Deal – is divided from Walmer Castle and the land by trees on the beach planted by Lord Granville, who was Lord Warden towards the end of the last century. A great part of Walmer, particularly in Upper Walmer, below the Old Church and Walmer Manor, is planted with fine trees, and in fields round the castle even the hawthorn bushes look as though placed by design. William Pitt the Younger, who was Lord Warden from 1792–1806, was a great tree planter, and so was Lady Hester Stanhope, the beautiful and egocentric virago who called herself 'Queen of the Arabs', who had cared for Pitt during his last days and had laid out much of the gardens at Walmer Castle.

How greatly we need a man such as Pitt today. An MP at 22, Prime Minister at 24, his patriotism was such that his dying words were: 'Oh, my country! How I leave my country.' Incorrupt in an age in which corruption was rife, he took on the premiership for a disillusioned country in great peril and with a national debt of £245,000,000 (as against a revenue of £25,000,000).[15] He strengthened the economy (he was the introducer of income tax, but sought to free manufacturers from crippling taxes, and when assessed taxes were introduced, led voluntary contributions by donating £2,000 from his comparatively small income; he waged war against smugglers by lowering the tea tax and increasing window tax, and stopped other frauds occurring); he reconstituted the Navy, so that by 1786, England was safe from her enemies, and by this maritime revival also increased merchant shipping and overseas trade. A man of the eighteenth century, who believed it was a man's duty to work (sometimes children's also), he supported Wilberforce in his fight to free slaves, and took a wide view of the brotherhood of man: 'To suppose that any nation can be unalterably the enemy of any other is weak and childish.'

Amid the wreck and misery of nations ... our still higher exultation ought to be that we provide not only for our own safety, but hold out a prospect to nations now bending under the iron yoke of tyranny ...

and that at least in this corner of the world the name of liberty is still revered, cherished, and sanctified.

His oratory was unequalled, perhaps until England's next great hour of danger.

Events forced Pitt's hand to war, but he died leaving the country buoyed up by Trafalgar. 'England has saved herself by her exertions, and will, as I trust, save Europe by her example.'

When invasion by Napoleon seemed most imminent, Pitt and Camden had the Military Canal dug from Hythe, to protect Romney Marsh, the most likely landing place of a fleet from Boulogne. (It is interesting to note that, as Lord Clark remarks in his biography, *The Other Half*, a copy of the German plan for the invasion of England, now in the Greenwich Museum, shows the same area designed for Hitler's army.) This was backed up by the line of Martello Towers, stretching along the coast. Pitt was very popular in Deal and Walmer, and local boatmen promised that they would man fifty gunboats. And because of his efforts in Kent, the Volunteer movement spread rapidly. He drilled his local Volunteers himself, and was determined to lead them into battle if need arose. However, when he asked Sir John Moore, commander of Shorncliffe Camp, what part the Volunteers would take in an invasion, the General pointed to rising ground and rather unfairly answered: 'I would post you there while we soldiers do the fighting on the beach.'[16]

Wellington, the greatest general of them all, was Lord Warden from 1829–52, and died at Walmer Castle. Elizabeth Longford's biography, *The Years of the Sword* and *Pillar of State*, is worthy of the great man, who although revered as a national hero, could refer smilingly to himself as *the Shew* whom crowds flocked to see in the streets, and who never lost his simplicity. When asked what it was like to be a hero, he finally replied, 'I feel I am but a man.'[17] She draws a delightful picture of him romping with his grandchildren at Walmer, playing the 'cushion affair', giving them tea in his saucer and writing minuscule letters to children who received none; and of him writing to a small boy to say that his pet toad was well.[18] His room in the castle is as when he died, with the armchair in which he died and his camp bed, whose narrowness caused him to say: 'When it's time to turn over it's time to turn out.' In an adjoining room are mementoes – his handkerchief, his Lord Warden's coat, and a pair of Wellington boots. A million and a half people lined the route of his funeral cortège. Among the mourning coaches and vast funeral car was the Duke's horse, led by his groom, with reversed Wellington boots hanging on either side. The sight brought tears to the eyes of the crowd, including those of Queen Victoria.

The Duke's favourite tree at Walmer was a lime. He was no gardener, but hired as one an old sergeant of the Peninsular War who had written to him to say he had no pension. When the Duke asked, 'Do you know anything about gardening?' the man replied, 'No, Your Grace.' 'Then learn, learn, and come here this day fortnight . . .' And when a fortnight later, he was told, 'Take the place of gardener at Walmer Castle', the poor man reiterated, 'I know very little about gardening.' Wellington replied, 'Nor do I, nor do I . . .'[19]

A simple conciseness shown also at times by Churchill, who when an epaulette came loose on his Lord Warden's uniform at his Installation, merely tore it off. And who in notes for a speech made in June 1940, wrote on the subject of night bombing: 'Learn to get used to it. Eels get used to skinning.'[20] (At the same time he wrote: 'This supreme battle depends upon the courage of the ordinary man and woman.') Two days earlier he had made one of his great speeches in the House of Commons:

I expect that the battle of Britain is about to begin. Upon this battle depends the survival of Christian civilization . . . Let us therefore brace ourselves to our duties, and so bear ourselves that, if the British Empire and its Commonwealth last for a thousand years, men will still say, 'This was their finest hour.'

It is fashionable to demythologize heroes today. Churchill refutes such attacks, not only by what he was, but by what he understood. Speaking in tribute to Neville Chamberlain (whose policy he had spoken against after the Munich Agreement), he said:

Then again, a few years later, when the perspective of time has lengthened, all stands in a different setting. There is a new proportion. There is another scale of values. History with its flickering lamp stumbles along the trail of the past, trying to reconstruct its scenes, to revive its echoes, and kindle with pale gleams the passion of former days. What is the worth of all this? The only guide to man is his conscience;

the only shield to his memory is the rectitude and sincerity of his actions. It is very imprudent to walk through life without this shield, because we are so often mocked by the failure of our hopes and the upsetting of our calculations; but with this shield, however the fates may play, we march always in the ranks of honour.[21]

*

Walmer Castle is a habitable rather than a warlike place, despite being partly shaped like a gun turret (one of Henry VIII's), and with cannon on the terrace. (Despite, too, having been called an ancestral dog-hole by Lord Curzon, when he was made Lord Warden. Lady Curzon called it 'that darling old castle'.) It has a typical 'Kentish Onion' cupola, of which another example is on the attractive seventeenth-century red brick and flint tower of Ringwould church (Ringwould was a Non-Corporate Member of the Cinque Port of Dover). Pitt's furniture is still at Walmer; also prints preserved by W. H. Smith of the book firm when he was Lord Warden. The proportions, with not very high ceilings, are pleasing, and windows let in plenty of light, particularly the one cut in the fourteen-foot wall by Wellington, to make Queen Victoria's room more pleasant for her visit there.

The gardens are Walmer's chief delight. The clipped yews planted by Lady Hester Stanhope are still there, although a little time-worn. The present Head Gardener, Mr Pond, rightly thinks it would be sacrilege to have them out. We talked to him during the time he was preparing the gardens for the Installation of Her Majesty the Queen Mother, who surely of all recent Lord Wardens can best appreciate the gardens at Walmer. He showed us the site where she would plant a Turkey oak, in the tradition of famous tree-planters there, such as Mr Asquith (a lime, 1914), Lord Queensberry (a box elder), the Marquess of Reading, Lord Curzon, Sir Robert Menzies and the present Lord North, to whom Sir Robert Menzies was godfather. Churchill planted a tulip tree, but it has not yet flowered – it doesn't like the cold winds.

The soil is medium loam over chalk, with deep topsoil. Round the moat of the castle are fig trees, bamboos and pear trees, with sun-loving shrubs and plants such as hebes, cistus, choisya ternata (Mexican Orange Flower), potentillas and roses. Stone lions stand among wallflowers in the spring and long herbaceous borders lead up to two terraces with, in summer, delphiniums which Mr Pond described as 'spectacular', which came from Regent's Park in London.

For the Queen Mother, he and his staff of three were planting red, gold, silver and blue flowers on one terrace, to echo her standard – double red Geranium Gustav, French marigolds, lobelia and cineraria maritima with regal small palms. Other beds had pink geraniums and blue petunias. There are also wild areas at Walmer, and espaliers of apples, some so old that they can't now be named. Among the trees are pines, cedars and a sumach, probably part of the pinetum-craze of the Edwardians and Victorians who loved to collect foreign species. Mr Pond is reinstating wood anemones and bluebells among the distant trees, with silver birch trees, and more shrubs to give shelter to birds. He is, he says, not even entirely against squirrels – 'Wildlife gets less and less every year ...' And he is wholly against pruning – 'When you start pruning, you lose the natural shape ... to me there is nothing between formal and natural.' He regretted the fact that while elm disease and hard weather had taken 150 trees, they had not affected a flowering cherry, which dominates the top of the terraces, and that there are so many copper-leaved trees, 'even purple-leaved hazelnuts'. The Turkey oak is a step in the right direction.

6 Dover

'... the Nobilitie of that time were fully persuaded, that both the safetie and daunger of the whole Realme consisted in this one Castell ... And to it finally, the countrey men in all times of trouble have an especiall eie and regarde.'

William Lambarde

'I saw the clifts and hills plaine, but in some cleer dayes towards the evening you may see the towers and buildings of Callice ...'

Celia Fiennes

It was Matthew Paris who in the thirteenth century first wrote that Dover was the lock and key of the whole realm of England (*'Clavis et Repagulum totius Regni'*[1]). It remains so today; the only one of the original five of the Cinque Ports that is still a major seaport; impregnable despite two World Wars; vital despite recurring rumbles of a proposed Channel tunnel and the cross-Channel air traffic that began when Blériot landed on a slope below Dover Castle.

A small concrete outline of Blériot's plane marks the place where he landed. 'After making the first Channel flight, Louis Blériot landed at this spot on Sunday 25th July 1909.' It is on a downhill slope, just short of the Castle hill, which would have made a more unpleasant landing. In the town museum a coloured newspaper, *Le Petit Journal*, shows under the headline *'Blériot atterit sur la falaise de Douvres'*, two men in plus fours running towards the plane with the French and English flags. Photographs show a crowd of men and boys, in boaters, surrounding the fragile-looking craft and its indomitable aviator.

The *Daily Mail* had offered a £1,000 prize for the first man to cross the Channel. Two men, Latham and Blériot, were finally in the running, waiting for a gale over Calais to die down. They behaved with gentlemanly courtesy, calling on each other and admiring one another's planes – Blériot's in fact rather battered after a recent flight, and having to be drawn to its take-off point by an old white horse. Blériot himself was on crutches, having had his foot scalded by petrol from the engine on this earlier prize-winning cross-country journey – one of many accidents which he suffered while flying the monoplanes, which he had built himself, with undaunted enthusiasm – it seemed he had a charmed life. He got up before dawn on 25 July. The gale had abated, but there were still gusts of wind and it threatened to become squally again, so at 4.10 am Blériot handed his crutches to his mechanic, and performed a test flight. At 4.35 am he took off, without a compass or map. 'In which direction is Dover?' he asked some spectator ... 'Thank you' as they pointed towards the mist shrouded coast of England. The Blériot XI vanished straight as a dart into the weather. And someone ran to waken Blériot's rival.[2]

After a difficult flight, Blériot saw the green fields of England. He turned west, and flew over the Home Fleet, and then made towards Shakespeare Cliff. He saw a figure running across Northfall Meadow with a French flag, as a sign that he could land there, and glided down, but was caught in a sudden downdraught and pancaked hard from about sixty feet. Across the Channel his rival burst into tears, then sent a congratulatory telegram.

Blériot returned to France with his wife, who had followed on an escort ship and, as he walked down the gangway, he was handed a telegram telling him he had been made a Chevalier of the Legion of Honour. He also received orders for over a hundred aircraft.

No pilot of today, it has been said, no matter how great, could repeat this exploit in such a frail aircraft, with such an engine.[3] And a new era had dawned, although few would recognize it. The *Daily Mail* commented:

The British people have hitherto dwelt in their islands because they have attained at the price of terrible struggles and of immense sacrifices the supremacy of the sea. But locomotion is now being transferred to an element where Dreadnoughts are useless and sea power no shield against attack. As the potentialities of the aeroplane have been proved, we must take energetic steps to develop a navy of the air.

Parliament reacted by planning four new superdreadnoughts. Five years afterwards, victory at the first Battle of the Marne was to depend on the Royal Flying Corps, who by the end of the war were the finest air arm of their day.

*

The great earthworks on which Dover Castle stands are Iron Age in origin. The Roman Pharos beside the castle was built in the first century AD (it is probably the oldest man-made structure we have). But it was King Harold who built a fort round a well on these eastern cliffs, in accordance with a promise made to William of Normandy, and it was Henry II who later built the great castle keep and massive stone walls. Richard Coeur de Lion stayed here while equipping a fleet to sail to the Holy Land; Henry V used the castle as his base and returned here in triumph after Agincourt; Henry VIII set out from Dover to the Field of the Cloth of Gold ('never in the memory of man was seen so vast a multitude so bravely arrayed and adorned'); Charles I fitted out the royal apartments to receive his bride Princess Henrietta Maria from France; Charles II landed at Dover on his restoration and tèn years later celebrated here for a fortnight with his beloved sister Henrietta (Minette); Cromwell's men had earlier infiltrated the castle, and perhaps it is noteworthy that it was an Englishman who achieved this, for the one and only time; French prisoners were guarded here during the Napoleonic wars; here the evacuation from Dunkirk was planned, and the castle in the 'Hell-Fire Corner' of Dover, remained solidly standing. Did Hitler, like William the Conqueror, want it for his own?

I first visited the castle on a day of torrential rain and hail, a freak storm. I took refuge in a taxi. Thunder crashed overhead. 'You could see the Blériot memorial from the castle when I was a child,' the taxi-driver said. Now trees hide it.

Nothing hides the castle. On its clifftop, from along the coast, the square keep and great walls, with small flag flying, appear a perfect symbolical castle, in the county of Kent whose motto is 'Invicta'. Nearer to, it becomes a towering fortress, grey and granite-hard on the Eastern Heights, daunting and inconceivably rock-like. The road to it winds steeply up the near-precipitous hill, and the outer towers and curtain walls rear massively above you. No one could ever take this stronghold; it reduces the on-comer to the proportions of a midget, tilting spears at the might that was – and perhaps is – England. Symbolically too, until recently there was near the castle entrance, at this 'lock and key' post of the kingdom, a prosaic but significant notice proclaiming 'Immigration Office'. You go on through one of the towered gate-ways into the inner bailey, and the keep, with walls that are seventeen to twenty-one feet thick, ninety-five feet high – strengthened with buttresses and built of dark Kentish rag with Caen stone – stands square above you, with a small Union Jack streaming from the ramparts in the wind, 469 feet above sea level, compelling your 'especiall eie and regarde' and moving you, in a moment of unguarded emotion, face-to-face with this old guar-dian on its rock.

*

In a thunderstorm the castle was superb – lightning playing round the clifftop and thunder breaking like cannon-fire between the dark bastion walls, under a black sky. I hurried inside the keep, which is protected by a forebuilding with three towers and three flights of steps, originally barred by three iron-clad doors, and a drawbridge at first-floor level. No wonder no foreign enemy ever got in.

The entrance way leads into the second storey of the keep, where there is a well shaft which descends into the chalk of the cliff far below, and at whose head are leaden pipes which (as early as the late twelfth century) piped water to other corners of the building. On this second storey are two great halls, which were the state apartments. Their timber roofs were replaced by brick vaults to take the weight of cannons above, during the Napoleo-nic wars. Leading off one hall is a small chapel of 1180-90 dedi-cated to St Thomas à Becket, one of two in the keep.

Robes of a Baron of the Cinque Ports are in a showcase in the state rooms and round the walls is an impressive collection of weapons. American visitors linger by the pikes and armour.

Statutes of Dover Castle (in the reign of Henry III)
   i. *At sunset the bridge shall be drawn, and the gates shut ...*

ii. *Any warder found outside the walls, or otherwise off his guard, shall be put in the Donjon prison ...*

iv. *...if a chief guard discover a warder asleep, he shall take something from him ... or cut a piece out of part of his clothes, to witness against him ...*

vi. *Either sergeant or warder using vile language shall be brought before the Constable ...*

The porters at the gate shall not suffer any persons to enter, until they have taken particular notice of them, and if they be strangers, they shall not step within the sill of the wicket ... but every person asking admittance is to receive civil treatment ...

If the King arrives unexpectedly in the night, the great gates shall not be opened to him, but he shall go to the postern called the King's Gate ...

'See the three holes in the seat, two large and one small ... because you used to get young ones ... one of the princesses from abroad ... Richard, the one on the crusade I think it was ... she was seven when he married her and she was a widow at fourteen ...' (Isabelle of Valois, who landed aged eight to marry Richard II).

The attendant wasn't using vile language, but it was vivid. He had drawn me aside to a 'garderobe', where there was one of the five lavatories of the keep, all using the same 'shoot and pit' leading to an exit hole at ground level where the pit might be cleaned out. 'They used to put quicklime and straw into the pit, and they hung their clothes up here – the fumes from the lime and ammonia killed the fleas and lice, you see. They kept their dirt on themselves to keep warm. "Never cast a clout till May is out ..." – that meant keeping your clothes on and two baths a year, one at Christmas and one in June. You know they talk about a June bride? Well [a close wink], ladies got married in June because they smelled sweeter, didn't they ...'

I climbed up to the roof for a bit of air. From here there is a magnificent view, out to sea, grey streaked with silver that day, with France clearly visible. Down into the dip of the town, and over to the Western Heights, beyond which juts Shakespeare Cliff with its jagged white edge. The keep is battlemented; the drop sheer. With lightning forking again, I returned to the bowels of the castle, where there is a model of the Battle of Waterloo, made in the 1830s by Captain William Siborne, who lived for eight months at the farm of La Haye Sainte to get the details correct. Small model horses lie on their sides on a turf battlefield; Wellington is there on his charger Copenhagen. The Info-Bar commentary is equally dramatic, with whinneying horses and the tramp of feet. Wellington: 'Before you send me more generals, let me see more troops ...' Gunfire and the sound of bugles. '... the squares like knotted ropes held tight ...' Then Napoleon leading out the Imperial Guard, and later, for the first time in their history, his Invincibles retreating, *'La Garde recule ...'* As the commentary ends, a cry of *'merde!'* goes up from the French troops.

French prisoners from this war were kept in the castle, within sight perhaps of the 'towers and buildings of Callice'. Their graffiti (and I realized gratefully, since my guide was conducting me again, that one tends to forget that graffiti does not necessarily have the meaning obscene) are cut into the walls. Messages of love, or despair, or hatred. One flowing carving incorporates the Cross, with symbols of roses, the crowing cock, the reed with a sponge, a spear, the dice thrown for Christ's clothing, the passion flowers of Calvary. Above, the incised words scribbled, reverberating round the gaunt walls of the castle, *'Dieu tout puissant délivre moi ...'*

*

Underground works were constructed at the northern end of the castle by Hubert de Burgh, after a siege by the French in 1216, as part of a series of new towers and defences. The underground works were adapted and enlarged later, with features such as a remote-control booby-trap, at the threat of invasion by Napoleon, when gun platforms and cannon emplacements were also built. Dover was seen to be the last stronghold of the English army, should Napoleon's troops land on Romney Marsh, assumed to be his chosen point of attack. There are also underground works in the East Cliff below the castle, first mentioned soon after they were built in 1539, as 'the new ramparts and bulwarks in the rock where the sea beats'.[4] These underground works, linked to the castle, were the site from which Operation Dynamo covering the evacuation from Dunkirk was directed. Here Vice-Admiral Bertram Ramsay, Flag Officer Dover, who was to execute the operation, had his headquarters. Some of the chalk tunnels had been extended into barrack-like rooms. A window opened on to an iron-railed balcony, and from here Ramsay, and Churchill, could look out across the Channel. (In A. J. Barker's *Dunkirk*,[5] there is a telling photograph of Churchill's backview, solid in tin hat, looking down over the harbour. C. Northcote Parkinson, who was a territorial officer there at the time, referred in a BBC radio interview recently to the traditional style of it all – 'Our helmets would have attracted no adverse comment at Agincourt ...'[6])

On a clear day, Cap Gris Nez was visible from the balcony; in May 1940 flashes from German artillery shelling Boulogne could be seen. Ramsay, who was 57, had had long experience of the Channel and had commanded a flotilla in the Dover Patrol in the First World War. He was in command of the Allied naval forces on D-Day in June 1944, and carried with him the same telescope with which he had watched Operation Dynamo carry out the successful evacuation four years before. Sadly, he was killed in a plane crash near Paris in 1945.

By 1 June 1940 four-fifths of the British Army in France had been saved, and the evacuation was completed on 4 June. Churchill had asked a week before to make a statement in the House of Commons on that day, thinking that 'it would be my hard lot to announce the greatest military disaster in our long history'. He was able instead to announce 'A miracle of deliverance, achieved by valour, by perseverance, by perfect discipline, by faultless service, by resource, by skill, by unconquerable fidelity ...' He continued by saying that the Navy had carried 335,000 English and French men 'out of the jaws of death', but added, 'We must be very careful not to assign to this deliverance the attributes of a victory. Wars are not won by evacuations. But there was a victory inside this deliverance, which should be noted. It was gained by the Air Force'.[7] Attacks on the scene of the evacuation had been routed by British planes fighting in the ratio one to four. In *The Struggle for Survival*, Moran notes that Winston told him,

Dunkirk was the turning-point. In a month after their return to England these men became a formidable army. It was one thing to plan an invasion of England before Dunkirk, with a hundred thousand men; quite another when perhaps half a million would be needed to break down the defences of this army.[8]

Only two days later,

June the 6th, 1940, was one of the most fertile days of my life. I put down on paper everything that we should need for a successful invasion of France. I did this two days after Dunkirk. Dr Johnson said: 'When a man is going to be hanged it concentrates his mind wonderfully.'

(He had in fact described the landing craft and the Mulberry Harbours in a paper to Lloyd George on 7 July 1917, nearly thirty years before the Normandy landings – to be used in a scheme for the capture of the Friesian Islands of Borkom and Sit.)[9]

Perhaps at least four of the virtues Churchill lists as making the miracle at Dunkirk possible are no longer fashionable, to some perhaps intangible, or even incomprehensible.

They know that they have behind them a people who will not flinch or weary of the struggle – hard and protracted though it will be; but that we shall rather draw from the heart of suffering itself the means of inspiration and survival, and of a victory won not only for our own time, but for the long and better days that are to come...[10]

Perhaps we should be glad that he cannot see now, what we have made of those long and better days, which he always bore in mind.

*

'I've got a corner of the church, all of that thing ... and you –' Tourist photographing his wife, in tracksuit, in front of the Roman pharos.

The Church of St Mary-in-Castro was possibly built on the site of Roman barracks; it incorporates Roman tiles and a Saxon doorway. It was restored in the Victorian era. John Newman in his splendidly eloquent North East and East Kent volume of Pevsner's *Buildings of England* styles the Victorian mosaics 'quite exceptionally unsympathetic'.[11]

So old, near the edge of the castle cliff, the little church is dramatically atmospheric, buffeted by wind and weather. Beside it, the Roman pharos, or lighthouse, tapers towards the upper storeys. The seemingly frail structure holds two millennia of history within its hollow beacon walls. Together, the two small buildings huddle as outposts by the sea, against time, against modernity.

On the Western Heights, on the other side of the town, was a twin beacon. Fires of brushwood were lit in the base of each open-topped tower, so that flames and smoke streamed skywards, lighting ships into the safety of the harbour between them, and serving as landmarks for navigators at sea. The Western Heights were fortified too, at the time of the Napoleonic wars, or rather hollowed out in a series of impregnable chambers, with gun-slits and a citadel – now a Borstal – from which to cover the whole valley. The size of the undertaking was monumental; much of it is intact; when he visited it in 1823, Cobbett found,

a hill containing, probably, a couple of square miles or more, hollowed like a honeycomb. Here are line upon line, trench upon trench, cavern upon cavern, bomb-proof upon bomb-proof ... scandalously disgraceful, more brick and stone have been buried in this hill than would go to build a neat new cottage for every labouring man in the counties of Kent and Sussex!

These hills by the River Dour were a natural stronghold. Neolithic tribes lived here and Bronze Age spear-heads and armlets can be seen in Dover museum. But before the colonization of Dubris, Roman Dover, the area had been largely sweeping downland. The Romans used the large, natural tidal harbour in the Dour estuary as their main base across the Channel. They already had a base and harbour at Boulogne, marked by a large lighthouse. Their fleet in British waters was known as the *Classis Britannica,* and during the conquest period was used in a support role, ferrying supplies and troops along the coast and rivers, and on northern campaigns. Inscriptions show that units of the fleet helped build Hadrian's Wall. During the later, peaceful period, the fleet was probably employed at times in mining Wealden iron, because tiles stamped with CLBR *(Classis Britannica)* have been found at nine sites in Kent and Sussex – Richborough, Dover, Folkestone, Lympne, Cranbrook, Beauport Park, Bodiam, Bardown, Pevensey – of which the inland sites are all iron-working areas. An altar found at Lympne, suggests a secondary base to Dover; an arm of Watling Street finished there, as at Dover.

In 1970 possibly one of the most exciting archaeological finds ever to have been made took place. Mrs Joan Nelson, who is a member of the Kent Archaeological rescue unit, told me about it when she showed me round the site. She also gave me a cup of tea, in a manner typical of hospitable Dovorians, and told me about the exercise book in which she is writing down her experiences while at the site, for her granddaughter. Sir Mortimer Wheeler, she told me, was always convinced that there must have been a second Roman lighthouse at Dover – only a few stones remain. He was equally convinced that there must have been a Saxon Shore fort here, and spent some time excavating what he estimated to have been the site, but found nothing. Then when plans for the new Dover bypass went through, Brian Philp had the chance to excavate the Queen Street area, and within twenty minutes of starting digging, found the *Classis Britannica* fort, and later, walls of the Saxon Shore fort. The latter was only a few yards from where Sir Mortimer Wheeler had looked for it. 'Sir Mortimer,' Mrs Nelson told me, 'always said it was his site!'

The naval fort was a large rectangular stone fort, with quays and a harbour wall. It is thought to have been built in the second century AD. Sadly, the naval fort is now covered by the bypass, but the Roman 'Painted House', which is Dover's leading tourist attraction at present (sign-posted almost from the motorway), is the finest Roman town house on show in Britain, having been open to the public since 1977. It is of the same era as the naval fort, probably the home of an official of the Roman fleet or for visitors crossing the channel. Cutting right through the walls of the house is a wall of the Saxon Shore fort, built later when auxiliary army units were moved to Dover to combat Saxon raids, and so overlapping the old naval fort and civilian settlement. The wall is massive, made of flint, chalk, and tufa, which is composed of millions of sea creatures, and is found in the Dour Valley.

The painted house itself is so called because the internal wall surfaces, in rooms heated by a hypocaust underground heating system, were plastered and painted in brilliant colour. The plaster is the most complete Roman plaster ever found north of the Alps and fragments are being most carefully reconstructed. There is a dado of dark green or red, above which are rectangular panels between painted columns, containing motifs such as trees, fronds and blazing torches. Its survival is due to the fact that the rooms were sealed into the walls of the fort.

There are also coins on show at the site (a particularly good profile of Trajan), figurines, a very tender Mother Goddess figure clasping suckling twins, and a fine marble head found in a drain just outside the naval fort, of a Roman matron who may have lived in Dover, fashioned in the style of Hadrian's Empress Sabina, but looking remarkably like Angela Rippon.

There are many buildings of later periods in Dover which are particularly interesting – some of them small in scale. Apart from the castle, and the docks, Dover appears almost homely in its proportions – attractively so. The Parish Church of St Mary-the-Virgin, in Cannon Street, is flint, with graceful pinnacles, and a western tower which is richly arcaded, an encrusted lace-like pattern of stone waves or scales contrasting with its solid flint sides. Perfectly fitting for this sea town, with the dignity of a cathedral despite its unpretentious size, it has inside a gallery used by the Pilots of the Cinque Ports. Then the little wayside chapel of Saint Edmund (the first divinity student at Oxford, founder of St Edmund Hall, and later Archbishop of Canterbury). Built by his old friend, St Richard of Chichester, who died only four days after achieving his wish to consecrate it to his memory. And the Maison Dieu founded as a hostel for pilgrims, which now incorporates the Town Hall, and town museum. In the Stone Hall or Great Chamber, are banners of the Cinque Ports Volunteers, raised in the emergencies of 1794 and 1803, and a portrait of Churchill by Bernard Hailstone, dominating those of other Lord Wardens. There are stained glass windows by Ambrose Poynter, and in the Council Chamber is the original Cinque Ports banner, the 'Ancient Banner of the Cinque Ports carried before the Bailiffs of the Ports at the Yarmouth Fair' depicting a shell above the Cinque Ports lions and ships. Among other notable portraits are one of George IV on horseback and one of Elizabeth I, which she let the town have for twenty-five shillings in 1598, the price she paid for it, because she felt it had been so badly painted. It shows her with a very pursed mouth, no glamour, a ruff which makes her neck goitrous and a wig too high and of the wrong colour. An understandable reaction on her part, one feels.

In a neighbouring room is the Dover Patrol book – the Book of Remembrance of 1914-18, of the famous Dover Patrol, whose headquarters was the outer harbour at Dover, successors in the tradition of the Cinque Ports, in protecting our Channel shores, and protecting also the mass of merchant shipping in the Downs, both Allied and neutral, from mines. Miles of mine nets were laid, from the Goodwins to Dunkirk, and to screen the shipping in the Downs. The Patrol kept the entrance to the narrows of the Channel open for the passage of troops and materials to France – about five million troops were transported to France during the war, and it has been stated that there was not a single casualty due to enemy action.

Many of the men were fishermen or civilians in the RNVR. At the beginning, the drifters and trawlers they worked from were entirely unarmed, and only later a rifle or small gun was issued, and the trawlers acquired depth charges and a wireless telegraph set. The trawlers swept for mines, in all weathers, and helped the drifters maintain the barrage net defence. Joseph Conrad paid them tribute:

In their early days some of them had but a single rifle on board to meet the three- or four-inch guns of the German destroyers ... without speed to get away, they made a sacrifice of their lives every time they went out for a turn of duty.... But in truth that which in the last instance kept the German forces from breaking disastrously on any dark night into the Channel, and jeopardizing the very foundation of our resisting power, was not the wonderfully planned and executed defences of nets and mines, but the indomitable hearts of the men of the Dover Patrol.[12]

In the belfry of the Town Hall is the Zeebrugge Bell, taken by the Germans from a Belgian church to give warning of attacks. On St George's Day the Mayor strikes 'Eight Bells' in memory of the men who died in the Zeebrugge raid of 1918, who are buried in St James's Cemetery. There is a Dover Patrol memorial at St Margaret's Bay.

Minesweeping in the Second World War also had a vital role to play, as had the work of life-boat crews. During the 'phoney war', from the outbreak of hostilities until April 1940, it was peaceful on land, but U-boats, mines and bomber planes tried to destroy Britain's communications at sea. In seven months more than three hundred ships were sunk, and during this time life-boat crews rescued nearly two thousand lives.[13] And this under great difficulties – maroons were forbidden so that messages had to come via telephone or bicycle; the younger men were in the forces so that crews were often over 60 or under 18. There were no harbour lights and very few lighthouses, and to cap it all the winter of 1939 was the hardest in living memory, with spray freezing as it fell and oilskins having to be chipped off.

*

Dover's museum is in the same Maison Dieu building. It has varied exhibits, including models of ships, fossilized ferns of the carboniferous period (250,000,000 years ago), and a fossilized sea-lily of 400,000,000 years ago. Also Victorian children's toys, and a complete set of carpet bowls (striped china) which belonged to the grandfather of Mrs V. Arrindell, who was at the museum when I visited it – 'Arthur Negus said recently that he had never seen a complete set.'

It is such domestic touches which make Dover appealing, and it is the townspeople's pride in them, in their town, and their friendliness, which make it a town perhaps different from others along the coast. Warmer, less inhibited, more open to exchange, as befits a town with such a past, both of history and of hardship, enlivened by the continual hubbub of cross-Channel traffic. A much used and welcoming town, like a warm friendly fishwife, standing with arms sturdily akimbo in the doorway to England.

Not a very intellectual town perhaps. There is no theatre; for that residents have to go to Canterbury's Marlowe Theatre. Some complain that there are few amenities, but in the opinion of one resident, 'If there was a theatre, they wouldn't go to it ... they prefer bingo ...'

Another historical building is the refectory of Dover College, which was part of a Benedictine priory, the Priory of St Martin. It is at Dover College that the Grand Court of Shepway is held to install the Lord Warden.

Here, on 1 August 1979, Queen Elizabeth the Queen Mother

was installed as Constable of Dover Castle and Lord Warden and Admiral of the Cinque Ports. Here she captured the heart of Dover, having already been given the keys of Dover Castle by the Deputy Constable (Brigadier Maurice Atherton, the 200th Keeper of the Keys of Dover Castle, who said that, now, no one had been able to find a lock to fit them).

In the morning, the castle had been shrouded in angry black mist, and the Royal Yacht *Britannia*, dressed overall for the occasion, was barely visible through squalls of rain, in the harbour. But with the naturalness that enabled her to wear a mackintosh cape as superbly as Churchill his miscreant epaulettes at the same ceremony, the Queen Mother arrived at Dover College in her carriage, preceded by a Captain's Escort of the Household Cavalry, despite rumours running ahead of her that all would be cancelled, or that she would arrive in a car.

The Barons (there are now four remaining) and Officers of the Cinque Ports Delegations were already in the grounds, in fur collars and cuffs, tricorne hats, white frilled stocks, red and black robes, decked with staves topped by satin ribbons and silver maces – enough falderals for twenty pantomimes, and yet worn with complete dignity and purpose, in this ancient ceremonial. Before the marquee in which the Court was held, a guard of honour, found by the 1st Battalion of the King's Regiment, with the band of the battalion. 'Those poor soldiers have been here two days, practising this ...' And the Queen Mother stepped forward, in a light, electric sea-blue floating dress and ostrich feather hat, that made every colour fade by comparison ('They have them specially dyed, you know'), and with her own unique smile inspected the guard of honour, and went into the marquee.

'I have summoned this Grand Court of Shepway to take upon myself the office of Lord Warden of the Cinque Ports ... I have great pleasure in assuming the duties of the ancient and honourable office ...' And the speech of Admiralty Judge Gerald Darling QC: '... I venture to doubt whether there has ever been a Lord Warden so universally held in high esteem, so much admired, so much loved by all ... courage and achievement during reigns of King George VI and yourself ... unfailing charm and grace ...' And having referred to the 'revolutionary change' of being the first woman to hold the office and, with a laugh, to the 'troublesome rider' of having to pay for the burial of 'fishes royal' such as sturgeon and whales (Sir Robert Menzies had received a bill for £99 2s 11d for removal of his whale from the Thanet foreshore), and having said, 'I feel both proud and humble to follow these great men (Churchill and Menzies)', the Queen Mother walked to a luncheon given by the Speaker of the Cinque Ports, Mrs E. D. Wells, Mayor of New Romney, through ranks of ex-servicemen proud with medals, old people in wheelchairs and children who ran forward with bouquets of flowers. There had already been a nineteen-gun salute from Dover Castle, and now, as she inspected a third guard of honour, by the Royal Navy (the first, of the 3rd Battalion the Queen's Regiment, just back from South Armagh, had been at the Castle), the band of the Royal Marines struck up and the Lord Warden's flag rose slowly up the flagstaff of the Maison Dieu, fluttering red and gold in the first bright shaft of sun of the day, to resounding cheers. It was an electrically exciting moment, eloquently moving.

The Queen Mother said later that it was 'the happiest day' of her life. And in the crowd they said, 'It's tradition ... it's our history ... it's England, isn't it ...'

*

Architecture of a later date than the Maison Dieu and St Martin's Priory can be seen in streets such as Castle Street, with its bow windows and small cafés, and in the intimately scaled seafront terraces and crescents.

Surprisingly uncluttered, Dover's seafront is not much spoilt, despite some new blocks. One's main impression is of the small terraces below wooded chalk cliffs, and beyond them the open harbour. Marine Parade is balconied, and has no shops or kiosks. It is a dignified sea walk, with the massive arms of the harbour opening beyond, on to a sea strangely turquoise, or changing from grey to a calm stretch of blue with the rapidity of an English sea-change. There is a statue to Charles Stewart Rolls, the motor-car manufacturer and sportsman aeronaut, one of Britain's best-loved airmen, the first man to cross the channel and return in a single flight, on 2 June 1910. (He was tragically killed in an accident at Bournemouth the same year.) And, with two dolphins for bosoms, below his moustachioed face, a bust of Captain Matthew Webb, who swam from Dover to Calais on 24 and 25 August 1875 – the first Channel swim (although a French historian has claimed that the credit should go to an Italian soldier in the service of Napoleon, who was imprisoned in a floating hulk off Dover after Waterloo, dived overboard and reached France guided by the stars.) Born in Dawley, Webb learnt to swim in the Severn, near the Iron Bridge, and had already performed feats of valour, walking across the railings of a high Severn bridge at Buildwas when a schoolboy, and receiving three medals for a gallant rescue attempt from a Cunard liner. He was welcomed home with rapturous enthusiasm after swimming the Channel, and has been immortalized in verse, while a booklet published in 1875 opens with terms strangely reminiscent of today: 'It has been the custom of late to moralize much on the loss of stamina and old English pluck, consequent, it has been said, upon the changes which have taken place in modes of living ...'[14] The heroic Webb, in need of cash, was defeated only eight years afterwards, dying in a desperate attempt to swim across the rapids at the foot of Niagara Falls.

A poem contemporary with his Channel feat (from the *Hornet*) runs:

His brawny arms the long waves cleave – immortal Fame inspires him;
The waters cannot chill the glow of ruddy Hope that fires him!

But I prefer Betjeman's:

Captain Webb the Dawley man
Captain Webb from Dawley...
...
Swimming along –
Swimming along –
Swimming along from Severn
And paying a call at Dawley Bank while swimming along to Heaven.[15]

So Captain Webb swims on, and the sun sets each evening over Shakespeare Cliff – after a storm, in angry gold and black clouds. The cliff juts a warning into the sky from its wooded hillside, like the fist of England gesturing a thumbs-up to the sea. '... here's the place' – as Edgar says in *King Lear* – '... the dread summit of this chalky bourn ...'.[16]

Or as Cicero wrote, in a letter to Atticus, 'it is notorious that the approaches to the island are ramparted by astonishing masses of cliff . . .'[17]

One looks up at the castle on its other vast, astonishing cliff. Dover is not for storming.

*

Our oldest great port. Older than London or Bristol. Dover, when it was built reputedly the largest artificial harbour in the world, is our second largest port for general trade and Europe's leading Ro-Ro port; for value of cargo handled it is our main port (about £9 billion a year). Through it pass nine million passengers a year, over a million cars and 500,000 freight vehicles. In this grey era for Britain it is successful, optimistic and expanding.

It would seem almost impossible for Dover to grind to a halt; the docks have the businesslike and hopeful atmosphere of a concern roaring into its prime – and without having lost a human aspect in the process. Of remarks by long-distance lorry drivers whom I questioned about the port – Have you been through Dover? – I still like best the reply, 'Yes, probably'. But the port has its individuality. During the recent road haulage strike, Dover remained busy because of its preponderance of unit loads, 'cowboys' (one-man-band drivers) and firms having a tie-up with continental lorries. Its site (twenty-two miles from Calais, twenty-five from Boulogne, sixty-two from Ostend) is unrivalled.

Dover has not been free from the setbacks, the silting up, which have attacked all the ports along this coast. Silt first split the River Dour into two channels, and then threatened to block the harbour with shingle. But whichever of the disputed Cinque Ports was the leading one initially, Dover soon became the leading port in practice – the headquarters of the Lord Warden, who was also the Constable of Dover Castle from the time of Edward I. Dover provided its quota of ships as did the other ports: Dover and Hastings provided twenty ships each until the thirteenth century, and then twenty-one; the other Head Ports provided five each – all for fifteen days in the year. At other times the Dover mariners ran the passenger service across the Channel. In 1495 a pier was built by John Clerk, to make what was known as Paradise Harbour; but this accelerated the silting. During the reign of Elizabeth I, a Kentish engineer, Thomas Digges, laid the basis of the modern harbour by enclosing the lagoon water inside the long- and cross-walls of a 'Great Pent'. The 'Great Pent' is today the Wellington Dock.

Digges's harbour was expensive to maintain, so James I transferred the running of the harbour from the corporation to a Harbour Board of 'eleven discreet men' – the eleventh to be the Guardian or Lord Warden with ten Assistants. The Lord Warden thus became a power in the harbour's affairs long after the decline of the Cinque Ports as such, and continued as president of the Board until George V when Prince of Wales became Lord Warden, but was relieved, as were future Lord Wardens, of this extra duty.

Further harbour works continued to be carried out. When by 1824, as a pilot recalled, 'not a nutshell could float in or out',[18] action was taken, and in time most problems were cured – by the enlargement of the Tidal Basin, deepening of the Inner Basin, then renamed the Granville Dock, and the building of the Admiralty Pier which runs out far enough to defeat the shingle. Later the Prince of Wales Pier was built, and in 1895 the Admiralty announced its intention to enclose the whole of Dover's wide bay with breakwaters – adding the Eastern Arm and central breakwater. In 1909 the Prince of Wales (George V) opened the Admiralty Harbour, which could contain the whole fleet.

The Harbour Board, which had been reconstituted, and to whom running of the outer harbour was handed back after the First World War, has today eight members. It is unique in being non-profit-making under its charter and must 'administer, maintain and improve' the harbour (with income from dues and revenue from property.) It spends £100,000 a year on the promenade, shelters, beach and sea defences, and for this reason, Waterloo Crescent (built 1834-8), where its headquarters are, and also the White Cliffs Hotel, is dazzlingly kept up, with gleaming stucco and flowers, and the same attention keeps the whole seafront attractive. The Board is clearly efficient, but one senses none of the knife-in-the-back atmosphere of a multi-million conglomerate, none of the lassitude of some state-run concerns.

'Every person is made to feel an individual,' Paul Youden, the Board's Publicity Officer, told me, and anyone can approach the traffic staff to get their particular problems sorted out. He is himself the best advertisement for Dover. He was born there, and went to school at Kent College in Canterbury and then outside Liverpool, where his family had moved. He got his first job two days after his fifteenth birthday. 'I left school on Friday and started work on Monday', with a local newspaper. On returning to Dover, he was with the *Kent Messenger* for five years, and qualified at college as a journalist. Eight years with the *Kentish Express* were followed by work on a ski-ing magazine and public relations. At the Harbour Board, he can enjoy his twin enthusiasms, for Dover and shipping, and for writing – besides his job in publicity, he is an author, editing *Continental Motoring Guide*,[19] and working on a novel. He says of Dover, 'In these depressing days ... it is nice to be involved in a dynamic organization like Dover Harbour Board ... you are part of a team. The port of Dover has a tremendous future.' As a journalist, he says, he wasn't the aggressive, arrogant type. 'As a journalist I had to upset other people ... I used to try to amend it ... you're not a true journalist if you suppress something.'

The good working atmosphere is felt throughout the port, he said. There had only been one dock strike in recent times, when during the national dock strike pickets came down; 'although people didn't really want to strike, they had to.'

A true Dovorian, he told me, can probably trace his blood strain to Continental strains. Dovorians have also traditionally been called, like Deal men, sharks. 'The number of true Dovorians is decreasing all the time. A lot of people are drawn into the port, a lot of foreigners work here.' But the port currently provides work for thirty per cent of the working population of Dover and Deal, and brings a great deal of wealth to the town. 'It is a shame the town has not grown alongside the port,' Paul Youden said. 'It will take time to catch up, and hasn't ever really recovered from the hammering it had in the war. I've seen the town change from a blitzed nothingness to what it is today ... yet it's incredible to my mind that there are still bomb sites.' Industry has lagged a bit compared to Canterbury or Folkestone, although, among other concerns, BMW have a centre here, and AVO (part of the Thorn Group) a large electrical company. Yet possibly this lack has helped Dover as a town retain its small-scale charm.

The harbour's growth-rate is 25 per cent a year in some areas, with ten acres of land just reclaimed; exports are as varied as 4000 tons of Bar Steel to Dubai, to 400 tons of torch batteries to Nigeria. There is a new hoverport now open, with three of the largest hovercraft in the world in use. Across the Channel, at the six ports served by Dover, developments are also being made, such as a projected new pier at Calais. 'But I think we can teach them a lot (Ro-Ro ports in Europe) ... They haven't got their back to the wall ... they've got plenty of space ...'

Dover hasn't looked back since it took off in the 1950s, when the first car ferries were introduced. Townsend Thoresen was one firm in particular which saw that people would want to take their own cars across, and invested in reclaimed land; it is now ahead at Dover because when the Channel Tunnel was last discussed, the firm decided there would never be one, and concentrated on Ro-Ro ships, of which it is now an extremely large intercontinental owner.

Will there now be a Chunnel? There is renewed discussion of the prospect (which was first put forward by a French engineer to Napoleon in 1802. Napoleon, however, had other things in mind). Paul Youden feels there is no certainty of a direct link in our lifetime, and that a single bore tunnel would have little effect on Dover. 'Developments will have overtaken the tunnel by the time it is constructed ... Ferries will be larger ... modern hovercraft and hydrofoils would overtake it.' It is also interesting that trains in a tunnel can only go at a certain speed before the wind pressure builds up to push them backwards. And that progress does not always bring more speed. Channel packets of the late 1800s crossed the Channel faster than modern ferries, in one hour fifteen minutes.

Paul Youden is one who clearly sees Dover and the Channel as part of the motorway system. 'With the port running efficiently, one should hardly notice one has left *terra firma* ... the Channel is no more than a wide frontier ... In time of peace that mass of water should be disregarded ...'

At this frontier, he feels, a British citizen should not be required to show his passport. 'I don't have to show my passport between the North of Denmark and Sweden.'

*

In the Dover Freight Drivers' Canteen, a young driver from Holland with tattoos on his arm, good teeth and looks, and a smart khaki shirt with white insignia, was tucking into baked beans, chips, egg, bacon, sausage, tomato and black coffee – but had time to talk to John and myself and to give an assessment of driving conditions over here (in English).

Two French drivers, in good anoraks, with red stripes on navy blue, had been to see the Castle and Park, but deplored the coffee, which they said (in rapid French) would be better in Calais.

Two English drivers in grubby boilersuits had cigarettes going, looked slummocky, and one, who was bald, was battering the other's ears with swearwords ... They obviously hadn't been anywhere except their f---- cabs.

But the standard of driving over here is much more generous, the driver from Holland told us. He comes over twice a week carrying phosphoric acid via Zeebrugge to Oldbury. It takes him one hour to get through Zeebrugge, four to get through Dover, which he spends eating and sleeping. With ten or twelve gears to change, it is important to him that the public here does give way to him, and that when he signals that he is about to pull out, the car behind waits while he does so, and can then overtake him without any bother. In Holland, as you pull out to overtake, any car that's coming up will not hold back, but will 'flash lights and 'ow you say, 'onk and 'oot and overtake while you're trying to get out, will *force* their way past ...' He also likes the many roundabouts over here, because if you've made a mistake you can go round again. Food, he said, was better in Zeebrugge, but cheaper here.

It is more varied in the Reception Building of the Eastern Docks, where we also found some drivers who had infiltrated, or felt their boilersuits were smart enough. (There seemed to be no firm ruling as to who could use the Reception Building, but it has a good bar, as here you are past customs and 'out of the country'.) It stands like an airport control tower surveying the ranks of brightly painted lorries and containers – 'Hall to Arabia', 'Jumbofret Containers', *'Transportes de Sacavēm Lda'*, *'Transports Menweg SA'*, or the clean white lorry of *Paul Predault, Charcuteries.* Line upon line, in reds, yellows, white and blue, creating an atmosphere of excitement, under the great, lit, boards listing departure times.

In the Reception Building, Sandy Shaw sings a winning Eurovision song of ten or so years ago, or 'Amazing Grace' is played. There are green plants and discreet announcements, a soothing blue floor.

'It's a living,' the English drivers on bar stools told me. 'We were just discussing the scenery and the knocking shops in Amsterdam ...' They agreed about English drivers. 'In England there are too many in the middle lane [lorries can't use the fast lane]. Different countries different laws ... In France or Holland if you don't speak the lingo, police will waive it if you're going too fast, if you don't understand them. In Germany they say, "We speak English," and nab you. Tachos? [Tachographs.] In Germany or Austria blokes "run legal". Anywhere else you forget about them. But it'll tighten up. Why do we do it? It's the money. You can't earn this money in England – we wouldn't leave home if you could. It's all ducking and diving here, isn't it. This way we get a better living than you get in anything else [£134 to £190 or £200 a week plus £13 to £20 a night – which you spend in your cab]. The kids can have shoes,' he added, humping his shoulders pathetically. With only one day off a week, and two weeks' holiday, I suggested that the better living might be for the wife and kids ... But as they said, there's always 'money in your pocket', and I left them happily downing their drinks. And grumbling about the time it takes to get through customs at Dover, which is a universal complaint (and not the Harbour Board's responsibility).

In other respects, the Eastern Docks, under the management of Mr John Whitehair, Terminal Manager, runs with smooth efficiency and is, as he says, more like an airport than a port, with speedy turn-rounds. 'We've got about twenty acres, so we've got to be efficient.'

He has the unassuming, practical air of a Maigret, and strides the docks in rather the same way, in belted macintosh, with hat pulled well over his brow. He started as a lighterman on the Thames, and knows his business, greets his staff with lack of pomposity. The port operates 364 days a year; in summer 600 cars an hour can leave. The freight offices are a hub from which the freight operation is directed. (Forwarding agents arrange all documentation for firms, make bookings and employ stevedores; there is a consortium for the 140 or so agents at Dover. Ships' manifests are telexed on ahead, listing each load, which must tally with the drivers' forms.) Speed is of the essence, at Dover. Ro-Ro ships may do four trips in twenty-four hours. Night time is the busiest time, so that loading can be done during the daylight hours. Lights shine down on the rows of lorries, gleaming perhaps in the rain, reflected on wet tarmac – row upon row of giant containers on wheels, bringing across this narrow divide chemicals and fruits, manufactured goods and meats, motor-cars and wines, and beside these, the tourists who long to go on pilgrimages.

*

Inland from Dover is some of the loveliest country in Kent. Travelling from Sarre down to Romney Marsh, you can pass through Preston, with its small twelfth-century church, near a place called Heart's Delight, in the thick of cherry and apple orchards where poplars act as windbreaks; then Wingham, with its broad High Street, copper beech trees and Spanish chestnuts, and a church whose pillars are formed from the trunks of chestnut trees; on to Adisham, and Elham, in the Nailbourne Valley, which in spring epitomizes the misty, white ethereal quality of Kentish scenery, with tall hawthorn hedges and white pear blossom, sheep and streams, a tracery of branches against pale hillsides. A land in which the past is in the stones, in water and trees – as at Preston, where the palace of the 'Infanta of Kent', Juliana de Leybourne, a fourteenth-century heiress, lies below the depths of a pond; or in the Nailbourne valley, where after a long drought, St Augustine knelt to pray, at which the Nailbourne stream sprang forth to bring relief and new greenness to the fields. On through Lyminge and Postling to Aldington, where there was a Roman beacon on Aldington Knoll, and from where there is a sweeping view over Romney Marsh.

Nearer Dover, too, is unspoilt countryside, with villages such as Barfreston, where the small Norman church is the supreme example of its kind in England – its south doorway as richly encrusted with glorious and grotesque carvings as a reef with coral – birds and bishops, branches and leaves, a monkey riding a goat, amphibious beasts and angels, medallioned and encircled with curling tracery. As worthy of a visit as the churches of Canterbury and, usually, more peaceful.

A little way off is Waldershare Park, the seat of the Earls of Guilford. The Queen Anne mansion, with its strikingly tall windows, was originally built for Sir Henry Furnese between 1705-12, with a park on a very extensive scale, with a Palladian, balustraded belvedere overlooking the parkland and the pleasure grounds. These latter alone were fifty-eight acres in extent, encompassing everything from bowling greens to carriage drives, shown on old prints and maps as formally set out with trees, avenues and walks, surrounded by the deerpark. The estate was a landmark, mentioned in a guide of 1810 as visible from Mount Pleasant, near Minster, 'the stately banquetting house of the Earl of Guilford'. Lord North (2nd Earl of Guilford), Prime Minister under George III, had been Lord Warden of the Cinque Ports, and in their day, Pitt and Wellington would drive over from Walmer to Waldershare to dine with the then Earl of Guilford, Wellington coming over on Sunday evenings.

The present Earl of Guilford, who is Deputy Lord Lieutenant of the County, has like other landowners found it impossible to maintain the mansion as a private house. He has, after some trial and error as he freely admits, found a happy compromise by which the aesthetic appeal of the parkland and grounds can be preserved without gimmickry, preserving the traditional nature of this piece of the country, of one piece of England. The mansion, which when he and Lady Guilford lived in it, they found to heat rather like 'stoking the engines of the *Queen Mary*', has been sold for conversion into flats, some for Eurocrats, and 'weekenders I think they're called.' A nice phrase; but Lord Guilford is not in the least pompous. The Guilfords themselves live in an attractive Georgian house in the park, with a swimming-pool that most people would exchange for all the bowling greens in England, and a thousand acres are farmed intensively in a very efficient operation (mainly arable, with 600 sheep and fifty Sussex cattle), while at the same time keeping the parkland trees and features intact. The magnificent lime avenue still stands, and Lord Guilford has started to replant trees, keeping to the species that are already there – Spanish chestnuts, limes, oaks, beeches.

Does he, as a landowner, feel that the EEC and its agricultural policy will succeed? 'I feel the problems can be ironed out,' he said regarding agriculture, and 'in the long term ... (the EEC) will help to form a tremendous European block against a possible Communist threat.' Lady Guilford added that she was very much aware, here near Dover, of the proximity of the Continent, and being partly French, felt very akin to that country; at the same time the nearness was emphasized by the old defences and Martello towers, 'a hereditary mistrust, a love-hate relationship'. 'It is nice to be ourselves,' Lord Guilford said, 'knowing we can be a part of somebody else, but' (and he explained that he would not want to lose the Channel barrier) 'that we can still lock the gates ...'

An Englishman's park is his castle ... as Dover is our lock and key.

*

Kent is not all citadel and harbour, however, not entirely hop-fields, fruit and fishing-smacks. It is also industry, and coal. In the triangle behind Dover and Deal, is the Kent Coalfield, with three collieries, one of which is Snowdown, in close proximity to villages as unspoilt as Barfreston, countryside as beautiful as that around Waldershare.

'If you hear any bad language, you'll have to close your ears ...' I was visiting Snowdown colliery. (The language didn't materialize).

In the 1880s, while boring for the Channel Tunnel at the coast, 2,240 feet down, a coalseam was found, which is the Kent no. 6 seam, still worked today at Snowdown, at a depth of 3,000 feet. (At another of the Kent Collieries, Betteshanger, it is worked at 1,900 feet, but the coalfield stretches from Ramsgate to Canterbury to Dover, and is 1,500 feet below the surface at Canterbury. It is the only concealed seam in the country.)

If one thinks of mining, as I did, as a matter of picks, shovels and wooden pit props, one is out of date. True, the headgear (machinery) at pits are the old traditional shape and waste heaps have a changeless appearance (*not* slag-heaps. I notice even George Orwell, in his *Road to Wigan Pier*,[20] which includes descriptions of mining conditions in the thirties that are shown in all their grimness in his classic work, gets this wrong). But air is circulated down an open shaft in one headgear, up a closed shaft in the other, thus keeping the mine aerated – besides their use in carrying water pipes, power cables, coal, machines and men – and picks and shovels went out in the early sixties; nowadays coal is cut by a 'ranging arm shearer – you can say it looks like a bacon slicer', and coalfaces are supported by hydraulically-operated powered supports, which can be moved forward and reset against the roof of the coalface. There are still hazards (heat at Snowdown is a problem, since the mine is so deep: at a depth of sixty feet the temperature is 50° Fahrenheit and it rises one degree for every sixty feet; most men still work in their underpants). Water must be constantly pumped out, and tragic accidents occur, as in Yorkshire in 1978 when eight miners were killed and nineteen injured in a truck accident – one forgets that miners often have to travel for two hours a day from the cage to the coalface, and back. Mining, I see, from a newspaper survey, rates below bricklayers, seamen, fishermen, foundry workers and, curiously, *domestic housekeepers*, as a risky job, and a little above publicans, but to me it seems to call for the highest courage. Even to allay my journalistic cravings, I couldn't force myself down a mine, and since I am one who gets claustrophobia in the Blackwall Tunnel, I was delighted when the Coal Board told me underground visits were fully booked for two years.

I talked instead to those who do go down.

'It's not a question of liking it – it's a job I've done all my life.' Jack Collins had just come up in a cage with his shift, and we sat in the yard while he talked. He left school at 15 and went into mining.

'Mining is extremely unique – a tremendous feeling that's got no parallel anywhere else ... comradeship ... you've known one another, worked together. I think with mining ... we went to school in a mining community, did all the things you do together – ran together – began working together ... You knew everybody's background – everyone's background was identical – it's no good anyone pretending his background's different to anyone else.' Besides work, the colliery plays Rugby football, has a colliery team, brass band, choir and the pigeon fanciers. But the main raison d'être of a miner, which I heard repeated by others, was 'A sort of chauvinistic pride ... it's a man-sized job (with swearing as part of the strong-man image) ... you take pride in filling the bill.' 'The feeling of doing a man-sized job in adverse conditions,' another miner said.

Was Jack Collins ever worried, I asked, or his wife? He was obviously philosophical about this, had come to terms with it if it ever bothered him. But he told me of a mother with two sons in the pit who used to be worried sick if her sons were five minutes late. 'Forty years ago,' he said, 'they carried them out on stretchers with heat stroke. They'd start on a Monday and leave on a Tuesday and walk back to Scotland or wherever.'

Twenty men come up in each deck of a cage. The banksman, who gets signals from below when the cage is ready, said he 'wouldn't go down there now if you paid me double.' He works one of three shifts, with two shifts when he changes over on a Saturday – six till two, two till ten, ten till six. A lonelier job is that of the man operating the shaft pumps below, pumping water out continuously. He was just going down at 1.45 pm, and wouldn't see a soul until 8.45 pm, although he does have a telephone.

'The job's going backwards – it was more enjoyable when we were working harder,' another man told me. Did he enjoy it? 'Not really, no.' And the pay? A sore point, on which management, at least, did not want to voice an opinion, since a forty per cent claim was then scheduled.

'It could be better', 'Very poor compared to other industries', the men said.

Yet many people, of which I am one, would consider that miners, although they no longer work in tunnels less than fifteen inches high, do a job which deserves higher pay than most. 'What about pneumoconiosis?' I asked (the 'dust' disease, in particular one from coal dust – called 'miners' lung'). 'Some still get it.'

The only man who seemed contented with the pay was a Midlander, who typically from that gritty region, seemed cheerful and nonchalant, with a bared chest and beaming smile, as if he alone could take mining in his stride. 'I'm quite *con*tented,' he said. 'Enjoy it? At times ... my job is a challenge.' And he reckoned that the mining community was only now being really established, that it would take another 150 years. 'They used to come from all the throes of the earth ... Scotland ... Yorkshire ... in the 1926 strike [the General Strike which had left many of them jobless], they all marched to London and then settled here.' In the old days, miners were regarded askance in the towns, and were called 'cherrypickers'. About 900 now work at Snowdown. Most are from mining families.

'Afraid we can't show you the showers ...' But I was given a mound of sandwiches and cakes in the canteen. A group of men were doing the weekly tote draw, in which metal tokens are drawn out of a canvas bag. They asked me to make a draw. There was about £100 in the kitty.

Holidays are three weeks, plus May week and Christmas week. Output from the three Kent mines is about 700,000 tons a year. Supplies from Snowdown go by road to the Kingsnorth power station at Northfleet, and to Bowaters at Sittingbourne. The other two collieries supply the steel industry. Ten per cent of low volatile Kent coal is also added to lower rank coking coals from northern pits, ensuring supplies of valuable carbonizing coals are used to better advantage. Waste is used for purposes such as hard core roads, and shale from the Kent pits was used for the hover-port at Pegwell.

'We're planning for the year 2000. We're not running out of coal in Kent.'

Nor, yet, in Britain. Technically recoverable sources should last more than 300 years at present rates of mining. And the British Coal industry is the only one in Europe with a strategy for expansion.

Coal for petrol? Coal from under the sea? Natural supplies lasting longer than those of oil? Thanks to the strength and endurance of those who mine this source of power, its future looks as valuable to us as it has ever been; and in Kent certainly, it has not scarred the countryside for more than a very short distance. It leaves no oil slicks, it poses no radiation threat. It seems, and is, close to the natural processes of the earth, and as such, we might wholeheartedly depend on it.

*

'So many things ... our life in England being whittled away ...'

This sentiment expressed by a member of the public at the

Installation of the Queen Mother as Lord Warden, was coun-
tered that same day on all sides. The ceremony had been a joy
to organize, said Ian Gill, Registrar of the Cinque Ports, because
the new Lord Warden was so popular, so much welcomed.

At the Hallowing Service, in the Church of St Mary-in-Castro,
to which the Lord Warden had been preceded by the Acting
Sergeant of Admiralty bearing the Silver Oar – symbol of the
Cinque Ports' authority – the hymn 'For those in peril on the
sea' was sung, and the Archbishop of Canterbury then spoke of
the Lord Warden as one to whom the nation and Commonwealth
owed more than they could ever repay, adding '... life at its best
is service, is ministry ... Queen Elizabeth has helped to teach us
that lesson ...'

And in her speech at the Court of Shepway, the Queen Mother
struck straight to the heart of the matter, speaking of continuity
rooted in geography: 'It is inevitable that the men of Kent and
Sussex should be in the front line of the defence of the realm ...
in modern times the little ships of this coast made a crucial contribution at Dunkirk ... In 1979 we still value the traditions,
obligations, privileges and duties of days gone by ...'

Did all Dovorians rise to the occasion? Excited. 'Not really,
no ... Everyone keeps saying it will put more on the rates ...'
'Excited is rather a strong word for us here ...' 'We're very proud
of the heritage ...' 'Nobody ever says yes, nobody ever says no,
in Dover – but it all happens just the same ...'

A new generation nicely summed it up. Ken Miles, Divisional
Youth and Community Service Officer (who is also deputy launching authority for the Dover Life-boat, now the new Life-Boat
Rotary Service, named in 1979 by the Queen Mother), had taken
a group of boys out canoeing, to salute the arrival of the Royal
Yacht on the day before the Installation. Authority, he said,
is no longer accepted for its own sake, but the same boys who
will say 'who do you think you are?' when told to do something are 'the same people who will respond to this kind of
heritage authority. The more we preserve this kind of thing the
better.'

The boys, however, did not at first respond. Respect had not
been won. As the Queen Mother embarked in a barge to land,
Ken Miles had appealed to the boys to stay and cheer, for his

7   Folkestone; Hythe; Saltwood; Lympne

'That general good humour which is a characteristic of the people of
Kent is heightened at Folkestone into a positive kindness ...'
Richard Church

Folkestone has been called the English Riviera. Its Undercliff
has won praise for Mediterranean grandeur, the walk along the
Leas above it having aspirations to be the finest in Europe. I
approached the town with mistrust. Our seaside resorts are so
overlaid with a cloud of unfashionableness, mixed with a miasma
of fish and chip oil, that one does not expect to find the Riviera
there. Perhaps it would be better for Britain if we did – if we
could shed our inferiority complex as to our ability to be cheerful by our native seaside with any sense of panache or style. True,
there are years of spoliation to attempt to undo, but as a nation
which is poorer than it was, inviting tourists, we have depreciat-
ing capital along our shores, in our often misused or abused
coastal towns.

On a wet winter day Folkestone appears a mixture of Just
William land and something more hopeful. One's spirit ebbs at
the expanse of mock Tudor beams, on red brick picked out with
white plasterwork, at grinning nouveau-Gothic gargoyles. A white
Court building, and Bouverie House, which resembles the curved
brown plastic upper section of a coffee grinder, do not alleviate.
Grand, peeling hotels, sport one basket of wilting plastic flowers;
an ex- (colonel? doctor? seed-salesman?) limps down the steps of
an AA recommended; a commercial gentleman grips his portfolio
tightly at memories of soup of the day; schoolboys pull their caps
down against the rain.

'We haven't gone comprehensive in Folkestone yet,' I was told firmly. There are the Harvey Grammar School for Boys, the Folke-stone County Grammar for Girls, the Techical High School, 'and a *motley arrangement* of secondary modern schools.'

Pensioners in Folkestone wear shoes, not boots, even in the snow. They pull the matted little fur collars tighter round their necks, and walk slowly against the wind past the Frogmore Tea Rooms, the War Memorial (also to the 'many civilian inhabi-tants of this borough who lost their lives as a result of enemy action ...' and 'many thousands from all parts of the Empire who passed this spot on their way to fight in the Great War ... for righteousness and freedom'), flanked on one side by the weep-ing yellow brick of the 'Welfare Life' block and on the other by palms and Morelli's ice-cream parlour – then past 'Flashman and Co, founded 1830 by George Flashman, Upholsterer to HM Queen Victoria'.

Along the cliff from the War memorial is the Leas Cliff Hall (Larry Grayson, concerts and the Senior Citizens' Talent Con-test), and a small bandstand. Looking out over the Leas is a statue of William Harvey, discoverer of the circulation of the blood, friend and physician of Charles I, and benefactor of the medical profession. He lived in the era when science was coming into its own, but could still write, in a set of rules for the student of anat-omy: 'the lower belly, nasty yet recompensed by admirable variety'.[1] He was a great drinker of coffee, before coffee-houses be-came fashionable, when the beans were an expensive luxury and in-creasingly in demand, and in his will made a special bequest of his coffee-pot. He stands at Folkestone with his hand on his heart, looking a little forlorn.

To his right, the road of the Leas sweeps round and along the cliff in serpentine curves. Below it the cliff-face drops sheerly 120 to 170 feet to a narrow beach of fine reddish shingle, beyond the lower road and promenade, and the whole steep drop, zig-zagged by paths, is wooded by pines, tamarisks and shrubs. A clear sea sucks on the beach far below, and Folkestone, sheltered to the north by a range of chalk hills, does here call to mind the Mediterranean, the Italian riviera perhaps, or a coastline where warm grass and pine-needles and winding paths fall away to an unspoilt beach. Out across the blue is France, and between the trees are the colours of boats, spiking the dense, light-filled air.

But back from the front, out of season, the paint flakes from gloomy façades, chairs are stacked in glassed boarding-house porches, and in an hotel lounge a girl whiles away the tedium to adulthood reading a novel, her shoulders bowed. The ennui of the seaside grips your throat, and you are assailed by vanished summers and vandalized vistas, by the loneliness of a resort past its prime.

*

There is another side to Folkestone, however, the workaday town of railway and harbour. Folkestone was early made a Limb of the Cinque Port of Dover, and was a fishing town, rivalling Ramsgate's catch. Defoe, who speaks with airy disregard of the Cinque Ports towns ('Sandwich ... an old, decay'd, poor, miserable town ... neither Dover nor its castle has anything of note to be said of them ...'), gives a more lively picture of the fishing smacks:

Folkestone, eminent chiefly for a multitude of fishing-boats belonging to it, which are one part of the year employ'd in catching mackarel for the city of London: The Folkestone men catch them, and the London and Barking Mackarel-smacks, of which I have spoken at large in Essex, come down and buy them, and fly up to market with them, with such a cloud of canvas, and up so high that one would wonder their small boats cou'd bear it and should not overset: About Michaelmas these Folkestone barks, among others from Shoreham, Brighthelmston and Rye, go away to Yarmouth and Leostoff, on the coast of Suffulk and Norfolk, to the fishing-fair, and catch herrings for the merchants there ...[2]

The easterly drift of shingle was the enemy of Folkestone, as of the other ports along this coast, and a harbour designed by Telford in 1807, was soon nearly useless. The town did not develop to any size until the coming of the railway in the 1840s, when the South-Eastern Railway Company bought the old harbour (for £18,000), cleared it and built landing stages for a steamer service to the Continent. The first boat crossed to Boulogne on 28 June 1843. After that the population doubled in under twenty years.

Deep-sea trawling was carried out here, as at Ramsgate, and in the years before the First World War fish to the value of £30,000 a year was landed (at Ramsgate it might be £70,000 in the 1890s[3]). There was more inshore trawling and drifting than at Ramsgate, and less prime fish. Before 1914, all the trawlers were sail-powered, and many of the crew were boys signed on from the workhouse as apprentices, who could work their way up to earn a good living or even to buy their own boat. Folkestone had about ninety-three boats, and it is interesting that the same problems beset fishing then as now: over-fishing, pollution, poaching and illegal fishing by foreign boats are nothing new. The Sea Fisheries Regulation Act of 1888 allowed the newly formed county councils to set up local fisheries committees to restrict and control fishing off their coasts and to forbid the dumping of harmful substances.

Today there are ten or a dozen boats, at low tide stranded on the harbour mud, so that they have to wait until the tide turns to land their fish at the Stade. This is under a railway arch (not the famous viaduct by William Cubitt, higher up the town), beyond barrows selling 'Jillied Eels', cockles and whelks. The fish market is here, in business when the tide brings in boats, and the ground is awash with ropes, boxes, fish-heads, barrows. Men swing in and out of the pubs, every other word a swearword, and a purple-complexioned retired captain and his camelhair-coated wife step round the puddles to glance in at Dick's Fish Shop, or one of the other fish shops where Folkestone people queue for whole fresh cod and other local fish sold at much lower prices than inland. Boards advertise oak-smoked kippers and haddock, and a wholesale fish merchant undertakes herring curing. (But not when I visited it, as no herring were being caught because of the quota. There was a complete ban on herring fishing in the North Sea in 1979 when I visited Folkestone, except for the limited amount in the one small Blackwater district. The question of quotas is one of the most vexed questions of the Common Market Fisheries Policy, the other being the question of fishing limits. Britain is due to open up even its six-mile limit to other EEC countries by 1982.) In the market sheds two men were working by a large galvanized bath, one of them handing out line with hooks, the other hooking sprats on to the lines and placing them tails up round the bath in a neat pattern as if lining a cake mould with sponge fingers. He told me that he was threading eighty-six sprats to a line, and about fourteen lines would go in the boat. 'Lining' in winter replaces summer trawling, and the catch is 'anything that happens to be there ... skate, whiting, dogs ...' The 'dogs', also traditionally known as 'Folkestone beef', may of course be cod or rock salmon by the time they reach London. When lining, you go on the tide, either ebb or flow tide, and most of the boats are 'on the same game'. Did they make a good living? 'Occasionally.' And a wholesaler told me, 'One day there'll be a lot, then two or three days, nothing.' But they enjoyed the work, the fishermen told me, which was the same answer that I received at Hastings when I asked there. 'Hastings?' they said at Folkestone, 'they're hobbledehoys, aren't they?'

There were also a great many scallops being loaded here, and in shops in the town. Only about four wholesale buyers come to the market, and some of these may take fish up to London, the others distribute locally. It does not seem a large-scale industry, although healthy. But as someone pointed out, 'There aren't many fish shops left now, are there?' The fish finger has taken over.

A 'punt' or dinghy was being rowed across to the Stade, laden to the gunwales with skate, their kite-shaped bodies and long tails smeared with blood. On each pile by the jetty a seagull waited expectantly. Orange nets were slung drying round the harbour. Pensioners looked out to sea and had time to stand and stare.

Also staring down at the harbour is about the ugliest piece of architecture I have ever seen, presumably built to 'match' a Victorian grey elevation to its left. Called the Motel Burstin, in two-tone grey, it juts its way skywards as barrenly as the diving plat-form of a thirties roadside swimming pool. This is sad, because the site deserves better. To the east of the harbour lies a curve of clean white sand, below the East Cliff with its grass and Martello tower, beyond which lies the Warren – an area of heathland and ferny caves, noted for its wild flowers, including orchids, and for butterflies.

And up from the harbour runs the most attractive street in Folkestone, the old High Street.

Exceedingly narrow, with an uneven surface and no traffic, it is lined with small shops – a barber, antique shops, a fish shop decorated with scallop shells, dress shops whose buyers have one eye on France, and Rowlands, 'Ye Olde Original Kent Humbug Shoppe', where humbug mixture is cut and rolled behind the glass windows, and stretched like iridescent chewing gum on a metal claw.

'Folkestone – *c'est pittoresque*,' a French family told me. A typical, relaxed *père de famille* on holiday from Calais, with his wife and two teenage daughters. They were over on a day trip, but had stayed in Folkestone in *January* of the year before for three weeks, and had come back now in February. They found the shops, they said, as good as in France, and loved the place. If we only knew it, perhaps we have as much to offer as Dieppe and Boulogne.

'I'm told they give you grey hairs,' the proprietor of the Elinor Restaurant in Tontine Street told me. He hadn't been there in the summer season yet. 'You're happy with your treacle tart and coffee (the treacle tart was home-made, spicy), but they want ...' he gestured in the air. 'Not all of them speak English, which makes for difficulties.' But he was prepared to meet the difficulties, and was having the menu written in French. The restaurant obviously had its winter regulars; it is a characterful street, with several Greek and Italian businesses, and at its foot, the dour faces of bingo devotees scowl up briefly from behind their cigs and headscarves – 'Come along nah, ladies and gents – eyes dahn for a full house – sixty-six, clickety-click ...'

Folkestone is prepared to meet the foreigner more than half way. The station buffet has a menu in French, even if it descends to *Pie au porc* and *Cake aux Fruits* and the inevitable *chips* (there is also the much more Continental sounding *Pie de Cornouailles* – Cornish Pasty). People in the street look up and smile as one passes, seeming to welcome strangers, an unusual trait in England. I found my impression that Folkestone people seemed exceptionally friendly confirmed by Richard Church; 'That general good humour which is characteristic of the people of Kent is heightened at Folkestone into a positive kindness. This quality of whole communities is a most unaccountable thing ...'[4]

Perhaps it is some element in the hospitable air and climate. Perhaps a blessing conferred by St Eanswythe, whose bones lie in the Parish Church above the High Street. During her lifetime she performed miracles as diverse as lengthening a roof beam which carpenters had cut too short, and banning 'ravenous birdes'. A granddaughter of King Ethelbert, who was baptized by St Augustine, she founded the first convent in England, at Folkestone. It is unusual for a saint's bones in entirety to be preserved; hers – those of a seventh-century thirty-year-old woman – were found in an ancient Saxon coffer immured in the wall of the church, in 1885. This was during the addition of alabaster arcading. It is a richly decorated church, with a Kempe window to William Harvey, and three magnificent lights by the same artist above the altar. Its surroundings are also pleasing, with the brick school buildings, the curve of Church Street, and nearby The Bayle.

How much will Folkestone residents profit – or lose – if there is a Channel Tunnel? As a spokesman for Sealink said, as with any new project, the advantages and disadvantages for the environment have to be weighed up. During 1979, about 1½ million passengers crossed by Sealink ferry to the Continent from Folkestone. The Channel would take up the growth in passenger traffic, while not detracting from roll-on roll-off freight. It would attract an increase in what is termed the 'classic' train / ferry passengers, and if freight were switched to rail, would prevent an increase in the numbers of juggernauts in the area. Employment in the Folkestone area would be helped if there is a service tunnel, which is one of the additional options under discussion; there would also be employment opportunities at rolling stock depots. As with so many new schemes, there would have to be changes and losses in the environment – new buildings, new approaches. Yet, in the long term, it perhaps seems an inevitable development in the history of this narrow expanse of water. Ever since the geological events of prehistory separated us from the Continent, our love-hate relationship has drawn us back. Individuals have been prepared to make arduous sacrifices in effecting a speedy crossing. Perhaps we should lay less stress on mammoth engineering works, and imitate Bryan Allen, who in June 1979 pedalled his Gossamer Albatross across the Channel from Folkestone to Cap Gris Nez, to be kissed on arrival by a French mayoress, and saluted by everyone who would like to see us exploit less disastrously the world's energy reserves, and more imaginatively man's crazy inventiveness ...

Meanwhile we cross the Channel by more conventional means, and tourists can ponder on the inventiveness of the past.

Between Folkestone and Hythe is Sandgate, where one of Henry VIII's castles is now half washed away by the sea. From Folkestone and Sandling, the railway runs on to Westenhanger, where Folkestone racecourse has an enviable setting in wooded fields. And here too is Westenhanger House; two ruined ivy-covered towers sheltering a later manor house, flanked by old barns. There was a Saxon palace and a Norman castle here, and it was here that Fair Rosamond lived – Rosamond Clifford, a Norman whose beauty and goodness were famous and who was the mistress of Henry II. When he acknowledged her, and imprisoned his Queen who had conspired against him, Rosamond met her death, possibly by poison. The beautiful *Rosa Mundi* Oldfashioned Rose is said to be named after her.

*

'Do you want to see the bloody Venetian fête, or don't you?'

The man was exasperated, having queued for one hour out of the two-and-a-half that would be necessary before he and his wife would be allowed along the towpath of the Military Canal at Hythe, for the biennial water carnival which has been held since 1860. It was a scorching August; his wife's morning button-hole of carnation had wilted; having travelled far to be there, I was in the same mood. Twenty thousand people crowded along the canal banks (the thoughtful two thousand or so had booked seats in advance) to see the event, which as this was 1978, cele-brated the 700th anniversary of the granting of the Cinque Ports' Charter, and would be particularly magnificent, with fourteen mayors in scarlet cloaks and cocked hats on the central stage. The set pieces ranged from a Crucifixion scene to Star Wars; the setting, illuminated and lit by fireworks later, is itself memorable, and worthy of the name Venetian.

The Military Canal has none of the forbidding atmosphere of the moment of threatening drama for Britain, when Napoleon was massing his troops at Boulogne (although gunfire from the Hythe Military Ranges – Cinque Ports Training Area – can be heard by day and – sometimes – by night). Napoleon is quoted as saying: 'With three days' east wind I could repeat the exploit of

Trinity House helicopter carrying relief crew, approaching
South Goodwin lightvessel in fog

Mr C. Hickman, the
oldest boatman on the
old beach at Deal, at
the site of Sandown
Castle

Interior of St Thomas Becket Church, Fairfield

Church of St Thomas Becket, Fairfield

Pylons leading to Dungeness Power Station

Ridged shingle at Dungeness

Fishing boats, huts and trolley at Dungeness

Snowdown colliery, near Dover

William the Conquerer', and 'Let us be masters of the Channel for six hours and we are masters of the world'.[5] A more unlikely rumour had the 'Corsican Ogre' landing at Dungeness in the disguise of a British sailor, to reconnoitre in person the possible landing ground, since Romney Marsh was indeed his chosen invasion point.

William Pitt, called on for a second time to be premier in the moment of danger, when defeat for England seemed likely, became not only Colonel of the Cinque Ports Volunteers, but also organized a complete line of defence. The Canal starts at Hythe, and runs for twenty-three miles along the northern fringe of the Marsh to Appledore, then down to Rye, ending at Cliff End a few miles from Hastings. It had sharp bends, planned as gun emplacements, and was backed by a military road protected by an earthwork. Animals were moved so that food for the enemy would be scarce, plans to flood the Marsh were laid, and a signalling system set up to signal messages from ships in the Downs to London within a few minutes. All windows facing the sea were to be blacked out at dusk, and evacuation would take place if necessary – supervised by the clergy. Road-blocks, landmines, and even man-traps were in readiness – and meanwhile smugglers happily sold information to both sides. In addition to the canal, the Martello Towers stretched from Folkestone to Seaford in Sussex (there were 194 in all, some of them on the Suffolk coast; some were also built in South Africa, North America and Ireland). The Folkestone tower was the first; others can be seen at Hythe, Dymchurch and along the coast, although not all of them have remained, and some have lost their warlike look (they were emplacements for twenty-four-pounder guns, with a garrison and openings for muskets) and have been tamed for domestic use. Their name comes from Mortella Point in Corsica, where twenty-two men in a tower had been able to withstand a British force for a long while in 1794. The design of the round tower was copied, with a spelling mistake by the British reporting officer incorporated. They were built of brick set in lime, ash and hot tallow, designed to be iron-hard when they had cooled, so that cannon balls would bounce off them.

Their effectiveness was not put to the test, as on 21 October 1805 Nelson's victory at Trafalgar removed the immediate threat of invasion, to be followed by Waterloo, in 1815. In 1806, Pitt, only forty-six but worn out by strain, died. The same year his Military Canal was stocked with fish.

On Sunday afternoon of 18 June 1815, the firing at Waterloo was heard in Hythe by the people who were walking up the hill to church. It is a fine church, set high in the town, which climbs steeply up the hillside from its lower levels by the canal. One of the original Cinque Ports, Hythe is the only one still to have its copy of Edward I's Cinque Ports Charter of 1278, and a facsimile is on display in the museum. But the sea has receded from the town, the silting up beginning in the thirteenth century (the resort area to seaward of the canal was once under water). Hythe developed as a market town, and has attractive old buildings and busy holiday traffic, to take advantage of the swimming, fishing, boating and golf, and the tree-lined walks along the canal. It is a little dusty and traffic-stormed at its hub, but up the terrace-like back streets, quiet and spectacular. St Leonard's Church is one of the most outstanding in Kent, with a very high chancel, considered the finest in an English parish church. There are some good modern silk hangings in the Calvary Chapel, and in the crypt-like ambulatory, a chilling collection of human skulls, and thigh-bones – about 8,000 thigh bones and 1,500 skulls – dated to between AD 1200 and 1400. They may have been moved from the churchyard when space was needed at the time when the Black Death struck the town. (This was in 1348; within a year England's population of five million was reduced by nearly half and the seafaring population were particularly hard hit, crews being decimated, a contributory factor to the end of the Ports' importance.) Or in 1400 when the Plague left the town even further bereft. But the skulls themselves are not British in type, and may be those of descendants of the Romans or other Europeans who came over in Roman days. They are roundish, the sutures clearly visible in the young skulls, joined after middle age. Many of the bones show signs of rheumatism, probably because their owners lived on the nearby marsh. There is a plaster cast of an immense giant's skull, which is now in the College of Surgeons, and which was described by Borrow in *Lavengro* – 'Only see that one; why the two young gentry can scarcely lift it ... One enormous skull, lying in a corner had fixed

194

our attention ...' He had seen the skull when he was a boy of under four, with his mother and small brother.

In the churchyard is the grave of Lionel Lukin, inventor of the life-boat, patented in 1785. It was a conversion of a fishing boat, and boats of his type, and of another specially designed type initiated at South Shields, carried out many heroic rescues. The south-east has seen some of the bravest life-boat feats on record, but it is a nice touch that in the land of wreckers and smugglers, the man who tried out Lukin's first boat for him couldn't resist using the splendidly unsinkable craft which he had got his hands on, for smuggling.

*

To the west of Hythe is Lympne, and Lympne – now Ashford – Airport. The airfield is the oldest which has been in regular airline service; it was used by the Royal Flying Corps in the First World War, and it was from Lympne that Amy Johnson set off for her record flight to Cape Town in 1932 and from which other record-breaking flights were made. It was an RAF front-line field in the Second World War.

To the north of Hythe is Saltwood.

The magnificent square elevation of the Archbishop's Audience Hall at Saltwood Castle rises above surrounding walls and the peaceful green dip of its moated valley. We walked towards it with Lord Clark, whom we had come to see.

'What part of the castle is that?' I asked.

'That's my library,' Lord Clark replied crisply.

Saltwood must now be one of the most peaceful looking castles in existence. On the day we saw it, in the Indian summer of a late October, evening sun was catching the middle row of windows in the library, and two white doves sat face to face on top of a tower which has at its base the Roman stones of walling from the time when Saltwood was a subsidiary Roman port, near the harbour at Portus Lemanis. Then, the sea covered parts of Romney Marsh; Lord Clark feels that this part of the marsh was probably covered by water until the thirteenth century.

The castle has not always been associated with tranquillity. Possibly a stronghold of Aesc, the son of Hengist, in 488,[6] Saltwood Castle was refounded by the Normans and rebuilt in about

1160. A manor house of the Archbishops of Canterbury, ten years later Saltwood had been confiscated from Thomas à Becket by the King, and it was here, on 20 December 1170 that the four knights met, having sailed from France, to rid Henry of his 'turbulent priest'. They laid their plans in the dark, without candles, realizing the magnitude of what they were about to commit, and next day galloped along the dead straight Roman Stane Street to Canterbury and to the Cathedral.

The castle was restored to the Archbishopric in a later reign, and it was Archbishop Courtenay who had the present gatehouse built by Henry Yevele in 1390 – one of the earliest examples of Perpendicular work and among the most beautiful gatehouses in existence. Its two towers rise with a staggering perfection and impact on each side of a portcullis; beside them, now, part of the moat has become a pond round which hens and peacocks strut in a French country courtyard setting. Roses and creeping ivy flourish on the walls on all sides, although Lord Clark tells in the second volume of his autobiography, *The Other Half*,[7] how when walking some civil servants round the wall walk they disparagingly referred to the roses as 'vegetable growth'.

Saltwood Castle is now the home of the Hon. Alan Clark, MP for the Sutton Division of Plymouth, the elder son of Lord Clark, who had decided to move from the castle to live in a house across the valley moat, built for him by the architect John King, a lecturer at Bournemouth School of Art, although it was Lord Clark who had the idea of forming the house from three pavilions, in the Japanese style – one for living in, one for eating, one for sleeping.

The house is of white boarding, covered with roses – expertly pruned to form a scrollwork across the brilliant white. Round it, before the ground dips away to trees and the sheep-filled moat, are rose hedges filled with birds and long borders overflowing with flowers; inside the house ('I am lucky to have the things to put in it,' he said; 'modern houses tend to suffer from having one painting by . . .') one is met with an equally brilliant profusion of works of art – flashing colour from a Sidney Nolan, gleaming porcelain, sculpture as diverse as pieces by Rodin and a sacred Egyptian hawk; a Samuel Palmer; Italian and French paintings; vases in the Delft style from Venice; a carved Madonna and

Child of immense tenderness by Agostino di Duccio ('one of my favourites,' Lord Clark said); masterminding one wall, Turner's 'Rough Sea Off Folkestone' ('It has come home.'). The perfect setting for the man who made civilization at its best accessible to several generations, who has written of himself with great humility: 'A success like this is always hard to explain. I believe that the average man (and I know that there is no such man, but the expression is irreplaceable) was pleased when someone spoke to him in a friendly, natural manner about things that he had always assumed were out of his reach.'[8] To see works of art chosen with inspired admiration and arranged with affection is to see them at their best, and I remembered that in the first half of his autobiography – *Another Part of the Wood* – Lord Clark writes of himself arranging china as a child, and how he still arranges small pieces as if in conversation with each other.

At present, or rather when we visited him, Lord Clark had two television programmes scheduled, but apart from that had renounced the medium because 'communicating with an audience depends on physical attributes' (I quote from his autobiography) and he felt the time to retire had come.

'There are several books which I ought to be doing.' He patted some manuscripts on a windowseat. He was working on a book on self-portraits for one publisher, and also – he smiled – 'one on the concept of female beauty'. He has made no secret in his autobiography of his admiration for this concept, on canvas or out of it.

Over tea, Lady Clark, who is a Frenchwoman whose style, charm and looks are a brilliant match for the *objets d'art* around her, talked to us with humour and zest.

Switching to her native language, she laughingly told us a story of one tourist calling to another in some foreign hotel, to come out to see a superb sunset, and the classic reply, '*Je n'ai pas mon appareil.*' (I haven't got my camera.)

Lord Clark was equally humorous about camera mania. We were discussing the Japanese. 'For the last twenty years all they've thought about is taking photographs.' (His autobiography is remarkably outspoken without being derogatory. I wondered about libel cases. 'A few widows were upset, but they came round.')

Clearly, as an outstanding television performer, and also as ex-Chairman of the Board of the Independent Television Authority during its important initial period, he values the medium, as he does all visual media. As a writer, I am glad, however, that writing does not take second place. I asked him of which of his achievements he felt most proud.

'I think my best work is *The Nude*.'[9]

And of future aims: the books he is working on, 'and I would like to do an article on Iconophobia.' He also had by his side a small notebook on the subject which in his autobiography he mentions as a major work he has not written, and which intrigued me – the states of mind which lead to a particular creative experience.

'One would need to know so much about medicine,' I said, although I was hoping perhaps to be contradicted.

'That shows how little I know about the subject,' he said with his own brand of irony.

Since this chapter is about Kent, which as he has defined civilization as a sense of permanence, could rank among the most civilized areas, I asked him if he felt an affection for Kent. He had first got to know it, he said, when playing golf at Littlestone, and at Rye, and had seen Hythe and thought how agreeable it was. In 1932 he rented a house at Lympne, but gave it up at the outbreak of war, rightly surmising that Romney Marsh, towards which Napoleon had aimed to bring his great flotilla, the only place in England where an invading army could conveniently be deployed, would also be chosen by Hitler. After the war, he and the late Lady Clark, saw Saltwood Castle, across its valley in the afternoon sun, and fell in love with it.

He is also fond of Canterbury Cathedral, particularly of the nave and choir. 'When the Gothic was less liked, people always dwelt on the choir.' But as a man of such wide knowledge, he looks outwards. 'Have you seen Chartres?' 'Charlemagne's Aix-la-Chapelle was a light in the Dark Ages ...'

He is a great man for heroes, so I asked if he had any modern heroes. General de Gaulle – 'he had a wonderful mind, was a pupil of Bergson ... a wonderful man – saved France, made France ...' And, 'the man who is everyone's hero at present, Henry Moore' (a lifelong friend). 'A man of wonderfully noble and straightforward character ... most people would agree the greatest living artist ... The English are very bad indeed at sculpture, so he is a strange chance, a freak ... it shows one should never be dogmatic.'

Although he has the humility and accessibility of all really great personalities (if one telephones to speak to a secretary a voice may ask 'Will Lord Clark do?'), Lord Clark has himself carried many banners for our age. He saved (with the help of a railway addict assistant), the National Gallery paintings during the war; he has been Director of the National Gallery and Chairman of the Arts Council; he played a leading part in the founding of the National Opera at Covent Garden; he has spotted or promoted new artists (Sidney Nolan, Graham Sutherland) and bought countless treasures for our galleries; he is the author of outstanding books and enabled us to see civilization through his own keen eye.

It is fitting that he should live in such surroundings, among treasures. On a day just before the war, some rolls of grimy canvas were discovered in a vault in the National Gallery. Before having them thrown away, Kenneth Clark took a scrubbing brush to one, and a Turner emerged. They are now among the most admired of Turner's work in the Tate Gallery. 'An extraordinary moment to have lived through.'

Turner made a Folkestone sketchbook, and as he often crossed the Channel, he also did a beautiful Normandy sketchbook, Lord Clark told us. (Turner's sketchbooks, often small, even $4\frac{1}{2} \times 3\frac{5}{8}$ inches in size, which he carried everywhere in his pocket, contain some of his most telling work. In the 'Jason' sketchbook is a Margate Hoy; in the 'Wilson' sketchbook, 'South Coast Luggers coming in to the beach', with swirling sail and wave sweeping towards Deal (?) shingle.)[10] He didn't paint Saltwood. 'I think he was always looking out to sea ...'

And one Turner has come home. As we left, the evening sun lit his painting of the sea off Folkestone, and caught the gilt of the frame round Turner's sublime mass of light and waves.

*

We drove on up the hill to catch the sun going down like a crimson comet over Romney Marsh. Between Saltwood and Lympne, on Lympne Hill, is the Shepway Cross, and from along this ridge of hill there is one of the most sweeping views[11] of the whole Marsh, laid out like a map, with shimmering silver flats towards Dungeness, the cuts of water inland catching fire from the sun.

Shepway, Lambarde says, was so called 'because it lay in the way to the Haven where the ships were woont to ride'. From there a road may have run directly to the Roman Stane Street, from Lympne to Canterbury, which in the Roman era was lined with magnificent villas, taking advantage of the mellowness of the area, and the south-facing hillside at Lympne. This range of hills was, earlier still, the primeval coastline of England, and ran round in a wooded crescent from Hythe to Appledore, a half-moon completed by Rye on its promontory. It is not certain at what date the Marsh became habitable, nor where the River Rother, or Limen as it was called, originally ran into the sea, although this was probably at Appledore in Julius Caesar's day (the river is mentioned as having its mouth there in the Anglo-Saxon Chronicle). The Rhee Wall, which began the 'inning' (or reclamation) of the Marsh, is thought by some to have been built in pre-Roman days by the Belgae, but is more likely to have been built by the Romans, experts conclude, as the Marsh was still flooded at spring tides by that date.

The position of the Roman harbour has also been much debated. Rice Holmes, the authority on Caesar, in proving that Caesar did not land at Hythe but at Deal, also conclusively proves that the Roman harbour was not at Lympne as is often said, but was a pool harbour extending from West Hythe to a point nearly opposite Shorncliffe.[12] Creeks cut through the hillsides from this sea inlet, with streams running into the creeks bringing down shingle to meet the shingle of the easterly drift in a shingle bank, broken through at the harbour entrance, and continuing on down along the line of the Dymchurch wall as far as Winchelsea. The streams also scoured the harbour by an inrush of water, so that it did not finally silt up until about 350 years ago. The Roman harbour of Portus Lemanis was therefore in this sea inlet, and the great Saxon Shore fort built to protect it was at Stutfall Castle, covering about ten acres. Huge masses of masonry lie at the foot of the cliff here, having fallen during landslips, but the cement is so firm, after seventeen hundred years, that the stones and bricks can't be separated. A Roman altar was discovered in Stutfall Castle, erected by 'the Admiral of the British fleet' (*praefectus Classis Britannicae*), so it was clearly an important naval base.

Lympne Castle is a medieval building, on the foundations of an earlier Norman castle. There was a Roman watch tower where the East Tower stands, a lookout for the fort below. (The sole of a Roman shoe was found in the wall of the tower, during restoration work. The ghost of a Roman soldier is said to walk here.) The castle was later owned by the Archdeacons of Canterbury, including Thomas à Becket, for 800 years; it was restored in 1905.

The Shepway Cross, near Lympne, marks the meeting place of the original court of the Cinque Ports – the Court of Shepway. It was quite common in the Middle Ages for courts to meet in the open air, with the participants on horseback. The court would be summoned by the Lord Warden, writs being sent in advance to the Head Ports and Corporate Members, as, in a fishing community, townsmen might be absent at sea. Town officers of the Ports were the judges and sat on either side of the Warden, who was the sole presiding judge and pronounced the judgement.

The Court of Shepway was a royal court, 'the Kynges high court of Shepway', a link between the ports and the central government. It was above individual town courts, but was in fact primarily concerned with the King's interests, and his only means of keeping in check the high-handedness of the Portsmen, to whom so many privileges had been granted. It was recognized as early as 1150, but its powers only properly defined in the thirteenth century. It provided a source of unity to the Barons of the ports (Barons were initially all Freemen, but later only those who attended a coronation), as did the office of Warden, who was installed, as now, at special sessions of the court. The proceedings of the court had to be completed in a single day, and judgement carried out immediately. For felonies such as treason, the punishment was death, the condemned man being first drawn round the place of Shepway and then hung publicly on the spot. For other crimes there were fines and imprisonment, or offending communities could lose their franchise. Other towns, such as Yarmouth, might lay claims against the Portsmen, or merchants claim for goods stolen at sea.

In the early days, the Portsmen felt themselves to be strong, and had both power and immunity; the Warden swore an oath to uphold their liberties, and indeed, as the ports diminished in importance, he pleaded for them at Court. He managed to blind the government's eyes to the fact that by the time they no longer made up the central core of the Navy, their privileges had ceased to bear any relation to their duties. As the Warden increased his powers, much of his business was carried out at Dover, at the Court of St James's, which was also an Admiralty Court for the Ports. As such, it dealt with such things as wrecks, captures at sea and the punishment of deserters. All finds on sea or shore were traditionally the King's property, but in time this was limited to things of value, such as whales or porpoises. Wrecks were of course a tricky subject. The Portsmen had their special privileges with regard to them, but were inclined to practise piracy when they were ostensibly salvaging wrecks. Aiming to prevent this, a charter of 1236 stated that if any man or beast remained alive, a ship was not a true wreck.

Two later courts, of Brotherhood and Guestling, became incorporated eventually as the Court of Brotherhood and Guestling. They were not held by officers of the King but were set up by the Portsmen to defend their common rights and privileges, and were the most interesting federal feature of the Ports, the most original feature of their constitution.[13]

The Brodhull was the earlier court and became important in the fourteenth century, when it was held at Romney (it was possibly an old court connected with administration of the marsh, annexed by the Portsmen for their own assembly). The Barons used the court to regulate affairs such as their presence at the coronation ceremony, and the clothes to be worn there. The regulation of the Herring Fair at Yarmouth was a major concern – in the Middle Ages the Portsmen were nearly all fishermen, and in the herring season all other activity ceased, no town courts were held, bread could be baked in any size instead of adhering to regulations, and probably the whole male population went off to Yarmouth. In the eleventh century Yarmouth was a small fishing settlement, and would be flooded by an influx of fishermen from the Ports and elsewhere as far afield as Bordeaux and Germany. Bailiffs from the Cinque Ports maintained order and fair dealing – no armour was to be worn and all crews were to be aboard by sunset, which gives an idea of the tense situation. As the town of Yarmouth grew in size, there was frequent conflict between the Yarmouth men and the men of the Cinque Ports, so that by the thirteenth and fourteenth centuries they were fighting not only at the fair, but anywhere they met at sea. No holds were barred; crews were killed and boats burnt. (In the reign of Edward I, for instance, the Portsmen claimed they had lost 184 men.)

The Brodhull was adopted as the general assembly of the Confederation by an agreement of 1357. Minutes of meetings and of those of the court of Guestling were kept and are preserved in the *White* and *Black* books of the Cinque Ports. The Guestling was a court which provided the Head Ports with links with their member ports, since the members kept their independence of government, but had to give financial and other support to their Head Ports. The original place of meeting may have been the village of Guestling, near Winchelsea. It was at first a special court for the Sussex ports of Hastings, Winchelsea and Rye, and was held at one of these ports. Later it became general to all the Ports and their Members, and was eventually usually held after the Brodhull.

Nowadays, the Court of Brotherhood and Guestling is called when needed, as for instance for the appointment of a new solicitor, for ceremonial occasions such as offering felicitations to the Queen on her silver jubilee or to celebrate an anniversary of the Great Charter of the Cinque Ports (as for the 700th in 1978). It is held in the town of the Speaker of the Cinque Ports (an office which is held for one year), and is attended by the mayor of each town with four members of the council, and by the town clerk, the town sergeants, the major's chaplain and honorary recorder. In addition a Standing Committee meets once a year (the mayor of each town with one council member and the town clerk), to conduct the normal business of the Confederation, such as buying a portrait, and if speed is needed, to agree matters as for instance before an Installation, the seven mayors may meet on their own. The Grand Court of Shepway meets for the Installation of the Lord Warden.

*

The decline of the power of the Cinque Ports came about for several reasons. Even in its heyday, the Confederation, in a typically English way, had been a loose and not rigidly defined one. (It is in fact the only example of a federation of towns in England.) It had never provided all the ships for the navy – foreign mercenaries were used, and merchantmen. After 1327 there was no independent policy for the Ports and their ships were integrated into the fleet. By the end of the sixteenth century they were part of the general administration of the coast, except that orders to them were issued via the Lord Warden instead of direct from the Admiralty.

An Admiralty became necessary to watch over national interests, when the lawlessness of the Portsmen became overweening. Their supremacy at sea had depended to a large extent on their skill as pirates and their ruthlessness. They struck indiscriminately and inspired universal terror – attacking expelled Jews in mid-ocean in 1290, and in 1293 starting a pitched battle against the Normans on their own initiative. However, pirating was not dishonourable and was a recognized part of naval warfare. Nor was brutality an exception. Sir John Arundel, sent to help John of Gaunt against the French in 1379 and caught in a storm, 'lightened the load' in his ship by throwing overboard sixty women, including young girls, whom he had taken on board after violating a nunnery.[14]

Yet the Cinque Ports were the worst, or best, pirates of their time, and although their fierce reputation was useful abroad, it had to be checked. In 1294 William de Leybourne was made Captain of the Ports, and Gervase Alard, Admiral, in 1300 (admiral comes from the Arabic *Amiral-Bahr* – 'Chieftain of the Sea'). The admiral was keeper of the King's ships with executive responsibilities and was also Captain of the King's mariners in battle – 'Captain and Admiral of the Fleet of the Cinque Ports and all other Ports from the Port of Dover by the sea-coast westwards as far as Cornwall.' He combined the functions of First Lord, First Sea Lord and Commander in Chief, and for this was paid two shillings a day.

At the same time, the navy was divided into three sections, Cinque Ports and East and West Ports. The use of merchantmen was regularized, and gradually marauding expeditions were replaced by regular patrols and formal engagements, for which larger ships were essential. The fishermen of the Cinque Ports in their small ships could no longer make a quick raid and then return home, and specially built ships took their place. By the time of Henry VII their ship 'service' was largely cross-Channel transport of distinguished travellers or troops, but they consoled themselves by adopting a uniform of 'a cote of white cotyn with a red Crosse and the Arms of the Portis, that is to say, the halfe lyon and the halfe shippe'.

Other factors leading to the decline of the ports were, above all, the gradual silting up of the harbours which was caused by the westerly direction of the prevailing winds and the force lent to the tide by the bottleneck at the eastern end of the Channel. Reefs made sheltered harbours, but then in time the rivers brought down silt and the harbour mouths became blocked so that the inlets were not scoured by the tide.

(Hythe was becoming silted up by 1230, and became so completely by the sixteenth century; Romney was stranded in 1287 owing to the river changing course after a storm, Winchelsea was lost after 1450, and the Wantsum Channel closed in the early sixteenth century, affecting Sandwich.) Then too, there were the losses caused by the plague and Black Death. When, in the fifteenth century, Southampton was made the headquarters of the new Royal Navy, the Ports, in practical terms, had had their day. But their spirit lives on. The people of Kent and Sussex are independent and value their customs and traditions. They are proud of their towns, and of their past, and doggedly determined to be what they always have been. And always, along their coast, is the sea, bringing invaders and change, danger and livelihood, shaping their destinies.

8 Romney Marsh; New Romney; Old Romney; Dymchurch; Littlestone

'The world according to the best geographers is divided into Europe, Asia, Africa, America and Romney Marsh.'

—RICHARD HARRIS BARHAM, *The Ingoldsby Legends*

The claim that Romney Marsh is the fifth quarter of the globe is probably no longer tenable. The era of inbred, exclusive farmers who would not take kindly to a stranger has followed the era of pressgangs, smugglers and wreckers into the very real mythology of the past. Before the Second World War, a farmer told us, there were still many people who had never been out of the Marsh, and you had to be careful what you said because 'everybody was related to everyone else'. You didn't belong until you had lived there for twenty years, and the variety of agriculture that can be found there today would have been unthinkable, the Romney Sheep being as exclusive as its owners.

Myths grow ... and looking back into the past one doubts whether the 'gentleman' smuggler was all that he is made out to be – a maritime Robin Hood backed by clergy and population alike, enabling people to get the brandy, tea and lace they craved at a reasonable price, as far afield as London, where the contraband was carried on a cheerful packteam of heavy-coated ponies. A myth sung by Kipling, and by R. H. Barham, who was a rector of Snargate, on the Marsh, in the early nineteenth century, before becoming a minor canon of St Paul's. 'Smuggler Bill is six feet high, He has curling locks and a roving eye ... And he laughs "Ho! Ho!" at Exciseman Gill.' (From 'The Smuggler's Leap' in *The Ingoldsby Legends*,[1] which contains a variety of spine-chilling or otherwise spirited jingles such as 'Catherine of Cleves was a Lady of rank, She had lands and fine houses, and cash in the Bank;' and ' 'Twas in Margate last July, I walk'd upon the pier, I saw a

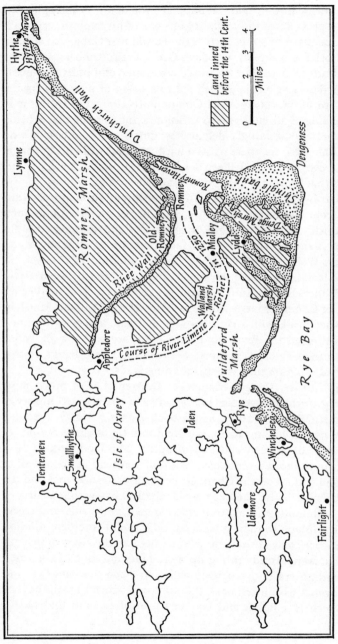

Map of medieval Romney, Walland, Denge and Guldeford Marshes showing the shingle
banks and land reclaimed before the fourteenth century

little vulgar Boy – I said, "What make you here?" ') Smuggler Bill, one suspects, from the brutality of some of his exploits, especially as perpetrated by gangs such as the Hawkhurst Gang, was at times as unsocial and shoddy as today's Great Train Robbers, and twice as difficult to catch. But the proud lawlessness and independence of his predecessors on the Marsh led to a strain of men that formed the natural backbone of the Cinque Ports character. In this most vulnerable of all our areas to invasion, lying in some places below sea level and seemingly defenceless, unless one counts men's destructible barriers, there exists a hardiness that will outlast change and stress. Men – and sheep – who can withstand the icy winter winds that blow across the Marsh can withstand anything.

What is loosely termed Romney Marsh (and pronounced *Rum*-ney, from the Saxon *Rumn-ea*, the 'marsh water',[2] or as some authorities have said, from Roman-ey or island, as opposed to the Saxon island or Ox-ney[3]) is in fact made up of Romney Marsh proper, Walland Marsh, Denge Marsh and Guldeford Level, the whole forming a triangular or arc-shaped section between Hythe and Winchelsea, running inland to Appledore. The smaller triangle of Romney Marsh proper, is divided from Walland Marsh by the Rhee Wall, which runs between Snargate and New Romney. The course of the B2080 and A259 roads are on the wall, which was a causeway or watercourse between two raised banks, so that the road is higher than the surrounding fields.

The further, shingle triangle of Dungeness is of much more recent growth, a newcomer in the long and complicated history of the area. Walter Murray, in his book *Romney Marsh*, describes the Marsh as having had since Neolithic times three periods of geological depression and two of uplift. The land sank in Neolithic times about seventy feet, as it did elsewhere in about half of England and across the Channel, in north-western France and the Netherlands. What had been a wide shallow bay within a curve of cliffs, with mudflats and sandbanks exposed by the tide, and creeks running inland to today's Robertsbridge and Tenterden, did not, however, become entirely deep water because the rivers which ran across it were already piling up more mud and sand. There then followed an era of geological oscillation when the land rose and was covered with forest oaks, the stumps of which can still be seen off Winchelsea Beach and Pett Level, in black mud underwater off Dungeness and in 'moor log', leaf mould and peat below the Marsh, which were buried there when the forest became submerged again, possibly in 2000 BC. The second era of uplift was before and during the Roman era, so that Caesar would have seen much solid land to the east of the Rhee Wall which was nevertheless marshy and subject to flooding, with prominent islands at Oxney, Rye, Winchelsea and Lydd. Finally the Marsh began to sink again, and some people think it is still sinking very gradually, at the rate of six inches a century. An added complication is the course of the rivers, the Brede, Tillingham and Rother, which ran into the arc of the bay. Winding through mud flats, their course often changed; they also broke through the shingle spits they had built up and which had been added to by the easterly drift of the tide. They scoured out good harbour bays, and then deserted them, so that the ports they had made rich were landlocked and ruined. The Rother may have changed course seven times, reaching the sea first at Hythe, then via Appledore to the Lydd, New Romney area, where its estuary was wide and changeable, and from whence it finally deserted New Romney for the Rye area in the Great Storm of 1287, changing course yet again later and with its mouth gradually moving seawards and being strangled with shingle at the new harbour mouth one-and-a-half miles from the town.

Rye now shares the fate of New Romney, so abruptly deprived of its river mouth in the Great Storm, when the waves thundered into New Romney harbour, burying houses in the town under mud, shingle and debris. The door of St Nicholas Church is still a few feet lower than the road, and pillars inside are stained green from the slime. No longer could ships sail into the harbour and tie up at rings in the churchyard wall. No longer was the great Cinque Port seaborne.

Man-made efforts have also changed the character of the Marsh. The people of New Romney tried to train the river back along the Rhee Wall to their town, but in vain. Smeaton attempted to create a new outlet for it at Rye, and built a new harbour which was in turn blocked by shingle. Earlier works had been more successful. The Romans first strengthened the sea defences on the line of the Dymchurch Wall, along which stage-coaches later bowled from Romney to Hythe, and which is today solidly impressive. 'Innings' or reclaiming of new land in the Marsh began very early and came about at first automatically, when shingle was left by the tide to make walls within which silt could consolidate. The Romans probably had no need, before the last period of depression, for extra dykes. It was the monks, those arch-cultivators of the soil, who began the series of man-made earth walls or 'innings' that would shut out the tide and make the marshland solid. The earth needed for the walls, left dykes or ditches that in turn drained the land. Canterbury, as the great Kentish landowner (besides being the centre of civilization and learning) led the way and, seeing the many small innings, Thomas à Becket made the first large innings west of the Rhee Wall, in 1162. Near Fairfield Church is a farm still called Becket's Barn. Later archbishops continued the work; one, Archbishop Boniface, reclaiming more than a thousand acres. This consolidation probably had its effect, along with natural causes, on the course of the Rother, which gradually moved westwards, while still curling back to exit by New Romney, with the result that the Great Storm could easily dislodge it. Between the thirteenth and fifteenth centuries most of Walland Marsh was inned, joining Romney Marsh proper as solid land.

The dykes, which curve to fit round areas of pasturage chosen as fertile from time immemorial, rather than running straight as in the fens, are unromantically called sewers and petty sewers. The Nock Channel, dug to link up dykes which had been severed by the Military Canal, is known to villagers at Stone as the 'Back Drain'. Water is pumped on to higher levels through the channels, and this is even more vital now, because the increase of arable land in the Marsh had led to the water table dropping. Nor is the regulating of the water all it was. 'In the old days a man would go round and regulate the water. Now they put boards in on the 31st March regardless of the weather ...'

*

'Nothing is new ...'

Tom Finn-Kelcey's family have been farming on the Marsh for three or four hundred years. They have farmed Newland Farm for about one hundred years – it is now run by Tom Finn-Kelcey's son Geoffrey. The land, near the ruins of Midley Church, was reclaimed 600 years ago, and lies below sea level. Beyond the grass mound of a sea wall is more recent land, reclaimed only 400 years ago ... As elsewhere on the Marsh, the soil is more or less as it was when the sea receded, with sandy patches which are good for potatoes, not so good for corn, and the more fertile fields like one at Newland Farm which has been pasture land for 300 years and never dries out. It was found that the hair roots of the grass go down eight feet. 'The permanent pastures they chose were the best.'

But within the old framework modern adaptations have had to be made, as Tom Finn-Kelcey, who besides farming has been a judge at shows and has lectured on the Romney Marsh or Kent Sheep, being in his retirement a skilled watercolourist (also in the family tradition), explained to us. His father told him: 'You stick to sheep over your lifetime – they'll never let you down.' However, arable land is paying; but with better drainage, better grasses, better vaccines and medicines, Tom Finn-Kelcey told us: 'We keep as many sheep on half the farm (the rest being arable) as my father kept on the whole farm.' He had to find a way to make sheep as profitable as arable because, simply, he was very fond of sheep. Twenty years ago he found a book written in 1805 by a vet at Appledore, mentioning a Mr Wood at Dymchurch who housed his ewes inside during the winter and saying how well they'd done. So he pioneered the indoor method, or reintroduced it, because, as he says, 'nothing is new'.

There is nothing of the battery-fed image about this in-wintering. The sheep in pens in their large, airy barns, with plenty of clean straw, look considerably more comfortable in a biting April wind than those huddling outside during this prime lambing month, which starts on 1 April. They are kept off the grass from January until lambing time, fed outside on swedes and kale grown after early potatoes, and then inside on barley straw or hay, barley and sugar beet pulp and some added protein. This gives the grass a chance to grow, so that during the summer twenty sheep can feed off one acre. 'The whole secret of grazing is keeping the grass very short'; the most goodness is in grass when it is shorter.

In the old days a 'looker' or shepherd would watch over the sheep, often riding round 'acre lookering' for two or three different people, since the land was split up higgledy piggledy. At Newland there is one of the small sheep houses where the looker would sleep during the lambing season – a house in miniature with door and tiled roof, although this one is being moved to a special site by the Romney Marsh Preservation Society. Lookers are rare today; no one wants to do a long apprenticeship; tractors and machinery are more fun. 'People who work with animals must be fond of them – seven days a week.'

As on many farms on the Marsh, there is no farm house at New-land. 'It's such a horrible place to live, particularly as one gets older,' said Tom Finn-Kelcey, and he and his wife used to live at New Romney. Even smaller farmers have traditionally not lived on their farms, being of the opinion, as was Lambarde (echoing Hesiod on his fatherland), that the place was 'Evill in Winter, grievous in Sommer, and never good', and people 'starke madde, that would dwell in an unwholesome Aire, were the soile never so good and fertile'. Now that the marshland is well drained, malaria is no longer a danger there; but that still leaves in turn creeping winter mist, a wind seemingly straight from Siberia, and burning summer sun.

The Romney Marsh sheep is a strong, large breed, probably of Flemish origin. The pure Romney has an open fleece of long wool, full of lanolin. 'In the old days it was used for army uniforms; now the Swiss and French, in particular, buy it for sweaters'. But to get a quicker maturing lamb for meat, cross-breeding is usual, particularly with the Down breeds, the Southdown, Suffolk and Dorset being most popular. And as the cross-bred ewe should not be crossed more than once, it has been traditional to run a pure-bred Romney flock alongside a cross-bred flock.

When we visited Newland, the first thing we saw was a cross-bred lamb wearing a 'jacket', the skin of a dead lamb, running beside a cross-bred Suffolk ewe, which would mother it because of the smell from its own dead lamb's fleece.

There is something miraculous about lambs. To call them toys is an insult, but to see a field of them racing in the sun, in pairs, or stretching their hind legs like cats, with such small, unguarded perfection is quite out of the harsh adult world.

A sheep is pregnant for only twenty-one weeks and after that time, this complete little animal, which can weigh as much as 20 lbs., is born, with strong lower legs looking a size too large, and an extra fold of soft skin round its neck, which it will grow into, and which epitomizes the crazy hopefulness of the whole enterprise. Romney lambs are a bit quicker to get on their feet than other breeds, and may be up and sucking in a matter of ten minutes.

We saw one being born. The Romneys are quiet indoors, and don't mind you walking about. When a ewe is about to lamb, she scrapes the ground with her forefeet, a habit from ancient times when she would have been out in the wild digging a hole for protection. The other sheep seem to move away to give her space and air, because she can experience pain and difficulties like other animals.

'It can be a heartbreaking business,' Tom Finn-Kelcey said. 'The weather ... lambing ...' He was watching the ewe sympathetically, but the head and forefeet of the lamb appeared in their sack quickly and the lamb soon dropped on the ground, was licked clean and was bleating within minutes, then trying to get up. The ewe had very much taken it in her stride, hardly stopped munching.

In another part of the barn was an 'adopter', which is a pen divided into cheese-wedge shaped sections, where a ewe has her head held in a stall so that she can't smell the lamb which is nuzzling up to her until she has got used to it. A ewe tells her lamb by the smell of its dung, and after twenty-four hours drinking her milk the adopted lamb will have the right smell.

The Romneys are fine looking sheep, bigger than most. The heaviest weigh 180 to 220 lbs. They are white with black noses and speckles on their ears, with a clean face and 'topknot'. 'I was always taught when a boy if you want sheep to get fat they want a clean head and clean legs ... All the old things they told you have proved true.' They are almost immune to parasites when matured, because they have been grazed so thickly over the centuries and have built up immunity.

In 1940 all the breeding sheep (lambs and ewe lambs) were evacuated at the thought of the Germans coming. In 1941 the farmers travelled far and wide to find them and bring them back, telling their own by their earmarks. More ploughing had by then been introduced, and this paying trend has increased, not entirely to the benefit of the soil. Hundreds of years of sheep manure made the ground fertile, and ideally at least a third of a farm should be grass, and plough returned to grass after four or five years. Probably no amount of fertilizer can compensate for the altered balance. And the Marsh in summer is not so green in dry weather now that it is so much better drained.

*

We travelled on over Walland and Romney Marshes. Past a farmer who, when asked about keeping sheep indoors, said worriedly as he walked out to his lambs in the field: 'I've got no time to mess about like that ... When the time comes to turn them out they get all sorts of complaints.' And waving his hand at his flock, 'I mean that's nature isn't it?' (But as Tom Finn-Kelcey said, if ever in-wintering justified itself, it was in such a hard winter and spring as that.)

The Marsh is not only sheep. It is also churches; and we wanted to see them all. We were staying at New Romney, where modern-day pirates make the pubs noisy with music at night, and overfed boarders watch television. It is a hospitable area but the best food, we found, was in the Oasis Café, a large pull-in on the A259 near Old Romney, where lorry drivers can have slices of homemade iced sponges and the only tea that is any good when you are driving long distances – and which can only be found at pull-ins. There is also homemade food at the old Woolpack Inn near Brookland, but this draws smarter cars and larger crowds. Some people *do* live in the Evill area.

One would often want to. It is visually superb, and varied. In August large fields of yellow corn stretch to the sky, with a heat haze rising, or evening sun clinging to the wheat ears, the long grasses beside dykes, the pale golden rushes. Sheep; the ruins of a church; the call of peewits; a burning warmth.

In mid-winter, sun reflects off the frozen dykes. Skeins of white snow lie across the marsh green; birds scatter in the mist; bare willows bend to the frozen cuts which are edged with rime. The hulk of a farm looms from the whiteness; two geese cut across the sky; loneliness is muffled. Sparse, bushy hawthorns; calling church spires; the orange globe of winter sun sliding down behind a crescent of cloud, shooting from the grey sky into the white-grey marsh, exploding in the rents of snow and water.

Then the first green shoots in the brown earth. Light on the white barkless sides of dead trees, on the rushes. Scorched yellow

lichen on barn roofs, on church roofs, on the split rails and concrete uprights of the Marsh fences and on the brick bridges of the
dykes. Rusty red willows turning to green; purple brown blackthorn hedges. And everywhere lambs, running, sucking, curled on
a bank like commas, or with the ewes round the feeding pen, the
evening sun silhouetting the shepherd's back and legs and making
the thick fleeces translucent. *Now the day is over* ...

Texts run through the Marsh like swamp fire. The churches
raise expectant towers from their clusters of trees on the horizon
on every side, or sit settled in the fields like plump partridges. New
Romney; Old Romney; Ivychurch; Newchurch; Hope, Snargate;
Snave; Brenzett; Burmarsh; Brookland; Bonnington; Bilsington;
Ruckinge; Woodchurch; Stone-in-Oxney; St Mary-in-the-Marsh;
Fairfield ...

St Nicholas, New Romney. A Norman church, enlarged later,
with a fine west doorway, triple-shafted, zigzagged and overlapped
with abstract beakheads, as used by William of Sens at Canterbury.
Strong, short piers, alternately round and octagonal, pre-dating
those at Canterbury. A church with a massive, five-staged tower,
richly arcaded and windowed, pinnacled; suited to the importance
of the old Cinque Port town that once had three churches and a
mint. A church with yellow lichened stone walls, the churchyard
dropping away to an orchard where the sea once broke against the,
now moss covered, churchyard walls. A church that escaped restoration work planned by J. O. Scott in 1880 because of protests by
the SPAB, which had been founded in 1878 with William Morris
as its Secretary. 'The Society protested. The vicar was hostile, the
architect silent.'[4] A church whose tower, with one pinnacle taller
than the rest, stands on the horizon, beckoning to the churches of
Old Romney and St Mary's, to the tall 'cathedral' tower at Lydd –
and where an Armada beacon was lit on the stump of spire, the
corporation sending up beer to the men keeping it alight.

Midley church ruins – a solitary west wall rising in fields amongst
pylons, near Newland, and Horse's Bones Farm ...

St Clement's, Old Romney.[5] Peaceful among lambs, among rook-
nested trees, among old cottages, untouched by its nearness to the
A259. Shingled spire, steep tiled side-aisles. Unrestored. Plastered
walls, uneven red-brick floors, a perfect plain arch beside which
'squints' let light play on the whiteness, on heavy beams. Rustic.

Inspired. Twisted baluster rails, complete eighteenth-century fittings, among the least spoilt in the country. A stone coffin lid with a tree emblem or sword of an unknown crusader. A gilded royal coat of arms. The ten commandments in curlicued gold within raised frames of a reredos. Two black oval Marsh text boards with gold lettering; four white square boards, with rococo surrounds. A village church of 175 years ago, within thirteenth century walls.

'*The Lord our God be with us, as he was with our fathers ...*'

'*Blessed is the man that heareth me, watching daily at my gates, waiting at the posts of my doors.*'

The ruins of All Saints, Hope. Raised fingers of masonry round which sheep contentedly eat straw.

St Mary-in-the-Marsh. A spire like a pointed bird's beak, its plump body nestling behind it on the Marsh. An even larger royal coat of arms. Black wall text boards. Box pews and a carved and gilded tryptych. A tablet to E. Nesbit, who lived near here and is buried in the churchyard Author of *The Railway Children* and of books such as *The Phoenix and the Carpet* and *The Wouldbegoods*, as sunlit, magical and capricious as the area itself.

I cannot tell you about all the windings of the stream; it went through fields and woods and meadows, and at last the banks got steeper and higher, and the trees overhead darkly arched their mysterious branches, and we felt like the princes in a fairy tale who go out to seek their fortunes. . . .[6]

Ivychurch. A beacon turret on its lofty tower, to watch for invaders. Its pitted stonework, as John Piper says, taking on the mood of the day.[7] Black oval text boards over each pillar.

'*Be ye doers of the word and not hearers only, deceiving your own selves.*'

A blocked window with flowing stone tracery. A jet black sheep in a field nearby. Lapwings. A 'hudd' to keep eighteenth-century parsons dry at the graveside. Black and solid by the altar, the creed, Our Father and the ten comandments. A brick floor empty of pews. A ticking clock in the silence.

'*Let us not be weary in welldoing, for in due season we shall reap, if we faint not.*'

The ruins of Eastbridge church. Fragments of a tower, of a nave and west wall.

All Saints, Burmarsh. Battlemented and buttressed. The cliff at

Lympne louring over it in bad weather. One of the earliest settlements; near 'Shear-way' and the Shepherd's Crook Inn, and a wooden bridge over a stream.

St Peter and St Paul, Newchurch. Of ragstone, with a tower which leans and gravestones in upheaval as if from an earthquake, and possibly because of one, or the sinkings of the Marsh. A wide and striking porch. Near 'Frostland Farm'; icy in the biting wind of spring.

St Eanswith, Brenzett; St Rumwold, Bonnington, plump as its name.

St Mary the Virgin, Stone-in-Oxney. Among trees, on its island cliff, with a distant view of Dungeness. Inside, a Roman Mithraic altar, with the faint remains of a bull carved in the stone – a pagan block, which holds its power in spite of having been used as a mounting block in the past. And near it the fossilized bones, found in a quarry at Stone, of the Dinosaur Iguanodon, which became extinct about seventy million years ago, and whose three-toed footprints have been found in the Wealden rocks of Sussex, hugely treading the primeval landscape – the biggest animal that ever walked the earth.

St Augustine, Brookland, with its separate and detached campanile, of shingled wood from top to toe like a three-tiered Christmas tree, which is said, such were the morals of the Marsh in times long ago (and later?), to have jumped from the church in amazement that the bride brought there by her bridegroom was a virgin. Rare as the virgin, the church's Norman lead font, like one at Saint Évrault-de-Monfort in Normandy, with the signs of the Zodiac and the Labours of the Months. In May, hawking; in June, scything; in November, knocking down acorns for the pig; in February sitting by the fire ...

And finally, and first, St Thomas Becket, Fairfield. The smallest church in Kent. Which has swum through the centuries in its bare sea of fields which are as fair as its name, and which swam in floods in 1960 when villagers rowed to the door. Reached by a grass causeway. Restored but unspoilt. A shingled bellcote and lichened roofs; beams from the original timber church, already there in 1294, incorporated by W. D. Caröe in 1913 with other beams into the massive crown-post roofs with tie-beams only seven feet from the ground, above pale plastered walls striped like a milkmaid's dress and darkened by black text boards. Holding within them white box pews spiked with black and a three-decker pulpit with flowering candlestick to match the delicate hanging lamps. A tiny altar within rails. Through the windows, the flat land, reminiscent of Ireland, with misty hills, windblown thornbushes and pools of water. Idyllic in the sun, when the sheep, and the moorhen church, are the only features on the green plain.

Inside the church is framed a poem by Joan Warburg.

> My parish is the lonely Marsh
> My service at the water's edge;
> . . .
> Where pilgrims and crusaders sleep.
> . . .
> So still I guard the coast and look
> Beyond the sea, across the Downs.
> I, that was writ in Domesday book,
> Have watched tall ships and towns
> Spring up as flowers and pass away
> Within the fading of a day.
> . . .
> I am nothing but Thy house,
> Empty stands the sacred porch. . .'[8]

And the texts echo across the Marsh.

'*Our Father, which art in heaven . . . Thy kingdom come . . . in earth as it is in heaven . . .*'

'*Suffer the little children to come unto me, and forbid them not: for of such is the Kingdom of God.*'

And in the sun the lambs race among the flowers which pass away.

*

In spite of its lost harbour, New Romney doesn't seem a dead town. Its broad main street has an imposing Town Hall and some fine porches, enough shops to keep it lively. In Church Approach are eighteenth-century Assembly Rooms, and the town has other eighteenth-century buildings and few modern eyesores. It was the half-way point between the Cinque Ports of Kent and Sussex, and as such eminent among them. Many of the meetings of the Brodhull and Guestling were held here, and for this reason the minutes of the meetings, kept in the historic White and Black Books of the Cinque Ports were kept in New Romney, but have now been transferred to the County Archives at Maidstone, except for the current minute book, which the Town Clerk, Mr D. E. Collins, assured us is still kept there except when it is away in use at a Court or ceremony.

Minutes were written from 1432 onwards. Some of the earliest entries were copied from old books into the White Book by a clerk, John Forsett, in 1560, who was charged to 'wryte out all the olde books into the cleane paper at the begynninge of this booke', being paid forty shillings for his work. In 1571 the White Book was closed, and from 1572 the minutes were recorded in the Black Book.

Typical entries are:

Brodhyll held at Romney on Monday, 2 May 1435. 'Ordered that John Grene go forthwith to London to institute proceedings on behalf of the Cinque Ports and to defend suit moved against them in the King's Exchequer ...'

1435–6 'Ordered that for defence against the enemy each Port shall warn the other Ports upon sight of the enemy and the Port thus warning shall receive 12d from each other Port on each occasion.'

1470. 'William Earl of Arundel at his admission as Lord Warden is to receive "a cuppe of sylver and gylte" of the value of 20 li. with the arms of the Ports thereon. John Westclyf of Sandwich is to labour for the cup and to have 20s for his pains. The 20 li. shall be paid at Shepway ...'

1488. 'The mayors of Dover and Sandwich with others of their towns are to meet with the King and the Lord Chancellor when they are next at Dover regarding the case of William Colyn of Birchington....' (Henry VIII)

1592. 'A complaint of Deal ... of hard dealing by some inhabitants of Kent nearby. Sandwich and Dover are to write to the Lord Warden seeking redress ...'

1726. 'A petition is to be sent to the Lord Warden regarding French fishermen who come and fish within the Admiralty of the Cinque Ports.'

1910. 'Alderman Jeal proposed and the Speaker seconded that the Lords of the Admiralty be notified of the serious effects likely to arise through the doing away with coast guards ...'

1937. 'Velvet caps were worn during the crowning ... and medals were given to the barons (coronation of King George VI).

1955. 'Bernard Hailstone was painting a portrait of the Lord Warden ...'

Many people, including some historians of the Cinque Ports, have written of the Ports as being the symbols of an outmoded and unreal pomp and status, with no power or reason for existence. Yet it is often the symbols and ceremonies of life which give it cohesion and continuity. To the small extent that we are not flowers of the field that pass away, we seek patterns and shapes within which to act, and to hand down to the next generations. The symbolism of the Cinque Ports, on a much smaller scale, is similar to the symbol of monarchy, and equally linked to patriotism and to a romantic love for place and country. And like monarchy, it has a practical side, engendering communication and understanding. The people of the Cinque Ports have a particular reason to be proud of their towns, and are the only ones to have a head start in friendly association and rivalry of the kind that 'link' towns of other countries can share with one another. Mr Collins assured us that when a meeting of the Brodhull and Guestling was held in New Romney to make a loyal address on the occasion of the Queen's Silver Jubilee, the meeting being held in the church and following a service there, it attracted a great many people, and much attention. The Cinque Ports being part of our heritage, not only the people of the modern ports would be sad if the tradition was ever to die out.

New Romney was also a centre for a famous cycle of Mystery Plays, with the collective title of *Le Playbook*, which were performed there and out in villages on the Marsh. Modern entertainment is more of the holiday variety, with seaside building of varying eras of ugliness spreading like a rash along the coast. Dymchurch, known for H. G. Wells's *Kipps*, and for the novels about Dr Syn, the smuggling vicar, by Russell Thorndike, is now known for caravans and chalets, although it has an older heart, with New Hall, where, until they had to relinquish their powers in 1951, the Court of the Lords, Bailiffs and Jurats of Romney Marsh sat – a body going back to the early thirteenth century, set up to provide the upkeep of walls and waterways, to hand the King his cup on Whit Sunday, or provide him with a sparrowhawk at Lammas. No longer are they enjoined to bother themselves with 'knockes, relayes, slattes, groynes, fotehegges and other necessaries for defence of the said walles', or to do likewise to 'the gutts of Sherlock and the watergangs of the same, Willop Wall and the

Grene Walls'.[10] The 'Dangers of the Sea' are bandied about by larger and some would say less caring bodies.

But the inroads of architecture or bureaucracy cannot spoil the quality of the Marsh, imortalized by Kipps's memories of his childhood, and excursions from New Romney to Dymchurch and Greatstone.

The sky in these memories was the blazing hemisphere of the marsh heaven in summer, or its wintry tumult of sky and sea; and there were wrecks, real wrecks, in it. ... The holidays were, indeed, very different from school ... In his memory of his boyhood they shone like strips of stained-glass window ... brighter and brighter as they grew remoter. There came a time at last and moods when he could look back to them with a feeling akin to tears.

And as a young man, it was surrounded by the Marsh that he pictured his future wife – 'and he saw her as he had seen her at New Romney, sitting amidst the yellow sea-poppies with the sunlight on her face.'[11]

Littlestone and Greatstone, once the sea markers to the great harbour bay of Romney, are now firmly of the shore, and resorts. Littlestone has some pleasant Edwardian style villas on the front and an 1890 water tower, an open beach. A concrete slab of Mulberry harbour lollops like a whale in the sea offshore, a reminder, as are concrete bunkers and other war detritus on the Marsh, that this area was in the forefront of activities at the time. We saw another shepherd's house near Old Romney, which with its small size, surrounded by day-old lambs, and dwarfed by distant pylons, seemed to stand alone in this vast, flat, sea-sunk level of land, open to invaders, symbolic of all that might need protection.

*

Protection in past centuries had rather a different meaning on the Marsh, an area where more smuggling was carried out than anywhere else in the country. It was by nature the ideal region for running illicit imports and exports – wild, watery, with creeks cutting inland and mist shrouding the most blatant lawbreaking.

The marshmen had piracy and smuggling in their bones, long before their privileges and status as men of the Cinque Ports gave an impetus to their feelings of recklessness. A Roman official, writing to an officer embarked in the Channel fleet which kept guard against Saxon pirates, put it concisely, and his words applied equally to the descendants of those pirates who settled round the coast.

Your foe is of all foes the most dangerous. He attacks unexpectedly.... And more than this, to these men a shipwreck is a school of seamanship rather than a matter of dread. They know the dangers of the deep like men who are every day in combat with them ... they gladly risk themselves in the midst of wrecks and surfbeaten rocks in the hope of making profit out of the very tempest.[12]

Profits from smuggling were worth the risk. Before the introduction of a permanent customs system under Edward I, trade was free and there was no need for smuggling. Edward I put a levy on the export of wool, our most important raw material until the Industrial Revolution. 'Owling' or wool running came into being, its name taken from the call of an owl used as a signal, and bales of wool, laden secretly on to pack trains, began making their way to the boats to be taken across to France. Later, other types of smuggling were added, as import duties on brandy, silks, lace and tea were introduced. The importing of wool had also been made illegal, while at one time the penalty for a second conviction for exporting sheep was death. In 1614, the export of wool was forbidden altogether, and owling became more wholesale and more desperate, when death was made the punishment for this offence too, after the Restoration, in 1662. Undeterred, the smugglers armed and consolidated themselves, and in the 1670s were sending some twenty thousand packs of wool annually to Calais.

By the eighteenth century up to twenty thousand people were concerned one way or another in the owlers' activities, while one smuggler alone, 'Captain' Joseph Cockburn, ran five boats regularly between Boulogne, Kent and Sussex, importing about six tons of tea and 2,000 half-ankers (four-gallon casks – the smugglers' handy-pack) of spirits a week. The Revenue would lose as much as £3 million a year from all smuggling, which would further push up taxation in a vicious spiral. Almost the whole population was involved, money changing hands and the smugglers having influence with magistrates, clergy, clerks and attorneys. 'The dearest lover of his country,' wrote W. S. Gent in 1656, did not dare to 'prevent that mischief which his eyes beheld.'[13] Smuggling was almost a recognized profession, and to the extent that they enabled people to obtain luxuries such as brandy, chocolate and coffee, the smugglers were regarded as public benefactors. The duty on tea costing 5s 9d in bond, in 1743, was 4s od, and by 1783 spirits distilled from corn were subject to eleven separate duties. The national debt was immense and had to be offset. Between 1739 and 1815, Britain had been at war for forty-five years – all expensive and partly maritime wars (the War of Austrian Succession, the Seven Years' War, the War of American Independence, the French Revolutionary Wars and the Napoleonic Wars).

Hiding places were legion. Nearly every inn and remote farmhouse in the Romney Marsh and Kent-Sussex border area, and in Thanet, has a smuggler's cellar or smuggler's secret hideaway. It was for this reason that so many houses had the reputation of being 'haunted': noises at night could be explained away by this means, and it was hoped that people would keep their distance. In boats, too, the smugglers' ingenuity knew no bounds. False hulls were built, so that tea, spirits and silk shawls could be stuffed within the lining. Ropes of tobacco were stained with rum to look like ordinary ropes; lace was hidden in cardboard apples; cargoes were sunk and weighted down, to be retrieved later at some convenient time, as when in 1829 the London barge *Alfred* caught a cutter off Birchington in the act of picking up 1,045 tubs of spirits with a 'creeping iron' – a five-pronged hook which was trailed along the seabed until it found the roped tubs.

The landing of goods was one of the trickiest operations. The boat would flash a blue light, and the 'land smuggler' would answer with sparks from a tinderbox visible for half a mile. Timing was essential. Then the goods had to be taken on the most dangerous leg of the journey, overland to London or elsewhere. The smugglers used lanes such as the 'hollow ways' of Sussex, cut deep by rain and overgrown with trees and bushes, so that they were almost invisible to the travellers on the main roadways. (In a large run in 1829, between 'Jew's Gut' and 'Ness Point', smuggled goods were taken through Lydd in twelve carts with eighty well armed owlers.)

Churches were smugglers' paradises, with their vaults and visiting country parsons. Stories are told of bemused vicars being told that it was the wrong week to preach, and being sent packing to their other church if it was not thought fit by the smugglers that they should enter. As at Ivychurch, where the rector was told by his sexton: ''Bain't be no service, parson. Pulpit be full o' baccy, and vestry be full o' brandy.'

As the authorities made more determined efforts to put a stop to this perpetual drain on the revenue, smuggling became less jolly altogether, and more brutal. Defoe has given a good description of the task of hunting the lawbreakers.

As I rode along this coast, I perceiv'd several dragoons riding, officers, and others arm'd on horseback, riding always about as if they were huntsmen beating up their game; upon inquiry I found their diligence was employ'd in quest of the owlers, as they call them, and sometimes they catch some of them; but when I came to enquire farther, I found too, that often times these are attack'd in the night, with such numbers, that they dare not resist, or if they do, they are wounded and beaten, and sometimes kill'd; and at other times are oblig'd, as it were, to stand still, and see the wool carry'd off before their faces, not daring to meddle; and the boats taking it in from the very horses backs . . .[15]

The preventive officers didn't stand a chance, and the Navy was too occupied elsewhere to be of much help. After the Napoleonic wars, a coast blockade was set up, which created great bitterness when it began to be successful. It was difficult to get recruits, however, and it was replaced by a 'Preventive Water Guard' which later became the Coastguard. With this, and the establishment of metropolitan and provincial police forces, and the reduction or abolition of duties, the position was altered. By the mid-nineteenth century, smuggling as a way of life had had its day.

One has to remember that if smuggling affrays were bloody, it was in a much harsher setting than today. During hard years and in time of war, the poor could and did suffer starvation. Bad pay and savage discipline in the Navy in its early days led to a lack of recruits and the setting up of the press-gang, which could seize men in the street and drag them on board ship either conscious or unconscious, punishing any attempt at escape afterwards by flogging or death. (Nor was the Army different. Just before the Nore and Spithead mutinies, the ringleaders of a mutiny in the Oxford Militia were sentenced, two to be shot, and two others to be given a thousand lashes – a sentence carried out where the Brighton and Hove Albion football ground now stands. The Army surgeon put an end to the punishment after three hundred

'For our time is a very shadow that passeth away' – clock and quarter boys on Rye Parish Church tower

Rye from East Guldeford

Lighting a charcoal kiln at Petley Wood near Sedlescombe

Ted Turner in trug-making workshop of Blackman, Pavie and Ladden Ltd, near Sedlescombe

John Bratby RA in his cupola studio at Hastings

Southease Church

Pevensey Castle

lashes.[16]) Some said that the end of smuggling also put an end to the winter employment of farm labourers, and so increased the hardship of the poor.

Nevertheless, during the eighteenth and nineteenth centuries, the smuggler ruled, as F. F. Nicholls has pointed out in his book *Honest Thieves* with 'a pervasive, Mafia-like network of crime, supported and protected (again like the Mafia) by corruption of officials, armed force, terrorism, murder, and occasionally torture.'[17] When forced to give up smuggling the men might take to highway robbery and housebreaking. Most notorious of the eighteenth-century smugglers were the Alfriston and Hawkhurst gangs, and in the nineteenth century the most dangerous gang was the Kentish Aldington Gang, called 'The Blues'. Abducting and maltreating customs officers, stealing horses, pegging revenue men to the shore at the low-water mark so that they drowned, shootings and beating-up, sometimes of mere bystanders, made these gangs a terror to the countryside.

The saga of the Hawkhurst gang is so bestial that it seems almost inconceivable, although it is well documented and has often been recounted. It is worth repeating because it did happen, and highlights the anti-social side of smuggling.

The gang literally terrorized the countryside. They had storehouses over a large area in Kent and Sussex, and preserved their immunity by rick burning, cattle maiming and other vicious acts against informers. The Mermaid Inn at Rye was said to be one of their headquarters, and so confident were they, that they were seen there after a successful run, sitting openly at the bar, 'carousing and smoking their pipes with their loaded pistols on the table before them, no magistrate daring to interfere with them.'[18] Tired of being molested, the village of Goudhurst, under an ex-soldier called Sturt, set up a band of militia, and defeated the gang in battle, killing three of them and wounding others. Still the gang continued its activities. A revenue cutter captured a cargo of tea they were bringing in, and lodged it in the Custom House at Poole. Thirty to sixty men, made up of the Kentish gang and men from Chichester and Hampshire, raided the Custom House and carried off the tea. On their way back through Fordingbridge, an old shoemaker called Chater recognized one of the smugglers, Jack Diamond, who threw him a bag of tea. Chater was a gossip, and when a proclamation offering a reward for information about the smugglers was issued, he had already let it be known that he recognized 'Dimer'. The customs officials arrested Dimer, and sent for Chater to go with an excise officer, William Galley, to make a formal statement. The two men never reached their destination. For seven months the authorities didn't know what had happened to them, and the terrified countryside didn't dare tell what they knew. While drinking at an inn, the White Hart at Rowland's Castle, Chater again grew boastful of his mission, and the innkeeper, a Mrs Elizabeth Payne, passed on the news to some of the Hampshire smugglers. Led by 'one of the most notorious smugglers living in his time', William Jackson, and William Carter, a group of smugglers, egged on by their women and the widow Payne, made the two old men drunk, and then Jackson woke them from their stupored sleep by rowelling their foreheads with his spurs. Bound on horseback, the two were beaten and dragged upside down until they were barely alive, and sadistically treated in the most brutal way, particularly by Jackson, who as Nicholls points out, probably had 'specialized tastes'. Galley was the first to die, or to appear dead, when he fell from his horse. He was later buried, possibly still conscious. Chater defied further terrible injuries, including having his eye slashed out, and was finally thrown, still living, down a well, with heavy logs and stones on top of him.

After an elapse of time, the murderers were traced and arrested, and hung. One of them turned King's evidence, and so we have the whole story. But it was not the end of smuggling, or of murders, although this particular gang was broken up. They had been forceful, virulent characters, clad in the legendary mystique of villains who capture, albeit fearfully, the public imagination. Some of them had names in the Billy the Kid, Bonnie and Clyde tradition, such as Little Sam, Smoaker, Little Harry, Coachman, Little Fat Back, Old Mills. A far cry from Smuggler Bill, of the curling locks and roving eye ...

*

'When did smuggling die out?' we asked Anne Roper, probably the greatest living authority on the Romney Marsh area.

'I don't think it's died out, even today ...'

But today the traffic is more likely to be in drugs, diamonds or watches. Recently, she told us, a man with several hundred watches stuffed behind a car's fascia board had come up before the magistrates.

But in other ways the Marsh has changed greatly since she came to live there fifty-two years ago. In those days it was still very much the fifth quarter of the globe, with cottages lit by candles and lamps, well water, no main drainage. People wouldn't tell the way to a 'foreigner', if he was a man, because they thought he might be an excise officer.

Anne Roper is a descendant of William Roper, who married Sir Thomas More's daughter Margaret, who so sadly bore his head to Canterbury. Miss Roper came to live at Littlestone for six months for the sea air, and has stayed there ever since. While at Cardiff University, doing an Honours French degree, she met with an accident to her spine playing hockey, and after being completely recumbent in plaster for two years, was told by her doctor that she would not be able to undertake any strenuous work. She was fascinated by the history, the archives and the archaeology of Romney Marsh, remained at Littlestone, and saw it develop in the pre-war years, when many eminent people in the legal and medical professions bought houses there. At the outbreak of the Second World War she was asked not to leave, when most of the inhabitants and children were evacuated, as her local knowledge was too valuable. She was appointed by the War Office as Assistant Army Welfare Officer and was able to brief successive commanding officers on local matters, as well as dealing with the soldiers' and airmen's personal problems, and the difficulties of ATS and WAAF personnel. She was told, 'Get into uniform or you may be taken for a canteen tout!' In 1944 she was awarded the MBE for her valuable and devoted work.

Today, eminent in her field, Miss Roper has been on the council of the Kent Archaeological Society for forty years and has recently been elected President of the Association of Men of Kent and Kentish Men. She is a Fellow of the Royal Society of Antiquaries and lectures tirelessly on Kent's history, particularly on its churches. She has written illuminating guides to many of the churches on the Marsh, and is the author, with H. R. Pratt Boorman, of *Kent Inns: A Distillation*, and of a short guide to Romney Marsh, *The Gift of the Sea*.[19] On the day we met her, she had

227

kindly hurried back from lecturing at Sandwich to talk to us, with what I am sure is typical generosity, at her house of white Kent weatherboarding which she had helped to design.

She told us how she had originally become interested in the archives and history of the Cinque Ports, and of the valuable work done by Major Teichman-Derville, Speaker of the Cinque Ports from 1931–7, and author of *The Level and Liberty of Romney Marsh*, whose unhappy task it was, in 1951, as Bailiff of the Lords of Romney Marsh, to announce that the duties and privileges of the Lords of the Marsh were to come to an end. 'Now it is Region 7 of the Southern Water Authority,' as she says. She also told us, how in the war, bungalows were gutted at Greatstone, because it was from there that 'Pluto' started – the fuel supply line to the Continent. The pumps were hidden in the gutted houses, so that the Germans coming over to photograph could see no change in the landscape. A transformer station was constructed under the shingle beach. (The Romney, Hythe and Dymchurch Railway, now a great holiday attraction with its line to Dungeness, was requisitioned by the Army also, carrying much of the material for Pluto along its fifteen-inch gauge rails.)

Anne Roper, who with her delicate features and pretty, searchingly intelligent eyes, must have made those years much less grim on Romney Marsh, summed up succinctly and with fervour on the occasion of a meeting of the Brotherhood and Guestling in 1978, the importance and the enduring meaning, of the Cinque Ports. In July of that year she stressed in an article how the Courts of Brotherhood and Guestling, showing as they do the strength of democratic institutions in medieval times, are a vital part of our English constitutional history. The Portsmen, summoned by their Speaker to regulate their own affairs, to a great extent laid the foundations of popular government, and their ceremonial should not be dismissed as a pointless anachronism. As Anne Roper wrote: 'Those who are privileged to attend the Courts on June 14th should lift up thankful hearts that they are heirs of so goodly a heritage and take heed to hand on to their children traditions no less worthy, useful and honourable.'[20]

9 Smallhythe; Tenterden; Appledore; Lydd; Dungeness

'Here the houses have gardens in front of them as well as behind; ...
and everything looks like *gentility*.'   William Cobbett, *Rural Rides*

'Neshe ... a Nebbe, or nose of the land, extended into the Sea.'
William Lambarde

A garden of roses and border plants surrounds Smallhythe Place,
which was once the harbourmaster's house when the sea ran in
to the port for Tenterden at Smallhythe; which was later 'The
Farm', when the sea receded and farmland replaced the shipyard;
which was finally the home of the actress Ellen Terry, from 1919
until her death in 1928. Her bedroom looks out over the marsh;
beside the timbered house is a thatched barn; orchards blossom
round the village, which is in a part of the country that even
the keen-eyed Cobbett labelled simply 'very beautiful' – bright
with mustard in its season, with old brick houses, chestnuts in
flower, sorrel, poplars, June grass rampaging over verges, pleached
apple-tree avenues. And as you approach Tenterden, the tower
of Tenterden church tall and imposing above the trees on the
skyline, visible for miles.

Ellen Terry's house was given to the National Trust by her
daughter, Edith Craig. It is full of her personal possessions, and a
magnificent theatrical museum in its own right. There is a carved
beam over the drawing-room fireplace from Nell Gwynne's house
in old Brompton Village; prints of old theatres; a life mask of Gar-
rick, and his engraved glass-handled knives; a death mask of Sir
Henry Irving; a handkerchief of Sarah Bernhardt's; a cast of
Eleanora Duse's long hand; a chain worn by Fanny Kemble;
Edmund Kean's swords and boots; Charles Kean's stage jewels;
prints of the inimitable Mme Rachel; a family tree showing how

John Gielgud is related to Ellen Terry via her niece Kate. There are enough mementoes, memorabilia and stage costumes for half a day's study; and everywhere the personality of the actress herself. In portraits, including a copy of one by her first husband, G. F. Watts, whom she married disastrously when she was sixteen (and who also portrayed her in the painting with red camellias, *Choosing*, now at Smallhythe); with her family in miniatures and photographs, showing her sisters Kate, Marion and Florence, the last of whom married William Morris and who looks even more striking than her sister (while Marion has the profile of the young Elizabeth Taylor); in her jewellery, trinkets, and simple make-up box, containing a small wig piece, a mirror, shoehorn, rouge and hare's foot, sponge, glass and pins in a German box. Ellen Terry had a necklace made from stones, each stone given by one of her friends; the richness of her life is as abundant here as the greatness of her acting. Oscar Wilde wrote, sending her the first copy of his first play: 'Dear Miss Ellen Terry – Will you accept the First copy of my First play – ... perhaps some day I shall be fortunate enough to write something worthy of your playing –'[1]. A print of Julia Margaret Cameron's photograph of Ellen at 16 shows her as an English rose. The later face is a stronger version of this, and in a review in the *Radio Times* in 1928, James Agate summed up her art, as being that of a natural actress, not excelling in tragedy, or artificial comedy – '... she was all the heroines of Shakespeare's comedies, who, it is convenient to remember, are all so many natural actresses ... And she was, of course, the only Juliet...'[2]

Ellen Terry's son Gordon Craig, the artist and theatrical producer, designed special playing cards for her, some of which are here. His talent is evident in one of the most telling exhibits, by the door of her bedroom – a dark watercolour of telephone wires and the moon, inscribed 'Mother from Ted', 1901.

In spite of failing eyesight and hearing, Ellen Terry was still charming and full of vitality in her seventies. In 1925 she was created a Dame. Her stage jubilee had been celebrated in 1906. (As a young trouper of nine she had played on with a broken toe after a trap-door fell on it, earning a double salary in recompense). Her funeral service was held at the small red-brick Flemish church of 1515, just up the road from Smallhythe Place, next to the Priest's

House, now colourwashed a dulled orange like its larger neighbour, and equally timbered, set off by a fine yew peacock.

*

The old repair dock next to Smallhythe Place has recently been excavated. It would have been in use since before the thirteenth century until the tidal channel which used to sweep round the Isle of Oxney below Tenterden silted up at the end of the sixteenth century (although even as late as this century, goods were brought by barge from Rye to Smallhythe wharf).

Some of the earliest references to ports, in the Patent Rolls of 1325–6, mention Smallhythe.

Jan 3rd 1326. Commission to: Thomas de Valoynes and Stephen Donet of the port of Redyng (Reading Street) and Smallidde, William Lang, Thomas de Goseburn and John le Tanner of the ports of Apeldre, Smallide and Neuenden ... to guard all places along the coast of the Thames etc, and search in all places where ships put in ... and to arrest all who are carrying letters prejudicial to the Crown and send all such letters with all speed to the King; ...

Feb 8th 1326. Mandate until All Saints, to the Mayors and Bailiffs of Wynchelse, Rye, Hastynges, Pevense, Redyng & Smalhide to let John Dyve, Master of the King's ship La Nicholas which he is bringing to the King, have as many mariners as he needs to man it ...

Accounts in New Romney records mention the launch at Smallhythe of the barge *Eneswithe* in 1400 and a fee of 3s 4d to the chapel there for the launching ceremony (the chapel was burnt down in 1514, and replaced by the church). It was a chapel of ease to Tenterden, but burials had to be carried out at Tenterden, with the exception of 'bodies of men who by shipwreck shall have been cast up on the sea shore within the town of Smallhythe'. Such a scene of shipwrecked mariners seems incredible today in the land-locked, sleepy countryside, as does the thought of Henry VIII arriving at Smallhythe to inspect the building of an important warship.

Tenterden's other industries are more likely ones. A 'den' was a pig pasture, and Tenet-wara-den was the pig pasture of the men of Thanet, one of the clearings in the Wealden forest. The name first appears in a charter of AD 968 conveying an estate from Queen Aethelflaed to a man called Aelfwolde, as 'Tenet-wara-brocas', the meadows of the men of Thanet. The countryside is fertile, and another of Cobbett's succinct remarks, actually as he left 'The Wells' (Tunbridge Wells) in 1823, obviously applied here too – 'The labouring people look pretty well. They have pigs.' They, the pigs, did best in woodland country, he said, and he also mentioned that it was a great '*nut* year', which meant according to the country people that four times as many babies would be born the following year (and presumably pigs also). 'The *Vice Society* too, with that holy man Wilberforce at its head, ought to look out sharp after these mischievous nut-trees.'[3]

Tenterden became a member of the Cinque Ports as a Limb of Rye in 1449, mainly because of shipbuilding at Smallhythe. But before that in 1328 Edward III had invited Flemish weavers to settle there to teach their craft. He allocated different types of manufacture to different counties and towns (with inspired interference that the state today might envy). Kent was to make broadcloth, and Tenterden became a booming centre, the industry only declining during the later half of the seventeenth century, when people wanted something lighter to wear than broadcloth. It was also a hub for the rich Wealden ironmasters, and the town with its broad central street edged with grass still tells of wealth in every finely set frontage of wood or brick. The Eight Bells is a fifteenth-century pub, later brick fronted; the timber and plaster Black Horse has been renamed the William Caxton, after the printer, who may have been born in Tenterden, although he himself only stated that he was born in the Weald 'where I doubt not is spoken as broad and rude English as in any part of England'; the Spinning-Wheel restaurant is timber-framed fifteenth-century; there are sixteenth- and seventeenth-century timber-framed cottages, but no stone buildings of earlier than the nineteenth century. The essential pattern of the town today is eighteenth-century timber, brick and tile, with a predominance of white-painted Kentish boarding that is airily attractive, and well kept, pointing to the fact that the town is certainly not in decline, with its shops, banks, schools, clinics and county commerce. It is even a little too busy for some, who will claim that it is 'not what it was', adding the rider 'supermarkets' in outraged explanation. But its markets must have been more bustling in the days of the weavers.

Coaches disgorge their parties at the Tudor Rose tearooms, a

Wealden hall house, which has an interior passage beside it opening on to the street – beamed, hung with meat-hooks and guarded
by a studded door – down which you walk to wash; one of the
best corners of the evocative past in Tenterden.

'Do you like coach parties?' I asked a scurrying waitress.

'You must be joking –' But she laughed, and smiles pass from
table to table among the intarsia-knit suits, tweed jackets and
arthritic legs; the teacups are immaculate rosebud china; outside
in the street a blonde young woman with an overlarge car and
two blazered and sullen children parks clumsily and calls crossly
to her dog. Tenterden is very English ...

'We get interesting people coming in here,' I was told at the
Tenterden Museum, which has only recently opened but is fully
manned by volunteers. There is a good variety of exhibits, ranging
from footwarmers and 'worm cake' jars, to Georgian reaping hooks
and a hop-picker's horn. (Tenterden is on the fringes of a hop-
picking region, and I have myself picked them by hand, when
this was still the method, not many miles away, in the 1950s.) A
photograph shows Churchill accepting his portrait at Hastings at a
Court of the Brotherhood and Guestling in 1955. There are
Cinque Ports Barons' coronation robes; the arms of Tenterden,
which incorporate those of the Cinque Ports; a collage tapestry
of the town's history made by children of the Church of England
Junior School in 1974; a copy of the title sheet and final page,
beautifully illuminated with roses and leaves, of Tenterden Record Book's own copy of the confirmation by Edward IV of the
Great Charter of the Cinque Ports of 1278. Also housed here is the
Colonel Stephens railway museum, and for steam trains which
still steam, down the road is the little station of the Kent and East
Sussex Railway, which runs along track bought from British Rail
by enthusiasts, and opened in 1974, with a new station reconstructed with the help of young people under the Job Creation Programme, at its Wittersham Road terminus, open since 1978. The
Tenterden Railway Company Ltd is a registered charity. In the
station office are ranged books, leaflets, old timetables and 'Steam
Trains at Tenterden' T-shirts. In the sidings old cream-and-brown
GWR buffet cars sit nostalgically, complete with glass sandwich
domes. The present timetable also savours of pre-Beeching days.
'Trains will also call at Rolvenden on request. Passengers wishing

to alight must inform the guard and those wishing to join must give a hand signal to the driver ...'

... To steam away through the countryside watched over by Tenterden's tall church tower, of the church dedicated to St Mildred, the Anglo-Jutish princess from Thanet, descended from Hengist via her mother Domneva, Abbess of Minster Abbey before her. The tower was built at the end of the fifteenth century. The nave is twelfth century, the south and north aisles thirteenth and fourteenth century. Of all its fine details, the wide, panelled barrel roof to the nave is perhaps most striking; while the roof outside is of wood shingles, the only one like it in the country. The tower has twin west doors, as does Lydd church, and besides them only four other churches in England which are not cathedrals or abbeys.

*

On one of our visits to Romney Marsh we stayed at Appledore, on the borders of the Marsh. 'Have you visited our blacksmith?' Jean Southwick at the Swan Hotel asked us. 'He's got the same name as you, although spelt differently.'

The Swan Hotel, I should add, is bright and creeper hung, and has an *à la carte* menu a London hotel would be proud of. 'I'm afraid there's no mussel soup,' our hostess apologized. But there was venison soup and smoked mackerel. Nor could I believe my ears when I asked how late we could eat, as we wanted to catch the sun going down over Dungeness. I was told 'any time.' 'But how late?' I repeated. 'When you like,' Mrs Southwick smiled. Rare in cities, such a relaxed atmosphere is absolutely unknown in country areas, where 'evening meal' usually means chips with everything but only before eight and never on Sundays. It is rare, in fact, for us to stay at hotels. Bed and breakfast boarding-houses are not only cheaper, but usually quieter and always cleaner. In a hotel your room will be cleaned by a sulky paid helper (I write as one who has done the job). Bed and breakfast landladies are keeping their own house tidy and pleasant, and if they favour plastic frills and nylon sheets, they also favour scouring powder and clean tablecloths to protect their furniture. Some of the best addresses are listed in the Cyclists' Touring Club handbook;[4] you will find cars parked outside, as well as bicycles; there is no need to appear in bicycle clips.

Mr R. Moseley, wrought-iron and general smith, has a forge opposite the Swan Hotel, in this village which is unspoilt, and which has even just eliminated, by a resale, one of its few 'week-end' householders, a tribe not generally much loved by villagers, particularly if they come from as far afield as America, and only a few times a year. The lawn of the Moseley house slopes down to the main street, opposite the church, and under the grass lie the cobbles of the old shambles or market area. The road then dips away between porched and half-timbered houses to where the tidal channel from the sea used to flow, as at Smallhythe, round the Isle of Oxney to the south. Now the Military Canal flows a little way below the town, through green meadowland flecked with black-and-white cattle, and mild-faced sheep.

In the forge was an astonishing sight. One of the large copper square sails of the four weathervanes of Tenterden church, being repaired. Another was having gold leaf carefully applied to it, which would withstand the weather of years. The vanes have been repaired three times before through the centuries, Mr Moseley told us, but no records show when this was done. So he has engraved his name on the metal, and the date, 6.5.1979, which also happened to be the twenty-first anniversary of his ownership of the forge. We realized too late that we had also recorded the fact; John had spent some time photographing Tenterden church the day before, without its vanes.

Mr Moseley has been a smith since he was fourteen. He is also passionately interested in local history. His forge is in an old wheelwright's shop, and behind it is the building which was the old tinker's shop, where the tinker would have worked on pots and pans and sheet metal work. When we visited him, he had recently bought a house he had been hoping to buy for seven years, along the village street. It was once the saddler's shop, and before that possibly a weaver's house, as the front room has Flemish weaver beams, ridged in the 'grape' pattern – in cross-section like a bunch of grapes. Some of the other beams are eighteen feet long and a foot across; the dowels or pegs, put in 300 years ago, drop cleanly out of them when pushed, so beautifully do they fit. (It was Henry VIII who stopped people using green oak for house timbers, Mr Moseley told us, reserving it for ships only.) Some of the walls are wattle and daub, the daub being straw plaster. In the back room is a little kitchen range and stone copper. 'It's got a lovely feel, this house,' Mr Moseley said, running his hand round a door latch, worn and smoothed by generations of other hands. The chimney hadn't yet been fully opened, although rooks' nests strewed the floor. Would it contain, as at a house in a nearby village, a witch's pot – the earthenware pot which used to be put in the chimney, with a coin, a thimble and other things to keep a witch busy so that she wouldn't come farther into the house? 'It put quite a funny spell on the woman who found it ...'

The saddler's shop will be restored, and will be made into a crafts' shop specializing in silversmith's ware and other fine craftware. It will be an added bonus to this village with its well-built houses, and church of a size to denote past prominence; a village with a present concern which has seen to it that telegraph lines have been taken underground, and that there are no street lamps. 'The village didn't accept them ...' quite simply. It also shows its pride in a display, started nearly ten years ago, of tulips and flowers down by the canal, with a notice proclaiming 'Appledore's Answer'. Answer to what? I asked. To the Dutch and other visitors who come there, to show that it is not only their own tulip fields that are worth visiting.

*

Lydd, too, has a church which belies the present size of the small town, or rather, large village. Often called 'the cathedral on the Marsh', All Saints, Lydd, has a pinnacled tower 132 feet high that was raised when Cardinal Wolsey was Rector of Lydd, and which can be seen with its one pinnacle larger than the others rising like a watchful talisman to guard the Marsh. There is a good view of it from the airport at Lydd, as planes glide in to land, but although it can be seen from far away, the church is no longer the only landmark. It is dwarfed by the multiple lines of pylons threading out from Dungeness, crisscrossing like a lunar cat's cradle over the shingle and patches of gorse, the paired pylons marching two by two inland from the power stations – giant robots, with drooping wires slung over their arms, engaging in their clumsy robots' dance.

In this landscape of contrasts that form a weird dissonant symphony, Lydd itself is quiet, unsmartened, windswept and rugged.

At its heart is the Rype – 'the locals will kill you if you call it a green' – where in Saxon times enemy ships were driven off by the men of Lydd with farming implements, so that the king proclaimed this piece of land should never be built on. The same spirit prevails today. Mr A. Parsons, who has a large-scale map of the area in the window of the barber's shop he used to run, told us about the Friends of Lydd, and how he and others make sure that footpaths are kept open. 'We guard the walks carefully. It may sound mean, but I don't like to see natural things disappear.' There is enough to contend with. Power stations; the natural easterly drift of the shingle; the removal of shingle, leaving great pits – 'for this new motorway to London – you can see the massive pits from the air'; the Ministry of Defence military training area, on ranges where in 1888 the explosive 'Lyddite' was first tested. Now troops are trained there for Northern Ireland, we were told. Red flags fly in the lunar shingle landscape and there is a sputter of small arms fire at the butts. 'They're fighting all night sometimes – they've got a rotten job those fellows. It's bad enough in a straight war, but they don't know what's what out there ... They have full-scale battles here, searchlights, helicopters, the lot.'

Lydd knows about war. The church with its long back, the longest church nave in the county, 199 feet from west door to altar, which looks exaggeratedly long and low from outside, received a direct hit in 1940, and was damaged again in 1944 by flying bombs. 'A soldier was playing the organ when the church was hit – organ practice – and two other men were on the roof fire-watching.' But the restoration work has been well carried out, with an entirely new chancel, its ceiling embossed and painted, striking modern altar rails by Anthony Swaine, the architect responsible for the restoration of the church; and new stained glass. There is some Saxon stonework in the north aisle; a notable font with a marble pillar pedestal of red and black; a table tomb round which the Jurats and Commonalty of Lydd assembled to elect the Bailiff and Jurats, a custom carried on until 1885 when the Bailiff became the first mayor of Lvdd.

Lydd is a Limb of the Cinque Port of Romney. Like Midley, and Stone in Oxney, it was once an island. On the other hand, Dungeness power stations might one day find *themselves* on an island.

This is because of the drift of shingle, to the east, so that while Dungeness 'grows' at a rate of eighteen inches a year, having left successive lighthouses landlocked, shingle must be swiftly lorry-loaded back to the western side of the power stations, from where it has been eroded.

'All the local people told them not to build there ... it must cost thousands to take it back across ... but they would do it ... had to have their pipes in a certain position ...'

I was talking to the widow of a man who had been a chief bird-watcher for the Dungeness bird sanctuary. Her house is one of the neatly painted, black, pink or white, tin-roofed, hut-like houses, with a boat at the side, and a ladder to the first floor, that face the sea and stand in an ocean of shingle on Dungeness point, where the chalets of Dymchurch and the seaside houses of Lydd-on-Sea have thinned out, to give way to beached fishing-boats, hawsers, winches, and trolley rails, upended iron anchors, tin sheds, drying nets, strange flowers and wheeling birds, and, under the shadow of two lighthouses and two power stations, the long ridges of stones. Dungeness is unique, a fantastic, but very human, landscape. Once very lonely, with its isolated communities of fishermen at Dengemarsh and Galloways, now decimated by sea erosion and by the fact that the Army requisitioned the whole of the area in the Second World War, it has a history of smuggling, of dauntless life-boat feats with a life-boat which women have traditionally helped to launch in emergencies, of fishing publicans who kept spyglasses trained across the beach to spot the representatives of the law who might have them up for breaking licensing laws,[5] and of its coastguard stations, since it is only twenty miles from France and close to one of the busiest shipping lanes in the world.

Less lonely now, it still has its fishermen, although there is not much seine netting in the summer as there was in the old days, when both the driftnet fishermen and the stake net fishermen (who used kettlenets) also used seine nets. Drift nets are still used here from October to December, I was told at one of the houses where fresh fish is sold at the back door, the fishing being for herring if the quota allows (and when there is not a ban), and then from December to February there is the spratting season. Some men use trammel nets, which is similar to drifting, but trawling is the most usual form of fishing, with lining in winter (the multiple hook system I had seen at Folkestone). The fish goes to Folkestone to be sold, or straight to Billingsgate, or is sold locally. In the old days, it was carted across the beach on wooden trolleys with large wooden wheels, like one which is preserved at the Britannia pub near the old lighthouse. The men wore 'backstays' on their feet – wooden overshoes like snowshoes.

The kettlenets of the Romney Marsh coastline were unique in construction, and used to account for the majority of the national catch of mackerel from fixed nets. These were staked in wide upright loops like a circular maze on the foreshore, into which the shoals of mackerel swam. As the tide fell, the fishermen scooped up the fish in draw nets, or even bowls. One man recalled getting 700 stone of fish on one tide. And a single horse had to draw the heavy boxes up the shingle.[6] The staking out of the poles to hold the nets, in the spring, was a skilled operation, as they were sixteen feet high and had to be swiftly dug into the beach while the tide was out. Nor was the fishing always good; weeks could go by without a catch.

Dungeness is a triumph of man's adaptability, and of nature's ingenuity.

I had started talking to the birdwatcher's widow because she had, impossibly at Dungeness, a garden. She was bending over vegetable seedlings, and there were potatoes shooting and a stunted apple tree in flower. Her eyes were reddened by the salt winter winds, but she had brought topsoil to lay on the shingle, had planted apple trees from apple seeds and an oak from an acorn (now five years old and three feet tall). She has tulips, spring flowers and a lilac bush, despite the north easterly gales and the dry shingle.

'Two or three showers, and they come all of a sudden. The beach changes colour all the time. First it will be all white with dolly bells, we call them, and then the yellow poppies, and periwinkle, and seakale – you can eat it, you're supposed to bury the stalks and then eat it – and then valerian, lilac coloured, I have a piece, we call it "French May" ...'

The clumps of seakale spring directly from the shingle, with roots that go down deep. There is vetch, thrift and sheep's sorrel, and in some more inland parts, gorse, foxgloves, stonecrop, sea pinks and even sea holly – said to be a powerful aphrodisiac. The road to Lydd is bordered with viper's bugloss, a sea of blue in the summer. And in the spring, ladders are up against the tin-roofed houses, while they are painted brightly, with stripes of green or white woodwork down the walls, and their curtains are freshly washed, and the women walk bent against the wind.

*

There has been a light at Dungeness since the seventeenth century, when it consisted of a tower with a coal-fire light. As the sea receded, and the shingle promontory grew, the light lost its usefulness, and has been replaced since by several others, notably that of Samuel Wyatt in 1792, over a hundred feet high and lit to begin with by sperm oil lamps. This tower was in turn replaced by today's old lighthouse, which is now open to the public, and which was superseded in 1961 by the new lighthouse, because the power station had obscured the beams from the old tower. The new light can be seen from seventeen miles away at sea.

It is too vital a station to be left unmanned, we were told by an assistant lighthouse keeper, although it is a semi-automatic light, with control panels at the base. Men do shifts of two days on, two days off, and it is a tribute to their public spiritedness that they also voluntarily man the old lighthouse, to show visitors round. Besides the view it offers, there is much interesting material in the old lighthouse, including charts showing the shipping lanes in the channel. For anyone who has wondered why their cross-Channel ferry makes a seemingly hairpin course, the reason becomes clear. Under current regulations, in our English inshore lane (and conversely in the French one on the other side) shipping can travel either way, north or south. Then follows a separation zone, before the English deep-draught lane where traffic must travel to the south-west. Then another separation zone, and the French deep-draught lane, where traffic must travel north east before entering the French inshore lane. Both the deep-draught lanes and separation zones must be crossed – if necessary – at 90 degrees. Ferries therefore travel diagonally, and then cross at right angles where permitted. The charts also show how the twenty-metre line is very close inshore at Dungeness, so that larger craft can approach close to the coast. It is even reported that small packets have been flung from ships to the shore, and vice versa.

240

The new lighthouse is floodlit, which as a side result prevents migrating birds crashing into it at night.

There has been a Royal Society for the Protection of Birds warden at Dungeness since 1907, and it is the Society's oldest reserve. There is also the Dungeness Bird Observatory, run by an independent committee, established in 1952, which among its other activities trains bird ringers and has many visitors from overseas. Dungeness is larger than any other area of its kind in Europe, and the areas of natural fresh water (the only ones now remaining being the Open Pits) are possibly the only natural fresh water on a shingle formation in the world. Round these Open Pits, many species breed, including reed buntings, sedge and reed warblers and shellduck. At times of migration, the bushes here are alive with birds. Altogether 270 species have been recorded at Dungeness in recent years. Among those which nest here, is the common gull, which first appeared here in the 1920s and does not nest regularly anywhere else in the country. There are now about twelve pairs nesting here each year.

This and other species, such as black-headed gulls and terns, were badly disturbed during the Second World War, when Dungeness was taken over and used for military ranges. The firing virtually wiped out the colonies of birds. After the war, they did not quickly become re-established, and it was thought that foxes, which had greatly increased in number, were taking the eggs. It was difficult to provide better protection, but some of the birds had already adapted to nesting on the islands made in lakes left by gravel extraction. When extraction became mechanized in the 1930s, the quarrying worked to depths of thirty feet and left behind freshwater pits, into which unwanted minerals such as sand and silt, were thrown back to form islands at the edges. In dry summers, the predators could still reach the birds, so the RSPB asked the gravel company Amey Roadstone if it would leave islands in the middle of a lake. The company agreed, and the ARC Pit of eighty acres, with six islands, was formed, which was immediately colonized by gulls and terns. The RSPB then realized it could make use of its own land, that had been depleted by military activity, by allowing pits to be made there under its own control, and with the gravel royalties going into its own funds. Work on the RSPB's Burrows Pit began in 1970 and was finished in early 1977. By the time it was finished, over 180 pairs of common tern and 160 pairs of black-headed gulls had settled on its specially made islands, and in winter over a thousand duck of various species were roosting and feeding in the area.

The warden of the Dungeness Bird Reserve pointed out in an article in *Birds* magazine, describing this exciting venture, however, that too much quarrying would threaten wild life, so that further co-operation was necessary between conservationists and industry.[7] He hoped that the example of Dungeness would show that the aims of an industrial society were not entirely incompatible with those of conservationists.

It is good to read of a success such as this, to set against the continuous sagas of the spoliation of our environment. A world without birds would be a sad place, and although the building of power stations at Dungeness has not meant the end of the bird population, as was perhaps feared, the presence of the Dungeness 'A' and 'B' stations in this most natural of environmental areas is a pointed reminder of the options open to us. The Central Electricity Generating Board's fifth nuclear power station, Dungeness 'A', was completed in 1965. The 'B' station was completed in 1968. Is this the direction in which our future lies? Looking at recent film of space shuttle experiments, and possibilities for developing means to capture and manufacture energy in space for our ever-more rapacious energy demands, one feels bound to hope not. At least those of us who feel that man, like the common gull or the sedge warbler, needs an element of calm in which to thrive, and the ability to plant his feet in unpolluted fresh water and cast his eyes over a world where sea holly can still grow, and salt winds lift his spirits.

Natural changes are mysterious and extreme in themselves. The reasons for the growth of Dungeness, for the easterly drift of shingle, are both complex and fascinating, basically the same as the reasons for the drift elsewhere along this coast, but accentuated and differentiated in a unique way. Walter J. C. Murray has given a clear description of this in his book *Romney Marsh*. Of the 'fulls' of shingle which are the ridges of beach piled up by the waves, so that Dungeness undulates like the sea; of how the shingle is broken down from flints which come from chalk cliffs, as the chalk is worn away and then washed away by the sea; of how the Eastward Drift caused by the waves driven by the prevailing south-west wind of the Channel, drives the shingle eastwards, to be met by waves from the east, driven by winds coming through the straits of Dover, which create fulls facing east, or shingle in ridges running north and south, and meeting the other ridges in a point. At this point of the Ness, there is a tip, or 'noodle', which itself moves eastwards – just as the remaining mass of shingle does – at a rate of roughly eight to twelve feet a year.

Will the Ness become an island? or could it send out spits to the north-east as Walter Murray suggests might be possible, as shoals in the sea become more marked and alter the tidal currents and force of the waves? Whatever happens it will, one hopes, remain a unique landscape, with its strange, almost horizontal light, beating up off the shingle ridges, casting long shadows, catching on the colours of flowers and timber, or bleaching everything to a dry lunar landscape, as the wind rattles off the stones and whines away inland along the draped wires of the pylons, to the bare zones where rifle fire crackles and unworried birds fly over the craters dug by nature and man.

10   Rye; Winchelsea

'...grass grows now where Winchelsea was, as was once said of Troy...'
Celia Fiennes, quoting Ovid.[1]

'You're in England now, and you can't see it until Easter...' The
man spoke wryly to two young Americans, standing, like myself, in
front of the closed Ypres Tower – now Rye Museum – on a fine
spring day, before Easter. It was my second visit, and like the Court
Hall Museum at Winchelsea, and many other small museums, I
had found it closed. When one questions people, the reasons –
difficulties of staffing, vandals, expense – arouse sympathy. Yet
tourist boards are meanwhile meeting in earnest seminar to discuss
how to win more visitors away from tourist centres such as London
and Stratford.

The Rye Museum is in fact excellent and won the Heritage Year
Museum Award for South East England. My two Americans had
travelled far, preferring the smaller towns, and like perhaps most
inquiring minded tourists, wanting to avoid summer crowds. In
the same month Winchelsea church had been visited by people
from New Zealand, Hong Kong, Tokyo, Cumbria, Skye, Guernsey,
Eire, Texas, Sydney, Canada, Belluno in Italy, Lyons, St Cloud,
Ozark in Alabama, Nepal, Papilliou in Nebraska. And all before
Easter...

Lamb House then? the home of Henry James, and surely not to
be missed by Americans. Open March to October. It was March, so
we were all right. Wednesdays and Saturdays. It was a Thursday.

'I'm going to have a drink at the Mermaid Inn,' I said, feeling
apologetic. 'Perhaps I'll see you there.'

We met there later, and the Mermaid didn't let us down. Un-
crowded at that time of year, we sat beside what is probably the

largest open fireplace in England, spanned by a beam and concealing a priest's hole, decorated with ironwork and a carved panel of cherubs, with a goat's head and gryphons on polished fireside chairs. The beef sandwiches at the bar were prime fillet, and as far as I was concerned would alone have qualified the Inn for the Queen's Award to Industry it won in 1973 – the only small inn to do so. Forty-two per cent of its visitors are from abroad.

It has been open since 150 years before Queen Elizabeth I visited Rye in 1573, and is on the site of a wattle and daub tavern existing since about 1300, with cellars carved from rock. It faces on to cobbled Mermaid Street, which must be one of the most attractive old streets anywhere. The Inn has fine oak beams, painted panels, and a secret staircase. 'We have to keep that door shut or we'd have fifty people ending up in someone's bedroom,' said the barman briskly. On the walls hang handbills from smuggling days: *I am of the opinion, after thirty years remarks on this trade, the best, and most certain method to prevent it, and to interest the revenue, is to lower the duties ...* George Bishop to Parliament in 1783 (not in fact done until nearly a century later). *'Persons assembled at any public or private houses, or shall be on any road or other place having load saddles, large whips or sticks, to be taken up and carried before a justice of the peace ...'* *'Persons making signals by ... fire by night, or smoak ... to be fined and imprisoned.'* *'Reward of £1000 ... £500 ... £20000 ...'*

The American couple loved it. They were clean-cut, Scandinavian-looking teachers from Oregon, who had come along the coast from Whitstable where they had stayed with a lecturer from Kent University. They had liked Whitstable immensely, but were surprised at the low living standards of our university professors as compared to those in the States. They were over for seven weeks, to see Scotland and Ireland as well. 'But we like England ... We like it out of season ... the quiet places. We love the little old ladies with their shopping baskets and determination ... Everyone's very kind.' They found us more eccentric than Americans, but had not noticed a sour note here as sometimes on the Continent, they said. They appreciated BBC television – 'We watch all the time; much better than in the States. England is so much smaller than America so perhaps you notice what is going on more. In the US one state is not aware of what is happening in another. Your history is part of our culture, whereas in Europe, in Austria for instance ... Our house in Oregon was built in 1940. We think that's old, but here ...'

Rye appears genuinely old, but not decayed. Perched on its hill with its capped church spire and weathervane, it looks in the distance like a medieval town, rising from flat marshland on the borders of Romney Marsh. One gate, the Land Gate, and some of the town walls remain – sea erosion destroyed the walls between the Land Gate and Ypres Tower, which gives an idea of the town's old situation. Bestowed by King Canute on the Abbey of Fécamp in 1030, Rye and Winchelsea were redeemed by Henry III, and under the Charter of 1278 these two 'Antient Towns' joined the other five Head Ports of the Cinque Ports Confederation. The Great Storm of 1287, having benefited Rye while at the same time drowning Old Winchelsea and stranding Romney, brought the town and harbour prosperity and by the mid-fifteenth century it was one of the most important of the Cinque Ports. But French raids on the town were ferocious during the fourteenth and fifteenth centuries, and in one raid in 1377, every building not of stone was burnt and the church bells stolen – to be retrieved in a retaliatory raid. But the town recovered. Its fish, one staple trade, was famous and was supplied to London direct by the 'Rippiers' of Rye and Winchelsea, the London fishmongers being prohibited from buying it to sell again retail. After the massacre of St Bartholomew's Day in 1572, Huguenot refugees brought new trades such as cloth- and paper-making. In 1573 Queen Elizabeth named the town 'Rye Royal'. Then the sea gradually receded, the great river estuary was lost, and Rye Harbour moved away from the town.

*

'... For our time is a very shadow that passeth away ...'

The words from The Wisdom of Solomon[2] are painted in gilt above the clock on Rye Parish Church, which is thought to be the oldest church clock in the country, made in Winchelsea in 1562. Two eighteenth-century quarter boys strike the two bells under the same canopy, sounding the quarter hours. The whole can be seen, with the church's magnificent north window, from the High Street, as you walk up Lion Street, past Fletcher's House tea rooms, where the dramatist John Fletcher was born. Looking back down Lion Street, is another impressive view, of the Old Grammar School, its seventeenth-century brick enhanced by giant pilasters and Dutch gables. 'It was built in the 1630s ten years after the Mayflower set out, which Americans find hard to believe,' I was told in Peacock's Home Interiors, which it now houses. 'Americans are proud of their history and sometimes a bit taken aback.' But naturally they delight in this shop, which has decorative craft goods – woven silk pictures, Polish carved boxes, art deco eggs – as in the other Rye shops, which are many, and varied. Antiques, iron wood-burning stoves, leather goods, pottery, bookshops, and an unimaginable number of shops selling besoms, patchwork, homemade fudge – not at all shoddy, although in summer the narrow streets, which make even delivery vans seem too large, are congested. And some of the foreign students, away from home, take to shoplifting. 'I dread some of them ... they're so loud-mouthed ...' a shopkeeper said. ('Student' can be an inaccurately used and disparaging term in any place or language, I have found.)

Other items which foreigners value are the four-poster beds in the hotels. John Pennington, the manager of the George Hotel, who has been nine years with Trust Houses Forte and one year in Rye, which he likes, showed me some of the rooms with renovated four-posters, and an even more genuine wig cupboard and ball-room with minstrel's gallery. Room 14 has carved beams which are said to be from Queen Elizabeth's flagship at the time of the Armada. The George has a medieval banquet every fortnight, and the everyday menu sports grilled whole Rye Bay plaice and Mill-wheel Steak, while a framed menu of a banquet for the Lord Mayor of London in 1850, lists *Tortue à L'Anglaise,* a choice of five fish, Pigeon Pie, *Homard à la Indienne,* Duckling, Larded Pea Fowl, Marrow Pudding and Ornamental Trifles. Another famous inn is the Flushing Inn, with its thirteenth-century barrel-vaulted cellar; a smuggling inn, since boats could in those days come up to and beach at the foot of the cliff it stands on. The carved panelling and wooden ceilings are outstanding, and in 1905 a sixteenth-century fresco was uncovered – magnificent in dark greens and browns, incorporating the arms of Jane Seymour, with deer, roses and herons. It is in the dining-room.

The passing of time, in the church, is stressed. The pendulum of the clock – eighteen feet long – moves to and fro with a resounding tick. This is the 'cathedral of East Sussex', dating in part to the early twelfth century. A memorial window by Burne Jones, a Kempe window, Caen stone pillars, unfortunately needing expensive repairs, and a memorable, glistening, carved mahogany altar table in the north chapel, which may indeed be from a Spanish ship, as it bears Spanish emblems and is of Spanish mahogany; it is probably of a later date than the Armada and may have been captured by a Rye privateer from a ship returning from South America. One would not want to give it a more pedestrian provenance. In Rye, history is believable, tangible; our own age the shadow that passeth away.

*

'The rivalry isn't oppressive. It adds a little sharpness to the occasion ...' To get the flavour of a modern Cinque Port, one cannot do better than to talk to Mrs Yates, who was Mayor of Rye when I met her in 1979, having been Speaker of the Cinque Ports in 1978. Born in Rye, she is an enthusiastic exponent of the Cinque Ports. Her grandparents owned a hotel next to the theatre at which Ellen Terry used to appear. The actress had a cottage at Winchelsea at one time, and there is a story of her stopping her pony and trap in Rye High Street while the local draper brought out hats for her to try on. Mrs Yates's grandmother had one of Ellen Terry's dresses, of watered silk. The family also owned the Railway Hotel, now the Cinque Port Arms, where Mrs Yates was born. This is close to the cattle market, which used to be much larger than it is today – Ashford market has now become the leading market in the area. Sheep would be brought there by train, and after the market the long tables at the hotel would be set for the farmers' luncheons. Mrs Yates remembers these spreads, and a Marsh farmer's wife saying that on market day her husband's horse had to know the way home.

Mrs Yates has worked in nursing (and as councillor, deputy mayor and mayor) and takes a keen interest in the proposed new District General Hospital to be built to serve the eastern end of Sussex. She would like to see a ring road or bypass round Rye to take the big continental lorries, the site of which would probably depend on the hospital site. Despite such competence, she is a gentle, most generously friendly person, who as mayor made time for the personal contacts that leaven civic life and officialdom, forming a vital link between people and communities. She took a bowls team to the Cinque Ports' bowls tournament at New Romney, where the friendly rivalry became apparent, and was followed by supper and drinking from a loving cup. She knows everyone (as one man in Rye said 'there are about seventy societies in Rye, and the poor bank managers run from one to another doing treasury work'); and as Deputy Mayor, she visited the City of Rye in the State of New York, on Long Island Sound – once part of the hunting ground of the Mohegan Indians and bought in 1660 by some pioneers from Rye and other places in Sussex, for 'eight cotes and seven shirts and fiftene fathom of wampum' (beads made from shells and strung for money or decoration). Today Rye, New York, is a place where many prominent men in American life have homes – a weekend place with a Georgian flavour to the houses. The inhabitants, and most Americans, are extremely interested in their English counterpart, and when I met Mrs Yates, she was giving a commemorative Rye Pottery plate to be taken to the American Rye by a woman from Tenterden who was going there. So these links are made, and traditions kept alive. There is a Flemish or French flavour to Rye, and attempts have been made to find sister towns in those countries. Bad Hersfeld also wants to establish links with the town. In this way, perhaps as much as in the higher echelons of diplomacy, countries get to know each other.

Rye is proud of its status as a Cinque Port and indeed there has been a resurgence of interest from towns that used to be Member Ports, who have reapplied; but they have been turned down, so that the number of towns is limited to the present fourteen. (See note 7, Chapter 1.) Rye, as one of the towns with an ancient charter, may call the chairman of its parish council a mayor. And in the fine town hall, Mr Sherwood, Serrient att Mace, or Sergeant-at-Mace, showed me two of the town's four maces, of 1502 and 1570. Silver covers the iron of the original battle weapon, which would also have had spikes, and which was used to protect mayors, bailiffs and kings. The two larger maces, of 1767, and four feet seven inches in length, have been described as the finest in Britain. Rye has a popular mayor-making ceremony, when the new mayor throws hot coins to be picked up by children assembled round the town hall.

*

For 109 years (1723–1832), the mayor of Rye, with nineteen exceptions, was a member of the Lamb family, or a close relation. Two of the Lambs were Barons of the Cinque Ports, bearing the canopy at coronations, but of all the family the one who is most often remembered is James Lamb, who built Lamb House, Rye, and entertained George I there in 1726. He is remembered not so much for that, as for the fact that as Deputy Controller of Customs in Rye, he aroused the hatred of a butcher, and proprietor of the Flushing Inn, John Breads. One night Breads determined to put an end to Lamb, but Lamb had lent his cloak to his brother-in-law Allen Grebell, and it was the unfortunate Grebell whom the butcher Breads stabbed with his butcher's knife in the dark churchyard that night, thinking his enemy Lamb was the wearer of the cloak. Grebell managed to get home, but bled to death although, strangely, his brother-in-law Lamb thrice dreamt that his late wife was calling to him to go to see if her brother (the stabbed man) was all right. On the third occasion Lamb did get up, and found Grebell already dead. Breads had meanwhile had too much to drink and had roamed the streets proclaiming that 'Butchers should kill Lambs'. He was hung for his crime, and his body displayed on a gibbet.

A ghost, thought to be that of Grebell, has been seen at Lamb House, and Henry James, whose house it was from 1898–1916, also saw there the ghost of an old lady in a mantilla. James was very fond of the house, and in the separate Garden Room wrote *The Ambassadors* and *The Golden Bowl*. This room was destroyed by a bomb in 1940. Henry James became a naturalized Englishman just before his death in 1916. He was awarded the Order of Merit, and there is a distinguished portrait of him by Sargent in the Town Hall. Fond of children, and devotedly cared for by Burgess Noakes, who was his houseboy and then butler, James had a great passion for bicycling, and even bought a bicycle for Burgess Noakes, so that he 'should have an incentive to keep his master's bicycle clean'.[3]

E. F. Benson, the author, later lived at Lamb House, and more recently it was the home of Rumer Godden, the novelist and writer of superb children's books such as *The Doll's House*.

Rye has long been associated with writers and artists. In Jeake's House, in Mermaid Street, named after Samuel Jeake, author of *Charters of the Cinque Ports, Two Ancient Towns and Their Members* (published in 1728 and a standard work), lived the American novelist and poet Conrad Aiken in the 1920s. T. S. Eliot, Julian Huxley, Dame Laura Knight, Paul Nash and Edward Burra visited him there, and a plaque in East Street commemorates the house where Paul Nash lived from 1889–1946. A book with Rye as its setting, which was written in 1907 but not published until after the author's death, in 1971, is *The Tale of the Faithful Dove* by Beatrix Potter, which tells of the adventures of Mr Tidler and his wife Amabella, who roosted on top of the Ypres Tower.

From this tower is a view over the Walland and Romney Marshes, across the Rother, and over watermeadows to Winchelsea. Millais' painting 'The Blind Girl' was painted in these meadows, with the rainbow arcing above Winchelsea in the background. (He also painted a study of high Victorian sentiment called 'The Random Shot', of a barefooted child covered with a soldier's cloak lying on the Gervase Alard tomb in Winchelsea Church.)

The Ypres Tower was built in about 1250, and was originally called Baddings Tower. It is the oldest fortification in the Cinque Ports, apart from Dover Castle. In front of it lies the Gun Garden. In its time, the tower has served as the town gaol. It is portrayed in copies of pen and bistre drawings on show in the Museum, made by Van Dyck when he was waiting here before crossing to France – drawings with sheep in the pastoral foregrounds. Among other exhibits are models of sailing trawlers, swords and uniforms of the Cinque Ports Volunteers (and of the Rye Sea Fencibles, a volunteer company fifty strong raised in 1794 and disbanded in 1814), a very good miniature of Nelson (whose daughter married a vicar of Rye and is buried in the churchyard), and a piece of the gold outer covering and silver lining of the canopy held by the barons over Queen Charlotte at George III's coronation, with a silver gilt bell from its edge.

The Museum opened on its present site in 1954, having had a balance of £6 carried over from its pre-war Museum Committee, so it has achieved an immense amount in a short space of time. The tower lost its tiled roof during the Second World War, but has looked out on worse damage – caused by raiding French ships of six hundred years ago, down to the air-raids, sea warfare and land mines of our century. Below it, under the east cliff, where the Rother curls round the town, are the old Town Salts, now a recreation ground, and also the fishmarket and Rock Channel, the traditional shipbuilding site. Keels have been laid there for longer than anyone, or any records, can tell.

Shipbuilding still thrives at Rye. Its origins probably date from Roman days or earlier, since the Romans used the old Ridge Way which led from the estuary at Rye through Netherfield and Heathfield to Uckfield, linking up with the Lewes-London way. It was the easiest route along which to bring iron from the ironworks at Battle and Sedlescombe, to the estuary for shipment. Rye ships were also used for fighting, fishing and smuggling. In 1189 King Richard I sailed in a 'fine large ship that had come from Rye'[4]; a Rye ship took supplies to Drake when he was chasing the Armada in 1588; in the mid-nineteenth century hundreds of men were employed in the slipways. The timber for the ships was Sussex oak from the Weald, which even the iron furnaces had not depleted. Defoe wrote that in spite of the great ironworks, he found Kent, Sussex and Hampshire 'one inexhaustible store-house of timber never to be destroy'd ... and able at this time to supply timber to rebuild all the royal navies in Europe ...' Many of these strong ships' timbers have found their way into the lucky houses and farmhouses of Kent and Sussex, where you can tell them by the old cuts for joins and dowel holes.

Today wood is spared, because most shipbuilders have turned to fibreglass. Versatility Workboats at Rye, the largest of the firms there now, is run by Mr M. J. Haynes, who was the first person to bring fibreglass boats into the fishing industry – his firm designed the first fibreglass boat to be passed by the White Fish authority, the Mk. I *Potter*. Since then Versatility Workboats have made twenty-five to thirty boats for the White Fish authority, and have sent four to Finland, eight to Africa, one to Barbados and several to the Mediterranean. In 1977 a purse-seine-net fishing vessel was built for the United Nations Food and Agriculture Organization, and was delivered to Senegal; now the FAO have asked Mike Haynes to conduct various feasibility studies to see if fibreglass boats can be moulded in Third World countries – the first study will be carried out in Pakistan. He knows his subject from the seabed up, having been involved with boats since he left school – two years with the Hydraulics Research Station at Wallingford, five years in a tug in the late 1950s, towing landing craft and other vessels, seven years with his own fishing boat, between Christchurch and Rye. He speaks with fervour of fishing conditions today – of Russians coming in with factory ships and decimating fishing grounds, while British boats have to follow Common Market regulations, a sentiment that is echoed everywhere among fishermen.

*

The River Rother flows into the sea between Camber Sands and a triangle of land between the Rivers Rother and Brede where the sea has retreated, leaving Camber Castle well inland. Along the coastal edge of this triangle is Rye Harbour Local Nature Reserve, where there is a chance to see a great variety of shingle flowers and vegetation (sea pea, reeds, curled dock, herb robert, wall-pepper, among others) and where more than fifty species of birds regularly nest, including the little tern, herring- and black-headed gulls, ringed plovers and oystercatchers.

Rye Harbour itself is still a smallish village community, with old houses and gravel workings, scoured by the wind from the sea. In the graveyard of the Church of the Holy Spirit with its wooden roof inside shaped exactly like a boat's upturned hull, is a large memorial showing the figure of a life-boatman, in front of which lie named stones, and bright, well-tended flowers. The evening we were there, the flowers were being carefully watered. Rye Harbour hasn't forgotten, and how could it, since on 15 November 1928 the entire crew of seventeen of the *Mary Stanford* life-boat were drowned in very heavy seas during a gale, while going to the rescue of the SS *Alice* from Riga. The life-boat had been recalled, since the *Alice* was no longer in danger, but was already too far out to get the message. All the crew were from Rye Harbour, and many of them were related. The stones spell out the desolation – Lewis Alexander Pope, Aged 21 Years ... Robert Henry Pope, Aged 23 Years ... Chas Frederick David Pope, Aged 28 Years ... James Alfred Head, Aged 19 Years ... And John Stanley Head, the coxwain's son of 17, whose body was never found. Round the memorial are the words 'We have done that which was our duty to do', and inside the church the text, 'Greater love hath no man than this, that a man lay down his life for his friends.'[5] Every year a memorial service is held on the first Sunday after 15 November, always at 3 pm. In 1978, the German who had been the cabin boy of the ship that came to the aid of the *Alice* attended the service.

We owe countless thousands of lives to the crews of the Royal National Life-boat Institution, and since a voluntary life-boat service was started in 1824, it has always been supported entirely by voluntary contributions.

*

> And you can pook
> and you can shove
> But a Sussex pig
> he wun't be druv. (Old Sussex rhyme)

The Sussex pottery pig was used at weddings in the country, to drink the health of the bride and groom. Its head could be taken off and used as a mug, enabling the guests to drink the traditional 'hogshead' of beer without the foreseeable results. Earlier still, a baby pig was the present for the newly married couple.

The earliest pottery pig is from the eighteenth century, and is in the British Museum. Sussex pigs are still made at the Rye Pottery, in Ferry Road, which carries on another of the area's traditional trades, and is the leader of several pottery firms now in the town.

Potters have been working in Rye since the Middle Ages, when potters were itinerant and moved where the job took them. At Rye they had the benefit of a high quality creamy white clay dug in the local fields, which is now unobtainable. (A council estate in the area has been named Potting Field Estate.) The Rye Pottery was an offshoot of an eighteenth-century brickworks and pottery at Cadborough Farm, owned by Jeremiah Smith, who was one of the largest hop-growers and flockmasters in Sussex and seven times Mayor of Rye; during the hopping season he would employ 1,500 workers. The hop patterns introduced in the next century, by the Mitchell family, who became managers of the pottery, were particularly popular. The 'sprigs' or applied decoration of hops, flowers and wheat ears, are made in moulds of baked clay or pipe-clay. The ware was lead glazed, either a rich brown or green.

Metallic oxides were added to the clay – 'pin dust' or powdered brass from the waste of pin-making produced a vivid green; manganese a thick dark streaking or mottling. The best pieces such as a wedding plate of 1872 are sumptuous, and smaller pieces abounded. In 1866 the Cadborough works were described 'manufacturers to HRH the Prince of Wales and the Queen of Spain of the celebrated brown and rustic fancy ware'. In 1868, the pottery moved to Ferry Road, where the present owners still work in Frederick Mitchell's Belle Vue works, a house with Mitchell's name proudly incised above the door, and tiles lovingly set in the brickwork, facing a cobbled forecourt.

The pottery had closed in 1939, because of black-out regulations. In 1947 it was bought by Walter Cole, with his brother. Walter's son Tarquin has now taken over the firm, allowing his father more time for his own ceramic sculpture. The pottery is very successful, selling at Tiffany's in New York among other of its sixty per cent export trade outlets, with the sister firm, Rye Tiles, selling about a quarter of a million tiles a year, twenty per cent to export, 'with a customer list like something out of *Who's Who* ... Arabian princesses ... the Sultan of Oman ...' Tarquin Cole was previously a naval officer, but obviously has clay in his veins and has been a potter for twenty-five years. Pottery is, he says, 'a disease you catch'. As striking as his enthusiasm and the efficiency of the firm is his loyalty to and affection for his father, who was, he told me, an innovator with Bernard Leach of the new trend in pottery. Pottery prior to the Second World War was studio pottery and highly priced, about £300 a piece. W. B. Honey from the Ceramics Department at the Victoria and Albert Museum asked, 'Why not make some pots that can be used?' Leach and Walter Cole set up commercial studios to make pottery people could use every day, and the new trend was born. At Rye, the Coles were lucky in finding Bert Twort, who had worked there before for sixty years, from the age of 12. They said to him, 'Make the things you always did ...' and the old patterns were reborn. But with stringent modern regulations as to lead glazes, it is not possible to equal the old greens and browns, so a new style has been evolved, in white majolica ware in the tradition of seventeenth-century English Delftware, using many of the traditional shapes, and with green hops on the white ground. (The old Dutch Delftware technique came from Spain where it was introduced by the Moors, who attempted to copy fine Chinese porcelain, but having no fine clay, put on a white glaze.) A special line at Rye is commemorative plates, many of which have won awards from the Council of Industrial Design. Pots have been exhibited in international exhibitions and at Prague in 1962 Walter Cole won the silver medal.

He was working for his 1979 commemorative exhibition when we met him. Sitting beside a large, smoothly sculpted terracotta bird form, he stroked it with affection. His own face has a craftsman's open eagerness, under white hair; an innocent eye.

Inspiration? Birds – 'The garden's full of them. As a student I spent every Wednesday at the Zoo – eight in the morning till five at night. Draw, draw, draw ... You'll get your inspiration anyway – I get a lot from the clouds ...'

He trained at the Central School under John Skeaping, and taught there before coming to Rye. He was, he says, influenced by Skeaping when a student, and by Henri Gaudier-Brzeska, who was only 23 when he was killed, and who was an admirer of Brancusi's work – both precursors in a sense of Henry Moore. Of commercial pottery he says, 'Obviously you couldn't give it all the thought you give to an individual piece.' And of modern trends such as the notorious pile of bricks – 'I'm all for freedom ... it's a case of seeing a thing; if a thing's got something, it doesn't matter what it is.' His own sculpted pieces and his lidded dishes have that indefinable element. Upstairs in the house, his wife has arranged, among green plants and framed sketches, a showcase of his smaller pieces, with others by noted potters and promising newcomers. Outside, through the window, are calm views of a windmill and the river, with Rye's old buildings. The perfect setting for this first, most earthy and yet most inspired of our crafts.

*

'Escapees from Pontins come in during the summer,' they had told us at the pottery.

Camber, between Rye and Lydd, is not beside Camber Castle (one of Henry VIII's circular fortress castles, now a massive ruin). It does adjoin Camber sands which are, as they sound, the sort of beach which can be pleasant, or according to the weather's mood a wind-wracked desert punctuated with striped and fractious canvas windbreaks. Here proliferate holiday 'camps', caravan 'parks' and tourist 'villages' of every description. The army terminology of camp seems suited to the whole concept of these enterprises, at least as seen by the native Ryers (let alone the quiet inhabitants of Winchelsea, who have settled there for reasons other than 'camping' or 'parking'). 'They come into the town in the summer,' the Ryers say, with horror as if of Caesar's invading armies. 'There'll be five to ten thousand of them at Pontins at a weekend ...' And one woman who had worked at the camp said: 'Goodness knows how many stay in one chalet ... they used to come past the gate and just say any chalet number ...' rolling her eyes at the thought of the ensuing saturnalia.

'MOD Out of Bounds to Troops' says a large sign by 'Pontin's Camber Sands Holiday Village', and on the other side of the road we noticed four 'For Sale' notices on the small seaside clapboard bungalows huddling together for protection. The camp appeared to be wired in by three strands of barbed wire at the top of a fence. A yellow and turquoise motif like a Neapolitan ice-cream ran through the architect's realized bank holiday daydream of the buildings. Another notice: 'Danger – Area Guarded by Security Dogs.' Next, Maddieson's 'Camber Caravan Park and Tourist Court'. We slowed down by the gateway. At once a guard, or cheery platoon leader came up to the car, no doubt to see if we were friend or foe. 'You could come and stay in a chalet, but no entertainment until Easter,' he said, leering, with the implication that we should not need entertainment. We drove on past the Silver Sands Caravan Park. 'It's got a guard house,' John said, disbelievingly. But this turned out to be the latrine block. The beach lay blond and empty, ready for summer drill.

*

Winchelsea is a very different matter. It has twice, and more, risen from destruction, and has about it an aura of the past that can be almost too real at times. '... a flourishing place before the sea left it [as any] that was in England ...' wrote Celia Fiennes; '... it's the ancientest Corporation in England, so that should Lord Major [Mayor] of London meet Mr Major of Winchelsea, he must give him place.'[6] But this was *new* Winchelsea, laid out as a new town at the end of the thirteenth century to replace Old Winchelsea, a shingle island in the Camber Sands area, being until the Great Storm of 1287 a flourishing port and trading centre and anchorage for ships of the Cinque Ports fleet. A town with two churches, a Franciscan monastery, and up to fifty taverns. In 1250, Holinshed writes:

On the first day of October, the moon, upon her change, appearing exceeding red and swelled, began to show tokens of the great tempest of wind that followed, which was so huge and mightie, both by land and sea, that the like had not been lightlie knowne, and seldome, or rather never heard of by men then alive. The sea forced contrarie to his natural course, flowed twice without ebbing ... Moreover the same sea appeared in the dark of the night to burne, as it had been on fire ... At Winchelsey ... there were 300 houses and some churches drowned with the high rising of the water course.

King Edward I sent his treasurer and the Mayor of London down to draw up a contingency plan, rather as we apprehensively watch the Thames for flooding. They recommended abandoning the town and moving it to the Iham peninsula, but before action was taken, the Great Storm of 1287 swept Old Winchelsea entirely away.

The new town was then built, on a grid-iron principle, with thirty-nine 'quarters', after the model of the stronghold of Monsegur near Bordeaux. The wine trade between Winchelsea and France was an important one, and in a good year Winchelsea imported 2,900 tuns of Gascon wine and the same amount of Rhenish wine. It was carried round the coast via Sandwich to London. Another important import and export trade was in pilgrims – to Canterbury via the Old Winchelsea in the thirteenth century, and to such places as the shrine of St James of Compostella in Spain during the fifteenth century. In 1434, licenses were granted for 2,433 pilgrims to be 'exported' from Winchelsea, and from the reign of Henry VI (1442–61) dates our earliest sea ballad of which there is a copy in Winchelsea church.

> For when they have take the see
> At Sandwyche, or at Wynchylsee,
> At Brystow, or where that hit bee,
> Theyre herts begyne to fayle.
> ....

Bestowe the boote, bote swayne, anon,
That our pylgryme may pley thereon;
For som ar lyke to cowgh and grone,
Or hit be full mydnyght.[7]
....

The Church of St Thomas the Martyr is strangely cropped, or
lopped. It was once very large and possibly never quite completed,
and its wide dimensions – only the chancel and side chapels remain – are topped with a small tiled cap with dormers, reducing
the grand design to a strange domesticity in keeping with the
white clapboard houses of the town. Possibly the new town also
was never quite finished, some plots not taken up. It was walled
and gated, and the gates still stand, one out in the fields, the others
guarding the town on its hilltop eminence, from where it used to
look down on a busy harbour in the old, larger River Brede.
Edward I promoted the town, and was perpetuated in a legendary
feat there. Come to review his fleet, he rode towards the walled
cliff above the harbour, by a whirling windmill, which frightened
his horse. It leapt over the wall and cliff, but somehow the king,
with superb horsemanship, kept his seat, and rode back into the
town. His thought-lined face is carved in stone above the tomb
of Gervase Alard in the church.

In the fourteenth century, Winchelsea, still reeling from the
Black Death, was subjected to savage raids by the French. The
buildings, of wood, were burnt down so that only the stone cellars
remained, and still remain, to form smugglers' hideouts in later
centuries, and the foundations for pleasant houses, each separated
from the street by a neat grass verge. The most vicious of the raids
was in 1359, when 3,000 Frenchmen sacked the town. They burst
into the Church of St Giles – which no longer exists – and mass-
acred or raped the people congregated there. Thomas of Walsingham wrote:

... after butchering many of the congregation and despoiling the
church, they met with one woman of more beauty than the rest of her
neighbours, and had come there together with them to her devotions;
her the brutes seized upon, and, in that very place, most grossly
assaulted, one after another, till the woman died.[8]

They were said to have killed forty townsmen, and drowned 400
who came to their rescue, and to have carried off thirteen ships.

The lane where the bodies were buried, near St Giles's graveyard, is known as Dead Man's Lane.

'Is this Dead Man's Lane?,' I asked a woman busily weeding her garden, after searching for it in vain.

'This is Spring Steps,' she replied, bristling. 'Dead Man's Lane? It must be in Rye ...'

I found it, shrouded by tall trees, among the cawing of rooks, dropping steeply to where the sea used to lap and French ships brought terror. I didn't walk down it. The hollow rasping of rooks, on a winter day in spring, seemed to follow one everywhere in Winchelsea, along the deserted streets, in leaf muffled fields; by the armless black windmill; where ruined stones lie unrecorded. Inside the church I could hear the wind moaning overhead, and this building too seemed full of dread, a quarter church, a remnant, but magnificent nevertheless because the walls are almost entirely formed of the stained-glass windows by Douglas Strachan, in winged deep blue and purples and sunburst yellows. Below the sturdy roof beams, hang shields put there to commemorate the Silver Jubilee of Queen Elizabeth II.

On one side lie, austere under encrusted canopies, three effigies of dark mottled Sussex marble, brought from Old Winchelsea, perhaps rescued from under the sea. It isn't known who they are, but the quality of the stone speaks more clearly than records about the town lost under the waves. On the other side of the church is the tomb of Gervase Alard, first Admiral of the Cinque Ports and Admiral of the Western Fleet under Edward I. He holds a stone heart in his praying hands, and has a lion at his feet. Beside him lies his grandson, Stephen Alard, also Admiral of the King's Western Fleet. On this same south side of the church is a window commemorating the Rye Harbour life-boat disaster.

In the sanctuary, the small north window has two panels of fourteenth-century glass which show, as does the town seal, religious buildings and features of the thriving port. All that remains of the religious houses are ruins. Near a later house on the site of the Greyfriars – which was one of the earliest Franciscan monasteries in England – are the impressive remains of the Chapel of the Blessed Virgin, with a turret tower and the twenty-five-foot span of a frail Gothic arch soaring up between branches, with at the other end of the chapel a view across marsh and sea to Dungeness.

The sea had receded from Winchelsea by the end of the fifteenth century. Sir Walter Raleigh said the town had 'gone to decay'. Defoe called it 'Rather the skeleton of an ancient city, than a real town'. John Wesley, who preached there and has a tree named after him, also called it 'that poor skeleton'. Smuggling brought trade of a sort. Thackeray's unfinished novel *Denis Duval* gives a powerful evocation of a boy only half aware of all the under-currents of intrigue and felony going on in his home town of Winchelsea, and of the mysterious Chevalier de la Motte's 'trading' links with France. In her introduction to the story, Thackeray's daughter writes of the impression Winchelsea made on her father:

He came home delighted with the old places; he had seen the ancient gateways and sketched one of them, and he had seen the great churches and the old houses, all sailing inland from the sea. Winchelsea was everything he had hoped for, and even better than he expected.[9]

Another who appreciated Winchelsea was Ellen Terry, who had her Tower Cottage by the Strand Gate, which overlooks Camber Castle. The town still has its mayor, jurats, town clerk and chamberlain, and is, with the exception of the City of London, the only unreformed corporation in the Kingdom. The mayor is elected by twelve Freemen and in a formal procession on Easter Monday walks to the old Court Hall, in a ceremony worthy of the Ports at their prime.

On my wintry visit to Winchelsea I saw only one visitor, a bearded artist with a cello, walking the lonely streets. There are a couple of small shops, in which the talk is of sheep, and behind the windows bright with flowers and curtains, no doubt life goes on most snugly, in this quiet place which is like a garden suburb, but much more attractive, more serene, or more spirit haunted.

*

To the west of Winchelsea is Icklesham, and where to the south of that the old carriageway from Winchelsea to Hastings used to run, is Hog Hill, with its old windmill. Here at Hog Hill is one of the most formidable smuggler's hideouts that can have existed – at The Elms, which overlooks Pett Level with its lakes, one of which a flamingo regularly haunts. The Elms is now owned by Ron Miles, who farms there. Earlier it belonged to the Martindale family, who had a herbalist's shop off Harley Street in London (in

1883 William Martindale helped to compile the *British Pharma-copoeia*, still used as a standard reference work). It is a seventeenth-century house, with open fireplaces. At the top of the stairs is a heavy trap-door which closes down to seal off the upper floors and could be secured with a cross-beam. A Captain Hog, a notorious smuggler, is said to have had his hideaway here, which seems likely, as he could have seen his own cronies or the revenue men approaching across the whole of Rye Bay.

It is a fine view and in summer, Mrs Miles sometimes provides teas in the garden. The whole of Pett Level was flooded during the Second World War, but it is now perhaps one of the least spoilt stretches of the south coast, with no buildings along the shore line. Ron Miles, who initiated us into some of the secrets of local farming, telling us of ewe lambs and hoggets and ewe tegs, fleeces and lookers, and Romney Marsh silt (the land at Hog Hill is better than Wealden Clay, not quite so good as Romney Marsh silt), is also the Chairman of the Publicity Committee of the East Sussex Branch of the National Farmer's Union. The NFU is, he said, 'vigorously campaigning to keep our shores free of rabies', which is good to hear, as was the fact that they felt this particular area felt itself ready to cope with an outbreak. All along the south east coast are, of course, posters warning about rabies, but local papers still carry stories of ships' captains exercising dogs ashore or of other prohibited activities. Horses, Ron Miles told us, can carry rabies in their hooves, a thing the public is probably ignorant of, as of many other rabies facts. 'People have champagne parties in London to discuss it,' he said, with vigorous scorn, standing large and strong as Captain Hog by his gate; 'they come and put a lot of placards on bedroom-type furniture on the harbour arms (as rabies defence measures), and imagine the gales won't blow it away ...' But he and his like are organizing defence strategy, and as ever, the bulwark shore may come to our rescue to ward off this menace.

*

Defence – and armaments. One material used in the manufacture of gunpowder, and still used in ordnance factories, is charcoal. Inland from Icklesham, at Udimore, the firm of Blackman, Pavie and Ladden Ltd have recently been burning wood for charcoal, but their main area of activity is at their yard at Petley Wood near Sedlescombe. Charcoal burning has been going on in Petley Wood for at least five hundred years, and the method has changed little, except that steel kilns are now used instead of the mounds or pits (pronounced in the Sussex dialect 'pet') of carefully arranged billets of wood built up round a central draught or chimney, or rather two chimneys, one triangular and one circular, in successive courses of wood, all covered with used straw, wood brushings and grass. (A record of 1424 notes: 'for the charcoal burners hired for making charcoal in Pettele Woods 6/8d; in the 8th year of the reign of King Henry, the Fifth after the Conquest'.[10])

The wood is still carefully arranged. A mixture of hard and soft woods can be used – the harder the wood, the better the charcoal (restaurants in particular like a slow burning charcoal for their grills). Inside the kiln, two half-burnt branches are laid diagonally, with smaller half-burnt branches laid across them, and on top of that the piles of freshly sawn logs. When the hearth is full, the steel cover is placed over it, and a paraffin-soaked rag pushed up the draught hole which has been left at the bottom. Smoke shoots out of the top of the kiln, and will go on drifting across the clearing for about twenty-four hours, when the charcoal will be ready to be cooled, sifted, graded and later packed. Several kilns are kept going at once, and the yard is full of activity – a shower of wood spraying over a kiln as men saw the wood to put in it; the heavy cylinders being heaved into place; smoke curling up as a fresh kiln is lit. Charcoal is used for barbecues, for the making of fertilizers, in copper refining and in case-hardening compounds for metals, for filtering, and among other things, for making carbon disulphide which is used for many purposes including the manufacture of viscose rayon. Blackman, Pavie and Ladden have been in the forestry business since 1888, and have been making charcoal here since 1939; the firm was particularly busy during the war. It is the only charcoal burning firm now in Sussex; there are only about six in the whole country. Very different from the days before coke when charcoal was used for iron-smelting (as well as for making knives and edge tools), when the whole Wealden district was dotted with, often small-scale, iron-foundries, taking advantage of local iron-ore and the oaks of the Wealden forest, which were ideal for making charcoal. Before the great iron foundries of the eighteenth century were established near coal-fields, and the introduction of coke to smelt iron ore, the Wealden district was the foremost producer of pig iron. Weaponry and cannon were supplied to the Tudor and Stuart navies, and naval contracts were not lost to other suppliers until 1769. Daniel Defoe, as acute in observation here as elsewhere, wrote,

I had the curiosity to see the great foundries, or iron-works, which are in this county, and where they are carry'd on at such a prodigious expence of wood, that even in a country almost all over-run with timber, they begin to complain of the consuming it for those furnaces, and leaving the next age to want timber for building their navies.... [11]

Later on, charcoal was still in great demand, for drying hops.

Blackman, Pavie and Ladden are also one of the three firms in Sussex still making the traditional Sussex trugs. In a light workshop behind their offices, Ted Turner showed us how trugs are made, with a wire-hard dexterity that looks deceptively easy; it must be very hard work – and he works from 7 am until 4.30 pm. Ted was taught how to make trugs by the grandson of the Sussex man Thomas Smith who invented the trug, and who walked to London to present one to Queen Victoria. They would certainly have been useful at Balmoral, and were originally used for every conceivable agricultural and domestic purpose – gathering potatoes and beans, fruit and flowers. Trugs are made from sweet chestnut wood, from the first clean branchless length at the bottom of a twelve-year-old or so tree, and willow – sally willow or cricket-bat willow. The wood is steamed in an electric steamer (a copper would have been used in the old days), so that it becomes pliable. The willow slats are bent by hand by pulling them through a frame, and the chestnut wood for the frames of the trugs is bent round a wooden gig or template. Ted has previously sat on a wooden horse to shave the slats smooth, and now he nails the framework together and the slats into place, using copper nails that won't rust. Finally, he trims off the ends of the slats with a knife so sharp that it cuts through them like butter, and then nicks them to finish them off at the same neat angle. His hands move with lightning speed, careful as a potter's, and he lifts the trug now and then to check its shape, with a craftsman's assurance and pride. Tangy fresh-cut shavings and finished trugs of every shape and size surround him. He is a master craftsman, and in a plastic age, workers in wood are increasingly rare. Perhaps Ted should walk to Buckingham Palace with a trug? Certainly we should all plant trees, encourage craftsmen, so that we don't leave 'the next age to want timber' ...

11 Hastings; Pevensey; Lewes; Seaford

'Here Harold stood, and England stood, that day!'
WILLIAM K. FLEMING, Senlac Field

'Lewis is a fine pleasant town, well built, agreeably scituated in the middle of an open champaign country, and on the edge of the South Downs, the pleasantest, and most delightful of their kind in the nation ... both the town and the country adjacent, is full of gentlemen of good families and fortunes ...'
Daniel Defoe

'It's the worst that it's been for fifty years ... for fish —'

George Rich was wheeling a trolley of ice from the Hastings fish market which is down on the shore, and closes at 7.30 am (having opened at six), to his shop, which is right by the market. It was January – the January of 1979, with haulage strikes, petrol shortages and the worst winter for sixteen years. A biting wind ran in gusts across the Stade, that part of the beach where the fishermen of Hastings may by right of a Royal Charter draw up their boats on the shingle. Mr Rich's face and hands were blue with cold, but he smiled, and his eyes were a crisp sea blue. He told me that most of the fish from the market was sold to Sussex suppliers, and some to London. His shop by the market is open every day. 'I've been here seven days a week for fifty years ... mustn't grumble ...'

Did he like Hastings? 'Yes, sweetheart, yes ... I've been here all my life ...'

The dogged tenacity of people who are so much part of their place that no tide could displace them. An unquestioned belonging. Undisturbed, in winter, by the summer crowds who swarm over the beach like flies. Under the gusts of snow, the Stade has a tar-rich salty independence; the shingle awash with sponge weed thrown up by the sea, with nets, nylon bottles, flung ladders, pulleys, hawsers, empty tins, gulls. Some of the nets are slung on poles to dry, because now that they are made of nylon, they are no longer dried in the tall net shops – about thirty feet high and eight feet square at the base, of black weatherboarding – which have been a unique feature here since Elizabethan days, possibly, with their Scandinavian elements, a design used since the days of the original settlement.

The huts are used for storing nets now, and there are fewer of them. Other sheds are being repaired, and rotten wood and rubbish send up warm flames and smoke from fires in braziers, or laid higgledy-piggledy on the beach. But the boats themselves are in ordered rows, nearer the icy sea. The crew of the *Shane* have just returned, from trammel fishing (in place of summer trawling). Nets are put out one day, picked up the next, up to six or seven miles out, 'going where the fish is', eight nets to a 'fleet', five 'fleets' in a boat. When the nets are brought ashore, they must then be sorted, the nylon untangled. A job, in the cold, which few would envy, and which would defy talk of differentials. But the two fishermen – young and obviously hale – seem cheerful. Is it being their own masters, that makes the job pleasant, or the actual trade?

'I enjoy it ... the fishing ...'

Could he pinpoint it for me?

'Well ... It's the nearest you can get back to nature ...'

There is nothing to add. Gulls wheel with a squawk overhead, the gulls that swoop and squabble everywhere you go in Hastings. The wind blows clean and the Old Town of Hastings shelters between its hills. The sea sucks at the shingle, where the boats lie at rest, and the tide makes civilization's worries seem insig....... as cockleshells.

*

There was once a harbour at Hastings, an important port in Saxon times. The name is derived from Haestingas, sons of Haestan, a Jutish pirate, who settled here in the fifth century. Later it became the territory of a Saxon chieftain, Ella. Under Edward the Confessor it was a maritime strongpoint, and was until the twelfth century one of the leading Cinque Ports, some claim *the* leading Cinque Port. William the Conqueror had a castle built here after the battle (the first tournament in England is said to have been at the castle here, with the Conqueror's daughter Adela, as Queen of Beauty); from here King John proclaimed the British Sovereignty of the Seas, in 1201. However, by the early thirteenth century, the port was already declining. Nine years after Edward I's Charter had made the Cinque Ports into a Confederation, the sheltered harbour in its river creek to the west of West Hill became blocked with shingle, and was abandoned after the great storms of 1287, which altered so much of the coast. Today the two streams which ran on either side of this rocky hill on which the castle stands are no more, the remnants of the River Bourne being piped into a sewer and outfall.

The Old Town, between the East and West hills, has kept its character to a great extent, although I was told, 'the heart was ripped out of Hastings when they put the main road through the Bourne ...' – the main road with its traffic cutting down between the two narrow streets of All Saints and High Street, with their Tudor and Georgian houses, stained glass windows, coloured tile windowboxes, narrow alleyways, pubs and curiosities such as the Piece of Cheese cottage, triangular and painted yellow, not much bigger than a good hunk of cheddar. Off All Saints' Street, in Tackleway, the Duke of Sussex had his summer residence in 1794. In 125 All Saints' Street lived the mother of Admiral Sir Cloudesley Shovell, who from being a shoemaker's apprentice, and then cabin-boy, rose to be Admiral of the Blue from 1650–1707. The Cinque Ports Arms is eminently old, and the talk inside when I was there was of shire reeves and charters, between two Hastings regulars.

There are three outstanding churches in this area. The Catholic Church of St Mary Star of the Sea, suitably encrusted with uncut flints; All Saints' Church below a wooded and bracken covered hill (as Charles Lamb, who had been 'happy many years ago for a brief week – at Margate ...' wrote in jaundiced mood – 'I love town or country; but this detestable Cinque Port is neither ...'[1]); and the oldest church in the town – St Clement's, the church of the patron saint of sailors, dating from 1390 but on the site of an earlier church destroyed by the French in 1377. (The French sacked Hastings in 1399 also, and the town never quite recovered from these two raids.) St Clement's is squat, chequered with black flint and white stone, with the Cinque Ports' arms over the door.

Pieces of the old rood screen are set into the wall inside, other pieces having been used to repair the roof after an attack by a hostile fleet in 1652. The roof is barrel-vaulted; the east windows were destroyed in the Second World War, but there is some good modern glass, and in the nave two fine chandeliers. There is also a sanctuary lamp, dedicated to Dante Gabriel Rossetti, and a sub-Rossetti print in his memory. He was married to Lizzie Siddal in this church, after ten years with this once adored model, but she was already by that time in poor health, and died less than two years later from an overdose of laudanum. Grief stricken, he had unpublished poems interred in her coffin in Highgate Cemetery, but this was too much for any poet, and he later dug them up.

A painted panel in St Clement's commemorates a bequest in 1721 by Archibald Hutcheson, one of the town's 'barons in parliament' – to repair the church and 'to build and increase the ships and vessels of this Corporation, for the benefit of the poor ... a perpetual fund to be lent without interest to poor fishermen to enable them to carry on their Trade ...'

Fishermen in Hastings today may not be poor, but they are beleaguered. In summer, the town has one and a half million day trippers and a quarter of a million long term visitors, including foreign students. Although they congregate along the front, in easy reach of the fish-and-chip stalls, and whelk and jellied eel stands, the Old Town is promoted, even recently on television, as a historical curiosity. It is well preserved (there is an Old Town Preservation Society), but in danger of losing its working identity.

'There baint a fisherman lives in All Saints' Street now ...,' I was told at the Fisherman's Institute and headquarters of the Winkle Club, in that same street. And indicating the fishermen in the room, Councillor Bert Northwood, at that time about to contest the Old Town ward, said, 'These are the aristocracy ... Old Town families are the descendants of families who came over with the Vikings ... If you look at the youngsters, they start off with absolutely blond hair – that's the sign of real Old Town youngsters ... and bright blue eyes.' Even if a fisherman married a woman from outside the Old Town, she would become Old Town. 'They don't recognize you easily if you're not ...' Many people who belonged there would intermarry.

We were sitting at a table with Jack Edmunds, who was coxwain of the life-boat for twenty-seven years, now bald with the rakish Hastings gold earring in one ear, and Wilf Adams, Secretary of the Fishermen's Society and who has also served for eleven years in the life-boat – Viking-featured, with two gold earrings and piercing blue eyes. No one there knew how the tradition of gold earrings originated – at a guess at about the time when Hastings men were known as 'Chopbacks' from their habit of chopping an axe down their enemies' backs ... Wilf Adams told me the system for drawing boats up on the Stade, the territory jealously preserved against gypsies and others, but which does allow a car-park and anglers to encroach. It has increased in size, as the old harbour arm has accumulated more shingle. The boats are registered at Rye, an incredible fact which happened over the years, since Rye is still a port. Anyone wishing to become a fisherman must be elected for a probationary period by the committee of ten of the Fisherman's Institute and Society, who are themselves elected by the fishermen in general. After six months, the new fisherman may apply for a place on the beach. 'It was a bit too easy in the past ... "cowboys" came in (and those, not regulars, who thought they would try their hand, and bought a boat).' Wilf's blue eyes look steely. 'And the East Sussex Fisheries Committee rely on our Committee to keep a tight rein on the regulars ... they need all the information they can get as to what fish are caught. It's illegal for outsiders to buy a boat, and flog fish.'

But how are the fishermen to keep too many new *residents* out of the Old Town, if it is not too late? Blocks of old buildings have been pulled down and the land sold to private owners. The Council have not concentrated on council housing here. The people who really belong are in danger of being driven out.

I was shown with pride a photograph of all the fishermen who served in the Second World War. And met an official of the Winkle Club, whose members meet at the Institute and whose annual dinner is famous, raising a great deal of money for charity. Its most famous member was Sir Winston Churchill. Sir Alec Rose was made a member and given a silver winkle in 1970. Past members have been the Duke of Windsor and Richard Dimbleby, and the Duke of Edinburgh is today a member.

In the Institute women smiled warmly from their corner tables – it was a cold day and they made me, although an outsider, welcome. The main road of the Bourne may have tried to rip the heart out of Hastings, but it is still alive here. For how long?

*

The rest of the town has its own character. It provides good shops for tourists, and off the beaten track are antique shops where pretty china can still be found for a matter of 10p. The Town Hall is stained glass Gothic Victoriana; Pelham Crescent has bow-fronted balconies and the Louis-Seize portico of St Mary-in-the-Castle church at its centre, 'the only good building in Hastings', as one resident would have it; in Wellington Square is Regency ironwork; everywhere are pockets and corners of interest. Smugglers' tunnels and haunts abound, as in the Stag Inn, and the Hastings Arms in George Street, where hidden kegs were discovered as late as the 1960s. Even modern concerns have sometimes the air of contraband; Ellis Son and Vidler have a store in the undercliff, shaped like a smugglers' grotto, and here during the 1979 hauliers' strike I saw Nuits-Saint-Georges being hurriedly unloaded from a one-man-band lorry from Dover. The Haestingas are survivors.

A museum in the Old Town Hall has many relics of the Cinque Ports. Down by the Stade is the Fishermen's Church, which also serves as the Fishermen's Museum. There are old photographs, and the Hastings lugger *Enterprise*; also a stuffed albatross. No sailor will ever kill an albatross, the largest sea bird, which can have a wing span of about seventeen feet. Here it spreads its wings near a window which is in memory of Hastings fishermen who have lost their lives at sea.

Hastings Museum and Art Gallery is on the hill beyond the White Rock Gardens (the White Rock Pavilion is the epitome of a pleasure-dome, putting on everything from excellent concerts to wrestling by Big Daddy and Cry Baby Cooper), and beyond also the modern and streamlined Law Courts – which should, of course, be the Art Gallery. The museum houses East Sussex collections, including iron firebacks from the Wealdon iron foundries. There is majolica, including the largest piece of Italian majolica known, dated 1593-4, showing a boar hunt; and an oil by C. Powell of 1790 showing the Old Town below its shorn green cliffs, the waves alive with white sails and shrimpers.

On the heights of West Hill is a small black-and-white directional light like an armless windmill, aligned with another below, and here are the ancient St Clement's Caves, probably made originally by a subterranean upheaval about thirty thousand years ago, enlarged later, and certainly used by smugglers. During the 1939 war they were used as a regular air-raid shelter for the Old Town. Today they can be rented for parties, at about £43 a night. 'Soundproof', as the custodian told me with feeling. Closer to the sea, are the ruins of the Norman Castle. From this hill there is the best view of the shore – the boats in amazing alignment on the Stade, with their masts pencilled black against the sea and ochre shingle. The black netshops, the irregular houses of the Old Town below the sloping cliffs, and a luminous light. A light which has haunted generations of artists, including Turner, in whose 'Hastings' (Tate Gallery) it fills sea, sky and shore.

Writers, artists, and distinguished men have all patronized Hastings, which became fashionable as a resort in the eighteenth century. Sir Arthur Wellesley (later Duke of Wellington) brought his bride here in 1806; Coventry Patmore lived in the town, Sir Rider Haggard in St Leonard's. Byron stayed in the same Hastings House where Wellesley had stayed, and in 1814 wrote to Mr Moore:

I have been renewing my acquaintance with my old friend Ocean, and I find his bosom as pleasant a pillow for an hour in the morning as his daughters of Paphos could be in the twilight. I have been swimming, and eating turbot, and smuggling neat brandies and silk handker-chiefs....[2]

Whistler often visited his mother here, in St Mary's Terrace, and it is thought 'The Artist's Mother' was painted at her window here; certainly it contains the soft grey light of Hastings.

*

And today?

'All along this south-east coast, from Folkstone and Sandgate to here, as far as Bexhill – is a philistine area.' The speaker, John Bratby, is quoting a remark made to him by a Canterbury art gallery owner, agreeing with it fervently, and expanding on it in reply to my questions as to how he finds Hastings, where he has moved from London. 'A cultural wasteland ... it's depressing to live in a philistine environment ... art grows and flourishes in the right climate ...'

Since the war, Hastings has probably lost part of its coterie of intelligentsia, although it has the Stables Theatre showing programmes such as Michael Frayn's comedy *Alphabetical Order* and an 'Evening with Ellen Terry' – and several art galleries. One doesn't need to ask, however, why Bratby, who took the art world by storm with his phenomenal success in the 1950s, and whose talent has not faded, has chosen to live here. His house, one of a quartet of houses 'based on Nash' by the nineteenth-century Hastings architect Joseph Kaye is called The Cupola and Tower of the Winds, and rises like an elegant folly of white stucco and glass on the hillside above All Saints' Church and the Old Town, with the best domestic view in Hastings.

The house is cluttered, but with no ordinary clutter. In the kitchen everyday things stand cheek by jowl with a letter from the Queen Mother's secretary thanking him for a painting of sunflowers (Bratby often paints sunflowers – David Frost has a painting of them by him – and also other flowers, and acknowledges Van Gogh's influence while stating that Van Gogh's sunflowers and his are not the same – his, Bratby's sunflowers, are his own). The wall is lined with other commendatory letters which offset the complete naturalness and lack of vanity of the artist, and his wife's charm as she pours large mugs of tea on a lacquer tray. A plumber is doing something to the heating arrangements. We perch in the sitting-room among Victorian furniture, books, green plants, our cups of tea and about thirty or so canvasses – portraits of Len Murray, David Rudkin and Leslie Porter of Tesco Ltd, with still-life paintings such as one of an animal carcase set among domestic objects, paintings of flowers, of the views from his house and the cupola studio, showing a blue sea, yellow sun and Bratby vegetation. Paintings of fishing boats, gardens, garden paths, sunflowers ... They are powerful, supremely painterly, unhackneyed.

In the 1950s Bratby led, with Middleditch, Greaves and Jack Smith, the movement that the critics named the 'Kitchen Sink School'. A realism that was then almost shocking, but now seems pastoral by comparison with later twists and permutations of the art scene. He had studied at the Royal College, and even *lived* in the Royal College for a while, having discovered some unused rooms under the roof, where he moved in with paraffin stove and camp bed, to save rent and fares, so that the smell of his kippers drifted out to mystify connoisseurs studying graceful antiques in the Victoria and Albert Museum. He was awarded an Italian government scholarship to travel in Italy (but didn't like the cooking), and represented Britain at the Venice Biennale in 1956; he has designed film sets, is an RA, author, and has paintings in the Tate Gallery and the Museum of Modern Art in America.

I had been wondering how he would feel about present-day trends, each successive fashion in art. He is not at all defensive; is, he says, with a trace of ruefulness, naturally aware of trends (on his last day at the Royal College he had asked his Professor of Painting how he could make money out of painting, an eminently practical question).

'I did a few abstract paintings ... but ... through no strength of will, I have just gone on doing my own paintings ... They are closely linked to my life – I find it very difficult to separate them from my own life, difficult to do that, as Cézanne for example could be detached ...'

This is his strength. His paintings are absolutely true. He painted, and the label 'Kitchen Sink' came afterwards. He still paints, and more strongly, in perhaps stronger colours, working outwards from his home, his own vision of his surroundings, which is not claustrophobic or introverted because his art is too sturdy, and much too fertile.

'Values that have been discarded are being restated again,' he says. Pop – Op – Abstract back to Representational Art. They come and go. His statement has not wavered.

He has expressed himself in print as well, his novels *Breakdown* (1960) and *Break-Pedal Down* (1962) being his best known fiction. *Breakdown* deals with an artist breaking out, rather than down perhaps, and has immense energy and physical descriptions of people which only a painter could realize:

The café was small, a worker's café, used by lorry-drivers and road-mending labourers. A bus-driver, a bus-conductor, and a grey-white-faced middle-aged man, sat at a table in the corner ... Suddenly there was silence. A poor poet stood outside. The silence was fierce ... But the poet wanted a cheap cup of tea ... Plumbers and carpenters, when in a crowd together, with union membership cards in their pockets, don't like single individualists, and like even less, sensitive-eyed and gentle-mouthed poets, in corduroy jackets, and high leather boots covered by pale blue jeans, smoking hand-made cigarettes with frightened elegant movements of the arms and hands. They had a name for them ... for chaps who mix concrete in the wrong proportions ...[3]

Dark straight hair cascaded down across her shoulders, and she had the frail pathetic body and arms popular in the art schools ... Bright red calf-socks contrasted with the wickerwork basket at her feet ... She was writing poetry, very personal poetry, bad poetry, incoherent poetry....[4]

Autobiographical?

'Prophetic in a way ... The arts are very strange ... all kinds of mystical aspects. It's as though we had a prophetic element in us that can be expressed in some art. I think I will do another book before I die [he was born in 1928] – rather important to do one. I was thinking as I came back from a walk this morning ...'

He likes walking, and is doing colour drawings of the Hastings area, of the ten churches, of garden landscapes, and of the coast as far afield as Whitstable. He is also engaged in painting a series of portraits 'that would celebrate individuality at a time when it was in jeopardy' – 'high achievers, individuals, persons of originality and persons with dynamic qualities'. Her Majesty the Queen Mother agreed to sit for a portrait to be included in the series, and the painting has recently been exhibited and shown on television.

He takes us on a tour of the house. The bedroom with a Bratby unmade bed, frilled woodwork framing the view through the window. Upstairs to his studio in the cupola, a blaze of light, with its dome and windows. He opens one of them, and we see what could be a Bratby painting of the white turreted house opposite. In another window the Old Town runs down to the sea in its sheltered cleft, with All Saints' Church on the hill on one side, the castle hill on the other.

But he has had to put up wire to stop vandals getting into the garden.

'Rather nasty. I came away from Greenwich to get away from vandals ... A philistine place ... inertia and letting it happen.'

He has often written to the local papers about it.

'The plumber said to me today, "You won't change Hastings – Hastings will change you."'

But it won't change his artistic integrity.

*

St Leonards, the sister suburb, now one with Hastings, was laid out as a resort by the successful London builder James Burton and his son Decimus, when Hastings had become fashionable, in the early nineteenth century. James Burton had been associated with John Nash in developing Regent's Park and Old Regent Street. He moved his own house down to Hastings by ship, and set it up there, lending it in 1834 to the Duchess of Kent and her daughter the Princess Victoria. The buildings which remain of his great plan are submerged by heavy seaside stucco and promenade, but the classical Assembly Rooms building (now Masonic Hall) still stands behind the Royal Victoria Hotel, which is regally the same as ever, providing an unhurried meal. There is a framed hotel register, with the signature 'Victoria' and remarks, in 1875, such as those by Lady Wolseley, 'extremely comfortable', or Miss Newton, 'much pleased with the quietness of the establishment'.

Where Hastings merges with St Leonards, Queen Victoria looks solemnly out on the Channel on the seaward side of Warrior Square, which is suitably imposing. Here in 1978 we watched the National Town Criers' Championship, which has been held at Hastings since 1952, and in 1978 honoured the 700th Anniversary of the Cinque Ports' Great Charter. Hastings takes itself seriously as a Cinque Port, and exploits the pageantry to the full. The Championship is sponsored by the *News of the World* and that year had among the judges the ubiquitous Freddie Parrot-Face Davies and a *Sun* Page 3 girl. The contestants' numbers were heralded by local beauties in togas.

Town Crying is a serious business, and its origins, we were told by a contestant, go back to the Fire of London when criers called to the inhabitants to bring out their dead. Belying that, we were also told that Hastings has never been without a town crier since 1205, Lyme Regis since 1080.

The criers are dressed in frilled white stocks, tricorns, silk waistcoats. Those of towns such as Rye bear the Cinque Ports arms on their coats. The Hastings Crier, Raymond Goode, told us that he got £132 a year for this honorary post, and worked as a beach inspector. He has travelled to a competition in Canada, and was soon off to Israel. He proclaims announcements round the town, and other functions of town criers are summonses to court leets, festivals, and carnivals 'when the tannoy breaks down'. Charles Tamplin, from Hillingdon, has been Town Crier since the Coronation; he told us he had been in the Royal Artillery in the war and had learnt to shout above the guns. He smokes, 'but you don't inhale, that's what does it.' Not all the voices are martially loud, and enunciation and carrying power tell. 'It's all from your stomach ... you've got to shout from your stomach,' we were told. A less Falstaffian crier had a small whisky bottle sneaked in his pocket. Some of the sables were wilted; but the music was stirring. 'We, the Town Criers ... in Hastings, the Premier Cinque Port, pay tribute to the member towns whose men and boats protected these shores over the years.' The winner, a young man, Ian Clarkson, from Chester, only appointed that year, was magnificent. His voice bowled over the square. Girls flocked round him; Freddie Parrot-Face beamed and the Mayoress handed over the trophy. 'There's no secret ... when I do a job I like to do it well,' he said. The girls fluttered their lashes.

Hastings is also the scene of the International Chess Congress, but another public draw, speedway, which was brought to Hastings originally, has now moved to Eastbourne, to the regret of some townspeople. 'There were two or three vandals so the council went against it ... we've a lot of retired people here. But I've seen more aggression in football than I've ever seen in speedway ... families go to speedway.'

And Hastings is also the home of that entertainment which claims us all, in the twentieth century. Tucked away in the small Queens Arcade among fish and veg shops and shops selling dusters and Maynards wine gums, is an unobtrusive plaque on a wall: 'TELEVISION first demonstrated by JOHN LOGIE BAIRD from experiments started here in 1924.' John Logie Baird was thirty-two when he came to Hastings in 1922, and tried, from a rented attic, to transmit single-handed a picture through the air. A hand-made replica of the first monochrome TV set called 'The Televisor' is in the Town Hall. The screen is approximately two inches by two inches.

*

'They call this progress ... we're a very slow town ... we change very slowly.'

I had bought some 'Winter Mixture' and 'Clove Humbugs' at the Rock Shop, down on the front, where the crowds will be in summer. Mrs Sheila Tutt and her husband talked to me about the town. He has been a rock maker for thirty years, the only one in Hastings now. 'The guvnor, D. C. Masters was a real character ... he got me interested. They're all his own recipes ...'

They deplored the loss of the clock tower memorial, which was set alight by vandals, and has not yet been replaced. The Hastings Muffin Club plan to build a new one. 'The clock tower was part of Hastings ... the students congregate around there and the police can't do anything ... old ladies can't get across. Trippers? Foreigners in the main are not too bad. They spend well, especially the Germans. Students aren't trade ... they go for clothing and discos. Over the years I've seen a hell of a change in manners ... to me manners go a long way ... but the pleasant ones outweigh the ones who come in and say "one of those".'

It could have been dispiriting down on the front in January, but the shop had been newly decorated, taking advantage of the off-season, and they clearly had not lost faith in Hastings, the place which has, as they said – less jaundiced than Lamb – 'the sea on one side and the country on the other'.

Which is the real Hastings? The Hastings of tar and gulls, of ancient churches and the even older trade of fishing, or the Hastings of the day tripper, with the newly painted smugglers' cottages and raffish boutiques? I think it is a little of both; a genuine, salty town, with its unspoilt corners, lack of cohesion, plates of cockles and bowls of jellied eel, winter quiet and summer carnival. The Chopbacks have adapted to less fearsome but not less inventive ways of winning a livelihood. It is not a booming resort, but less down-at-heel than many. And in what other English town would the following belief live on? That the Victoria Hotel was built on the site of a former 'Bulrush Pond', which was overhung by rocks, on one of which William the Conqueror ate a meal after landing in 1066 ...

*

It was William's town. But it was also Harold's town in death.

Leading his Saxon army, which was exhausted after defeating the Norwegian Harold Hardrada at Stamford Bridge near York, a short while before, Harold marched south. His brother, Gyrth, begged to lead the army instead of him, and also to lay waste the land between London and the sea, so that William would be in a desert. Harold refused to harm the property of those he had been appointed to govern. He drew up his men 'by the hoar apple tree' on the long ridge of Senlac where Battle Abbey now stands, seven miles from Hastings. The date was Friday 13 October. The next day the Normans attacked, with their mounted knights in heavy armour (William's chain mail coat weighed sixty pounds; three horses were killed under him). They had a tradition of killing everyone they captured. Harold was well protected by his house-carles with their shield wall that was almost impossible to penetrate, and the two-handed axes of the Saxons did fearsome damage, but after a long fight, the Normans made a feint retreat, and when the Saxons charged into the valley, defying Harold's orders, the Normans were able to storm the hill. Harold, it is now thought, died from blows to the head and body (a spear behind his head in the Bayeux tapestry was mistaken for an arrow in his eye).

After the battle, the Danish princess Gytha, the mother of Harold, begged in vain for the body of her son and offered its weight in gold in exchange. For some days the body could not be identified, among all those slain on the field. It is recounted that Edith the Swan-necked, King Harold's former mistress, finally recognized it. William had Harold's body wrapped in purple linen, according to one account, and buried on the cliff at Hastings. William's chaplain recorded that the Conquerer said: 'Let his corpse guard the coasts which his life madly defended.'[5]

So on this most English clifftop, the last of the Saxon kings looked out (his body was possibly later moved to Waltham) towards France, from whence the newcomers with their new laws, new culture, new ways of thought, came in this last successful invasion of the country to change our history. Yet it was a merging rather than an overthrow in some regards. If one looks at a map of the French possessions of Henry II, about a hundred years later, his territories of Normandy and Aquitaine appear almost to cover half the country, inland to Paris and down to Toulouse.

This can be clearly seen on the Hastings Embroidery, which was made by the Royal School of Needlework to celebrate the 900th anniversary of the Battle of Hastings, and which is currently on show in Hastings Town Hall. (The Bayeux Tapestry is also embroidery, rather than tapestry proper.)

The new embroidery highlights eighty-one events, as diverse as Henry I's son and heir drowning from the White Ship (the legend says his father never smiled again), to the Industrial Revolution and on to the Conquest of Everest. In the final panel Churchill's back view is shown solid in dark pinstripes and bowler, making the V sign to the boats in the Channel from the clifftop; beside him is embroidered the gold winkle which the Winkle Club gave him. A warrior looking out over the 'coasts which his life madly defended'.

*

William had vowed to build an abbey if he was victorious, and this he did. The high altar was where Harold fell. Battle Abbey today is part of later rebuildings; the tall gatehouse was built in about 1338. In 1538, at the Dissolution of the Monasteries, Battle was given to Sir Anthony Browne, who demolished the major part of it. The last monk to leave cursed Browne with the prophecy that 'by fire and water his line should come to an end and perish out of the land'.[5] Sir Anthony's son was the first Viscount Montague. In 1793, Cowdray House, the home of the Montagues, was burnt down and the 8th Viscount, aged twenty-two, was drowned shooting the falls in a small boat at Schaffenhausen, a month later. The land passed to his sister. Her two sons drowned before her eyes at Bognor.

It was not at Hastings that William the Conqueror had landed before the battle, but along the coast at Pevensey (some accounts say that some of his troops had been beaten off at Romney). Pevensey, and Seaford, became Corporate Members of Hastings in the Cinque Ports Confederation.

Pevensey already had a long history before 1066. Many Neolithic implements have been found there, and it was the site of Anderida, one of the mightiest of the Saxon Shore fortresses of the Romans. When the Romans left Britain, Anderida was occupied by Romanized Britons, many of them fleeing from Picts, Scots and Saxons. In 491 Saxons attacked Anderida, killing every man, woman and child inside: 'there was not even one Briton left there', the Anglo-Saxon Chronicle relates. They called the dense forest land that spread northwards into Sussex and Kent, for over a hundred miles between Winchester and Ashford, Andredsweald, or Wild, after the sacked city, and from this is derived the Weald.

In those times, the sea came inland to Anderida, but although it has receded, today the area is a watery area of dykes and meadowland, flat and grass tufted. In Saxon times there were other islands or 'eyes' besides Pevensey – the 'lost' town of Northeye; the lost village of Hydneye, once a Member of the Cinque Port of Hastings (below the sea, lies the vanished town of Bulverhythe; in Pevensey Bay fishermen used to call the action of waves on shingle 'the bells of Bulverhythe'); on the Pevensey Levels today, Horse Eye, Chilley, Mountney. And other names suggestive of the area's character – Marshfoot, Adam's Hole, Flower's Green. An area which was a perfect lure for Saxon or Norman invader, or indeed any other; in 1940 the castle was camouflaged and became a defence post.

The walls of the Roman fort are one of the finest examples of Roman building in the country, and in spite of sea winds, amazingly well preserved. They enclose a large area, and the stones are more regular than at a fort such as Wroxeter, having the streamlined horizontal bars of red Roman tiles, and pinkish mortar. Ten round bastions surge from the walls.

Inside there is an expanse of cropped grass, then a moat, and the Norman castle, built within the Roman defences. Sheep feed peacefully (in winter there are few visitors), doves coo from the ruins, the small towers of Westham and Pevensey churches – capped with spires, one tall, one squat – make intimate cutouts against the sky, between winter trees, lichened roofs, cuts of water, and beyond, the pale line of the sea (its chalet architecture too distant to obtrude), and a dark spur of the downs running into cliffs to the west.

I sat on a pile of stones inside the Norman castle, where stone cannon balls – from Roman catapults and Norman artillery – are piled up like marbles; inside the unprotected foundation stones of a chapel, fresh rainwater filled a stump of pillar or font; the grey and white doves settled on walls; February sun burnt on my back; in the countryside around were the first turned lines of reddish earth. The bloody deeds of Anderida, and of later battles, are buried deep under the tranquil Sussex turf, and are not felt here now.

Past one part of the Roman fort the traffic of a main road thunders (and on the A259 across the Pevensey Levels where it is dead straight and willow fringed, young bloods used to try out their cars' top speeds, in the 1930s); but Pevensey is still lined with old flint cottages, pubs and the Court House or Town Hall museum in which is an ancient seal (dated c. 1230), the oldest Cinque Ports' seal in existence, showing St Nicholas stilling a storm at sea. The church, which with its lancets and clockface has an air of a surprised owl, is dedicated to the same saint. Inside, green sandstone from a local quarry was used in the construction. During the seventeenth century, the chancel was completely walled off and used to keep cattle, coal and contraband brandy in. That at Westham, where there are also old houses among the new, is dedicated to St Mary, and dated to 1080 – 'the first church the Normans built' a notice proclaims. Whether or not, there are some beautiful stained-glass panels in the east window of the chancel, dating to the reign of Henry V.

Another Henry is associated with the Mint House in Pevensey. Here Henry VIII's physician, Andrew Borde, lived, and after Henry's death, the young King Edward VI, in poor health, stayed at the house for rest and recuperation. The house is open to the public, and antiques are also sold there – a very good collection of oak furniture, brass, pans, china, and curiosities such as an 1885 camera, a penny-farthing and a Victorian child's cooking range. The minting chamber is still in existence, where there was a Norman mint from AD 1076 – coins are in the British Museum. There is also a secret room, with a priest's hole behind a sliding ceiling trap – undoubtedly used for smugglers' contraband in the seventeenth and eighteenth centuries. But the house's most unsalubrious claim to fame is its ghost story. In 1586 a London merchant, Thomas Dight, was living at the Mint House with his mistress. One evening he came home to find her in the arms of another, had her bound and her tongue cut out, then forced her to watch while her new lover was hung from chains to the ceiling and roasted to death over a fire. Not surprisingly, the poor woman's ghost (she was left to die in an upper room) haunted the house, and was seen in lace headdress gliding in at the window. Does she still haunt the house? 'No ... I don't think I'd stay here if I'd seen her,' a young man told me among the antiques.

I hurried on to 'The Smugglers', for some homemade leek soup. Here piratical builders were ruminating, over heaped platters. 'How long will these houses we're building last? ... not long ... subsidence ... no solid beams ...' The constructor of the Mint House, on the other hand, was a believer in beams, and used an inordinate amount in his ceilings – which is perhaps why his house has lasted so well.

*

For a town where there are outstanding features of many ages, it would be hard to better Lewes, the County Town of East Sussex and market centre. It has a tourist information bureau in the middle of the High Street, with every conceivable guide, including the outstanding one by Walter H. Godfrey. Yet in some ways, of which the residents would no doubt approve, it has not adapted to foreign tourists. The smarter restaurants, and there are many of them, serve slowly, as if for the women with elegant grey chignons, leather boots and capes, who stride the streets, rather than for a visitor wanting a quick cup of coffee. For this, try the sleazier, friendly cafés, where the talk is of knitting patterns and prodigal sons, and the timeless subjects of country life.

Lewes is part of the country, especially now that the bypass has sheared off some if not all of the heavy traffic. The Downs invade the town, just as the town's outskirts invade hillsides, as at Cliffe; they are always present in the mind, in the ambiance of Lewes, and the town with its pale-bricked Georgian houses is filled with the same grey or bright shifting light that moves over their slopes.

I had never liked the South Downs before coming to live in Sussex. Seen briefly, or in one mood, they are dull, colourless and imbued with all the poor paintings of them one has seen – not to mention poems. Tamer than the hills of Shropshire or Wales, their secret is in movement, the movement of light. Sun and cloud shadows play over their sides and bring them to instantaneous life, for an instant only. White chalk gashes are illuminated, a line of brilliant sour green rushes up a field, a fire of light burns for a second behind a hill. Then the sun sinks, or the mood changes, and they revert to sullen grey-green whale-backed mounds rising from their over-domesticated valleys.

From Lewes Castle you can see a downland scene at its best, and possibly at its best in winter, or early spring. On two sides the scars of quarries mark the hills; behind you a gold weathervane shines under black snowclouds; in front of you sun shifts over the downs, white smoke curls up from the quarry chimney, the flat yellow grey Ouse winds towards the sea in snake-like coils, and silver pools of water lie inside the ring of downs, with blown willows, and birds circling in the fitful February wind. On the slopes are a hundred greys and greens, sometimes whitened like an old man's stubbly cheeks; by evening they are purple, brilliantly, metallically edged, under scudding clouds.

The castle itself is impressive. It was built by one of William the Conquerer's most powerful companions, William de Warenne, whose wife Gundrada was traditionally held to be the Conqueror's daughter. It has a double gateway – a Norman gatehouse and an early fourteenth-century barbican, which is remarkably solid, with cross-slit windows and arcading under the parapet. William and Gundrada also built the first Cluniac priory in England, whose importance can now only be judged from the ruins over its large acreage.

Lewes has, as the guide books say, a 'wealth of history' (which it celebrates enthusiastically on Bonfire Night – recording burning barrels of tar set alight at the defeat of the Armada, or more prosaically, the Gunpowder Plot). Even before the Romans, there was a prominent hill fort on Mount Caburn, which towers beside Lewes. By the time of the legions, ironworking was under way in the Wealden forests, where iron waste from Roman furnaces has been found (in the Barbican museum at Lewes are many Roman items, such as intaglios from officers' seal rings). It is possible, Walter Godfrey has suggested[7], that the rectangular entrenched position, now the churchyard of St John-sub-Castro, was a Roman defence of the Count of the Saxon Shore. Certainly the Ouse was used for barge traffic from the coast up beyond Lewes to Lindfield until the nineteenth century and the development of the railway, and much earlier the whole valley of the lower Ouse was an estuary, with a thriving herring fishery at Southease at the time of the Domesday Book. There were two mints at Lewes in Saxon times. In Edward the Confessor's day Earl Godwin was lord of the borough and when the fleet put out to sea, the citizens had to provide twenty shillings for munitions of war, thus linking Lewes to the coastal defences of the Cinque Ports. One of the most important dates in Lewes's history – in our history – was in May 1264, when, at the Battle of Lewes, Simon de Montfort overthrew the army of King Henry III, with the support of other nobles and with an army which reflected possibly for the first time the emerging power of the middle-classes and city merchants. As a result of the treaty after the battle, in which about 5000 men were killed, the foundations of our parliamentary government were laid.

In Henry V's reign, ships were fitted out with cannon manufactured in foundries in the Weald – made of latten, a brass mixture. By this time, too, English cannon had become articles of export. The first casting of iron cannon was at Banstead in the Weald of Kent, in 1543. The museum and Anne of Cleves house have examples of firebacks and ironwork. Iron founding was again stimulated by the Napoleonic wars, and there were two foundries in the Cliffe area of Lewes, that of John Every becoming the Phoenix ironworks, on a different site. In the castle grounds is an original panel of the cast iron railings of St Paul's, made at Lamberhurst.

Alongside this industry, it was as a market and transport centre that Lewes developed – with its traditional manufactures of brewing, engineering, printing and shipbuilding (merchant ships were built there until the 1860s). Agricultural produce was wheat, barley and sheep from the downland, and hops and cattle from the Weald. There was a wool fair from 1835, and an important autumn sheep fair.

In the 1880s, there were seven breweries in the town. Now only Harvey's brews – Real Ale (in this case traditional Sussex Bitter and Old Ale), also brewing for Beard's Brewery, another old brewery whose cellars once formed part of Lewes castle dungeons. Every nook and cranny of Lewes seems to have a pub. The sign of an old one, a white eighteenth-century lion, is maintained without its inn across the High Street from Keere Street, the near-perpendicular cobbled alley down which the Prince Regent is said to have driven in his coach and four at full gallop, a hair-raising feat, but no doubt unnoticed by him after some old ale at the White Lion.

Here in the High Street is the timbered Fifteenth-Century Bookshop, and Bull House, where Tom Paine, author of *The Rights of*

Man, lived as an exciseman and tobacconist from 1768–74. A brave and uncompromising rationalist, he was a self-made man who was well aware of what he had achieved through sheer force of intellect. 'At an early period, little more than sixteen years of age, I became the carver of my own fortune, and entered on board the *Terrible* privateer ...' Later, in America, his tract *Common Sense* was a prime inspiration of the American Declaration of Independence. 'I am proud to say, that I have ... contributed to raise a new empire in the world ...' His questioning of the accepted, and *The Rights of Man* which he wrote in answer to Burke's denunciation of the Revolution in France, led to an indictment for treason, but he escaped on being elected to be representative for Calais in the new French National Convention, narrowly escaping, by a lucky accident, the guillotine there. Pitt said of him: 'Tom Paine is quite right, but what am I to do? If I were to encourage Tom Paine's opinions, we should have a bloody revolution.' Yet in his prose, whether epigrammatic or musical and eloquent, he stresses the need for a responsible electorate, and man's responsibility to man. 'Government is no farther necessary than to supply the few cases to which society and civilization are not conveniently competent.'

The mutual dependence and reciprocal interest which man has upon man, and all the parts of a civilized community upon each other, create that great chain of connection which holds it together. The landholder, the farmer, the manufacturer, the merchant, the tradesman, and every occupation, prospers by the aid which each receives from the other, and from the whole.

His thoughts are perhaps as much to the point today as when he wrote them, and far-seeing, he gives our age a hope to echo. 'There is a morning of reason rising upon man on the subject of Government that has not appeared before ... For what we can foresee, all Europe may form but one great Republic, and man be free of the whole.'

Who could have foreseen, or who would have believed, that a French National Assembly would ever have been a popular toast in England, or that a friendly alliance of the two Nations should become the wish of either. It shows that man, were he not corrupted by Governments, is naturally the friend of man, and that human nature is not itself vicious ...[8]

He died in America in 1809, aged 72. William Cobbett had his body brought back to England ten years later, 160 years ago. One hundred and sixty years, and is his morning of reason yet rising upon man? He would have had an epigrammatic answer to that question.

*

The steep side-alleys running downhill from the High Street between flint walls are perhaps even more likeable than the street itself, with its outstanding Georgian brickwork and curving lines, updated by colourwash and by shops called 'Full of Beans' (wholefoods) and 'Bedtimes', by restaurants and bookshops. At the end of the High Street is St Anne's Church, peaceful inside beyond the rumble of traffic and cry of swifts. Its focal point is a heavy Norman circular font with basketweave design, and the curve is echoed in the beams of roof supports, and in solid round pillars and chancel arch. On the hillside below this church are modern Council Office blocks, faced with pebbles which blend well with the old flints of the church, the ochres of the landscape beyond Southover, which is down the hill by the Priory, and possibly the most attractive part of Lewes. Quieter, with more countrified houses, pollarded trees, the elegant yellow-white brick of Priory Crescent, and the public, formal, gardens of Southover Grange, where rocks strut among gnarled trees and arcaded walls.

Here in Southover is the Church of St John, chequered black-and-white in flint and stone, with the checked de Warenne arms and a fish weathervane above a cupola'd tower. Again there are massive Norman columns between the nave and side aisle, great simplicity. But the Gundrada chapel, in which she now lies with her husband, is labelled by Nairn and Pevsner in their invigorating *Sussex* volume of *The Buildings of England* – 'horrible neo-Norman s. chapel ... by J. L. Parsons of Lewes, who was advised by Ferrey who should have known better'.[9] When the railway line to Brighton was built in 1845, across the Priory site, two leaden cists or coffins were found by workmen, labelled Gundrada and William, with well preserved bones (although the cists are very small). The bones have now been laid beneath a beautiful twelfth-century black marble slab, which had covered Gundrada's tomb in the Priory before the Dissolution of the Monasteries and was later appropriated to cover a family grave at Isfield. It has a decoration of palmettes, thickly encrusted, most suitable for this thriving early settlement.

Typical of Lewes too, and redolent of the quality of the surrounding countryside, is a wooden block used by the printer John Baxter in the early nineteenth century, now to be seen in the entrance hall of W. E. Baxter Ltd, the Lewes printers in the High Street. So highly polished on its under surface that it looks like walnut, it depicts a pastoral scene with cows and sheep, beneath the downs – peaceful and timeless. There is also a copy of the wooden printing-press John Baxter used, similar to the one used by Caxton. The Baxter Bible is much sought after today, but Baxter's other bestsellers of the day were *Lambert's Cricket Guide* (with 'secret signs for the use of bowlers and wicket keepers'), almanacks and the *Farmer's Account Book*. He was proud to publish Lewes's first town guidebook, in 1805. He had left London in 1802 on the advice of his doctor, and opened a bookshop in Brighton, before moving on to Lewes. He was successful as bookseller and printer, and also experimented with typography, and with making paper from nettles – the supply proved unpredictable. A local tradesman made an inking roller to his directions which was later developed to a type still used today.

John Baxter's second son George was equally successful and played an important part in the development of the oil process of printing in colours. A talented artist, he produced colour vignettes for fifteen volumes of Mudie's *The History of British Birds*. His prints are invaluable as witnesses of all the important events of the early Victorian era. It has been said that he gave to colour printing what printing gave to letters, making it possible for anyone to take into his home good copies of works in colour.[10]

The firm is still active in Lewes, one of the largest employers in the town, undertaking a wide range of letterpress printing, and producing PVC binders and folders. It is now part of the Royles group. The shopfront at 35 High Street (housing Bredon's Bookshop and Sussex Stationers at present) has a preservation order, so that it will remain, even should the firm move to new premises because of expansion.

*

From Lewes the River Ouse winds its lazy course to the sea – holding within its banks the power that has contracted since earlier days when it filled this whole wide valley between the masses of the downs. Their slopes are vividly seen from the lovely village of Iford; then the road passes through Northease, and Rodmell, where Virginia Woolf lived at Monk's House, a place where she found a measure of peace after busy weeks in London, and sometimes reprieve from the mental illness that dogged her, although the cold in winter could be bitter. (In his biography of her Quentin Bell tells how a visitor to Monk's House, Morgan Foster, desperately warming himself at the 'Cosy Stove' in his bedroom, burnt his trousers.) In the late 1920s she wrote: 'I like driving off to Rodmell on a hot Friday evening and having cold ham, and sitting on my terrace and smoking a cigar with an owl or two.' Inspiration came to her here for her greatest novel, *The Waves*: 'It is done; ... the thing stated ... I have netted that fin in the waste of water which appeared to me over the marshes out of my window at Rodmell ...' And in these marshes, in the River Ouse, she sought final escape by drowning when she felt her madness would become too burdensome to her husband Leonard Woolf. 'I am doing what seems the best thing to do. You have given me the greatest possible happiness ... I can't fight any longer. I know that I am spoiling your life ... I don't think two people could have been happier than we have been.' Her death was, as she had written to Vita Sackville-West 'the one experience I shall never describe'.[11]

Farther along the road is Southease, a small village in the wide ring of downs that must be one of the most heartwarming hamlets in England. A bridge runs across the river a little way off, but in the days when the whole valley was an estuary, there was a wharf here and the herring fishery was the largest in the area. The harbour may have been where now a rushy pond lies below Southease Place. Herring and porpoise are recorded as far up as Iford in the eleventh century.

From the bridge there is the best view one can get of Mount Caburn, with Lewes on its left, the castle clearly visible, as in an old print. Across the green slopes of Mount Caburn cloud shadows move like black smoke. The wind lifts the rushes along the channels of water which bisect the flat levels stretching to the mountain; the river curls in its muddy banks; birds jet through the air.

One could sit on the stile by the bridge all day, watching the cloud patterns.

Up the hill beyond the pond is the church, in a flint-walled churchyard that seems the most sheltered place in Sussex. Between curlicued eighteenth-century gravestones, snowdrops lie thick as snow, with purple crocuses, and in the summer, moss roses. Birds sing, cocks crow deafeningly beyond the walled vegetable gardens of the mellow houses around, and the light burns on lichened roofs.

The tower of the church is round, with a pointed cap. Inside, the church is plastered white with pale roof beams. Badly faded thirteenth-century wall paintings nevertheless give an idea of their original dark reds and gold. The round tower is matched by towers at Piddinghoe and Lewes (St Michael's), and it is thought they may have been used as beacon towers, which is eminently logical if one follows the sweep of the valley inland from the sea.

The river did not originally have its mouth at Newhaven, once called Meeching. It turned abruptly left, parallel to the shore, and entered the sea at Seaford, which was a flourishing port (while Meeching was an agricultural village) and a Limb of the Cinque Port of Hastings from 1229, taking precedence over such places as Pevensey. (Another port loosely linked and mentioned in Cinque Ports writs in the thirteenth century was Shoreham-by-Sea, the next busy port along the coast.) Seaford was powerful until the fourteenth century, when constant attacks from the French, from disease and floods, decimated the townspeople and left them too poor to repair their port. Meanwhile shingle had also begun to pile up at the river mouth, which was almost blocked by the mid fifteenth century. It is now thought that a man-made cut was dug about 1539 through to the sea at the site of Newhaven harbour, diverting the river and leaving Seaford stranded.

The town had a revival towards the end of the eighteenth century, as a seaside resort. It returned two MPs to Parliament until 1832 (it was earlier the only Cinque Port Limb to enjoy this privilege with the Head Ports), and eminent MPs were William Pitt (Earl of Chatham) and George Canning. Lord Tennyson often stayed at Seaford House, and strode across Seaford Head in wide-brimmed hat and flowing cloak, no doubt stirred by the breaking sea 285 feet below, and the magnificent, wind-swept view across to the Seven Sisters, the seven white sections cut cleanly through the chalk cliffs as with a knife.

Modern Seaford is drowned in red brick and those cul-de-sacs which at the seaside seem to proliferate like sea clover. But it has its historical buildings, and its age-old defences, ranging from twentieth-century concrete set up when the area was a sealed off zone in the Second World War – mined, booby trapped and gun-turreted – back through the Martello towers of the Napoleonic era, the westernmost on this bit of coastline, to the great hill fort on Seaford Head. Built in the Iron Age, 2,000 years ago, the grassed-over ramparts enclose a vast area, and even so, only represent half the fort, much of which has fallen into the sea as the cliff has eroded. It also enclosed a burial mound, unusually sited inside a fort, and perhaps of the fort's original chieftain. The Romans probably garrisoned the camp site. Later, in 485, the Saxon prince Aella fought the Welsh at Mearcredesburna – the town on the banks of the river (Seaford) – from where six years afterwards he went out to sack Pevensey. (The coast from here round to Beachy Head is now defined as the Sussex Heritage Coast, and there is also a nature reserve on the cliffs. One more piece of Britain preserved – in the country as a whole, an area of green land equivalent to the size of Berkshire is being urbanized every five years.)

Seaford Head is a natural stronghold. To the north lies Firle Beacon, 718 feet above sea level and the highest point on this reach of the downs, from which a pre-Roman trackway runs to the Head via East Blatchington and Sutton. Tumuli and barrows abound. The South Downs Way runs parallel to the coast through Alfriston and Southease. The two valleys, of the Ouse and Cuckmere, spoke inland through dips in the downs, full of promise, opening up the interior. Seawards, there is a clear arc through which any approaching craft can be seen, coming from across the channel, or round Beachy Head, or from the west. From here beacon lights could spread like wildfire.

The downs are green, the valleys unspoilt. As at Richborough, you look inland to a scene full of promise, lying spread out before you, and from this height, conquerors or defenders must have felt invincible, able to see the first enemy boat to appear on the blue of the sea, or the glint of spears down a valley.

A warm or windswept countryside of downs, of flint, water and corn; of churches, ports and towns, some thriving, some declining; of people assimilated from many races into a nation. A land lapped by the sea, under the lonely cry of gulls, under threat of many invasions, from inside and out. Threatened by pollution and eager tourist hordes, erosion and inertia, lorries and population growth, new technology and age-old greed; even by time and our own history, by the future and unknown fears. But a land still open to change; still ours to safeguard.

Notes

INTRODUCTION

1. Speech to the House of Commons, 4 June 1940.
2. W. G. Hoskins, *English Landscapes*, BBC, London, 1973.

CHAPTER 1

1. J. R. Green, *History of the English People* (Vol. 1), Macmillan, London, 1878. He continues, 'No spot can be so sacred to Englishmen as the spot which first felt the tread of English feet.'
2. William Lambarde, *A Perambulation of Kent: Conteining the Description, Hystorie, and Customes of That Shire*, with an introduction by Richard Church, Adams and Dart, Bath, 1970. (First published 1570.)
3. Caesar: *The Conquest of Gaul*, translated by S. A. Handford, Penguin Classics, London, 1951, page 136. Copyright © S. A. Handford 1951.
4. *The Margate Guide, to which is prefixed A Short Description of the Isle of Thanet*, printed for T. Carnan and F. Newbery, jun. at Number 65 in St Paul's Church-yard; and J. Hall, in High-Street, Margate, 1775.
5. Monk's inscription, formerly legible on west-end of Monkton church (*Insula rotunda Tanatos, quam circuit Unda, Fertilis & munda, nulli est orbe secunda*).
6. John Pearson, *The Life of Ian Fleming, Creator of James Bond*, Jonathan Cape, London, 1966.
7. The list of ports as listed in the Charter of Charles II in 1668 is the list usually referred to. It is as follows (from *Charters of the Cinque Ports, Two Ancient Towns and their Members*, by Samuel Jeake, London, 1728):

Head Port	Corporate Members	Non-Corporate Members
Hastings	Pevensey, Seaford	Bulverheeth, Petit Iham, Hidney, Beakesborne, Grange, alias Grenche

Head Port	Corporate Members	Non-Corporate Members
New Romney	Lydd	Promehill, Old Romney, Dengemarsh, Oswardstone or Orwelstone
Hithe		Westheath
Dover	Folkestone, Feversham	Margate, St John's, Goresend, Burchington Wood alias Woodchurch, St Peter's, Kingsdowne, Ringwold
Sandwich	Fordwich	Deale, Walmer, Ramsgate, Stoner, Sarr, Brightlingsea
Antient Town Rye	Tenterden	–
Winchelsea	–	–

The ports today are: Hastings (Cinque Port), Sandwich (Cinque Port), Dover (Cinque Port), Romney (Cinque Port), Hythe (Cinque Port), Rye (Antient Town), Winchelsea (Antient Town), Deal (Limb of Sandwich), Ramsgate (Limb of Sandwich), Faversham (Limb of Dover), Folkestone (Limb of Dover), Margate (Limb of Dover), Lydd (Limb of Romney), Tenterden (Limb of Rye). The Local Government Act, 1972, made special provision to ensure the continuance of the Confederation by a provision that in the absence of Charter Trustees or Town Councils which could undertake the function, special Cinque Ports Trustees could be appointed. The Office of Speaker is the perquisite of the mayor of each of the five Cinque Ports and two Antient Towns, in succession. Towns have, from time to time, applied to join the Confederation (for instance, Gillingham and Eastbourne in 1937 and some towns more recently), but these applications have not been accepted.

8. K. M. E. Murray, *The Constitutional History of the Cinque Ports*, Manchester University Press, Manchester, 1935.
9. *The Journeys of Celia Fiennes*, edited with an introduction by Christopher Morris, The Cresset Press, London, 1947.

CHAPTER 2
1. The 'Ram is thought probably to be from 'Ruim', the ancient British name for Thanet.

2. Robert Edward Hunter, *A Short Account of the Isle of Thanet*, Ramsgate 1810.
3. *All About Ramsgate and Broadstairs*, 1864.
4. A. J. Barker, *Dunkirk: The Great Escape*, J. M. Dent, London, 1977.
5. *The Wreck of the Indian Chief. Full Account of the Gallant Rescue of Eleven Lives by the Ramsgate Lifeboat 'Bradford' and the Steam-Tug 'Vulcan' on Jan. 5th and 6th 1881*, Kent Echo Office, Ramsgate, 1881.
6. Michael J. Winstanley, *Life in Kent at the Turn of the Century*, Dawson, Folkestone, 1978.
7. Letter to Theo, 1876.
8. Letter from Dickens to Thomas Beard, 1842. At Dickens House.
9. Charles Dickens, *David Copperfield*.
10. *White's of Cowes – Shipbuilders*. Published by J. Samuel White and Co. Ltd, Cowes, Isle of Wight.
11. Reginald Hargreaves, *The Narrow Seas*, Sidgwick and Jackson, London, 1959.
12. Len Deighton, *Fighter*, Jonathan Cape, London, 1977.
13. *Ibid*.
14. Winston Churchill, speaking in the House of Commons, 20 August 1940.
15. Introduction by A. J. P. Taylor to *Fighter* by Len Deighton, see above.
16. Len Deighton, *Fighter*.
17. Richard Hillary, *The Last Enemy*, Macmillan, London, 1942.

CHAPTER 3
1. Gray, while staying at Denton in 1766 on visiting Margate.
2. Evelyn Joll, *Turner: A Special Loan Exhibition of 20 Rarely Seen Paintings*, Tate Gallery, London, 1977.
3. Quoted in Christopher Marsden, *The English at the Seaside*, Collins, London, 1947.
4. Charles Lamb, 'The Old Margate Hoy' in *Essays of Elia*.
5. Howard Bridgewater (Kent Archaeological Society), *The Grotto*, Margate (obtainable from Grotto Hill, Margate, Kent).
6. Charles Dickens, *David Copperfield*.
7. A. O. Collard, *The Oyster and Dredgers of Whitstable*, London, 1902.
8. Brian Hadler, 'The Rise and Fall of the Whitstable Oyster', Kentish Sail Association's 5th Swale Smack and Sailing Barge Match programme, 1977.
9. A. O. Collard, *op. cit.*

CHAPTER 4
1. Chaucer, The Prologue to *The Canterbury Tales*, translated by Nevill Coghill, Penguin Books, London, 1951, Page 19. Copyright © Nevill Coghill 1951, 1958, 1960, 1975, 1977.

2. The Venerable Bede, *The Ecclesiastical History of the English Nation*, with an introduction by Dom David Knowles, Dent Everyman's Library, London, 1965.

3. G. Le Baker: *Chronicon*, edited by E. Maunde Thompson, Oxford, 1889, quoted in Barbara Emerson, *The Black Prince*, Weidenfeld and Nicolson, London, 1976.

4. William Lambarde. *op. cit.*

5. John Boyle, *Canterbury Pilgrim's Guide – the Official Guide to the City*, Canterbury City Council, 1968.

6. HRH The Prince of Wales, KG, GCB, in Foreword to *Christ's Glorious Church: the Story of Canterbury Cathedral* by Derek Ingram Hill, SPCK, London, 1976. Prince Charles was made a Freeman of the City of Canterbury in November 1978.

7. Alfred Duggan, *Thomas Becket of Canterbury*, Faber and Faber, London 1967.

8. Froissart, *Oeuvres*, edited by Kervyn de Lettenhove, Brussels, 1867-77, quoted in Barbara Emerson, *op. cit.*

9. Froissart, *Chronicles*.

10. HM Queen Elizabeth II, at her coronation.

11. John Newman, 'North East and East Kent' in *The Buildings of England*, edited by Nikolaus Pevsner (Assistant Editor Judy Nairn), Penguin Books, London, 1969, pages 189, 190. Copyright © John Newman 1969.

12. Derek Ingram Hill, *op. cit.*

13. Derek Ingram Hill, *The Stained Glass of Canterbury Cathedral*, published by the Friends of Canterbury Cathedral.

14. Daniel Defoe, *A Tour Through England and Wales* (2 vols), Dent (Everyman's Library), London, 1948.

15. Lines from 'The Faerie Queene' on Conrad's tombstone at Canterbury.

16. The Reverend Christopher Donaldson, *A Short History and Guide of St Martin's Church*, Canterbury, The Church Publishers, Ramsgate, Kent.

17. Izaak Walton, *The Compleat Angler*.

18. *Fordwich, the Lost Port*, edited and published by K. H. McIntosh, Ramsgate, 1975.

CHAPTER 5

1. William Cobbett, *Rural Rides*, (in 2 vols with an introduction by Asa Briggs), Dent, Everyman's Library, London, 1966–7.

2. From 'Nepenthe' by George Darley.

3. Rev. Thomas Stanley Treanor, *Heroes of the Goodwin Sands*, London, 1892.

4. William Shakespeare, *The Merchant of Venice*, Act III, Scene I.

5. George Goldsmith, Carter, *Forgotten Ports of England*, Evans Brothers, London, 1951.

6. William Lambarde, *op. cit.*
7. G. B. Gattie, *Memorials of the Goodwin Sands*, 1890, in T. Rice Holmes, *Ancient Britain and the Invasions of Julius Caesar*, The Clarendon Press, Oxford, 1907.
8. T. Rice Holmes, *op. cit.*
9. *The Journeys of Celia Fiennes*
10. Margaret Brentnall, *The Cinque Ports and Romney Marsh*, John Gifford Ltd., London, 1972.
11. Edward Hinings, *History, People and Places in the Cinque Ports*, Spurbooks Ltd., Bourne End, Buckinghamshire, 1975.
12. George Goldsmith Carter, *op. cit.*
13. *Ibid.*
14. *All About Ramsgate and Broadstairs*, 1864.
15. J. Holland Rose, *A Short Life of William Pitt*, G. Bell and Sons, London, 1925. See also, J. Holland Rose, *The Life of William Pitt*, Vols I and II, G. Bell and Sons, London, 1934.
16. *Ibid.*
17. Elizabeth Longford, *Wellington: The Years of the Sword*, Weidenfeld and Nicolson, London, 1969.
18. Elizabeth Longford, *Wellington: The Pillar of State*, Weidenfeld and Nicolson, London, 1972.
19. Richard Church, *Kent* (The County Books Series), Robert Hale, London, 1948.
20. *The War Speeches of Winston S. Churchill* (in 3 volumes), compiled by Charles Eade, Cassell, London (Vol. I, 1951).
21. *Ibid.*

CHAPTER 6
1. William Lambarde, *op. cit.*
2. Arch Whitehouse, *The Early Birds*, Nelson, London, 1967.
3. Charles H. Gibbs-Smith, *Aviation – An historical survey from its origins to the end of World War II*, HMSO, London, 1970.
4. Letters and Papers ... Henry VIII, XIV, HMSO, 1894, in R. Allen Brown, Dover Castle, HMSO, 1974.
5. A. J. Barker, *op. cit.*
6. Desert Island Discs, BBC Radio 4, 14 July 1979.
7. Speech to the House of Commons, 4 June 1940, in *The War Speeches of Winston S. Churchill* (Vol. I) compiled by Charles Eade, Cassell, London, 1951.
8. Lord Moran, *Winston Churchill. The Struggle for Survival 1940–1965*, Constable, London, 1966.
9. Lord Moran, *op. cit.*
10. A broadcast speech, 11 September 1940, in *The War Speeches of Winston S. Churchill, op. cit.*
11. John Newman, *op. cit.*, page 279.
12. Aubrey de Selincourt, *The Channel Shore*, Robert Hale, 1953.

13. Len Ortzen, *Famous Lifeboat Rescues*, Arthur Barker, London, 1971.
14. J. Randall, *Captain Webb, the intrepid champion Channel swimmer*, 1875, facsimile edition published by Salop County Library, 1975.
15. John Betjeman, 'A Shropshire Lad' in *John Betjeman's Collected Poems*, John Murray, London, 1958.
16. William Shakespeare, *King Lear*, Act IV, Scene VI.
17. T. Rice Holmes, *op. cit.*
18. Rivers Scott, *The Gateway of England*, Dover Harbour Board, 1965.
19. *Continental Motoring Guide*, edited by Paul Youden, MIPR, published Dover Harbour Board (annually).
20. George Orwell, *The Road to Wigan Pier*.

CHAPTER 7

1. Richard Church, 'William Harvey', in *Kent's Contribution* (People of England Series), Adams and Dart, Bath, 1972.
2. Daniel Defoe, *op. cit.*
3. Michael J. Winstanley, *op. cit.*
4. Richard Church, *Kent*.
5. Margaret Brentnall, *op. cit.*
6. Keith Spence, *The Companion Guide to Kent and Sussex*, Collins, London, 1973.
7. Kenneth Clark, *The Other Half: A Self Portrait*, John Murray, London, 1977. See also *Another Part of the Wood: A Self-Portrait*, (Vol I), John Murray, 1974.
8. *Ibid.*
9. Kenneth Clark, *The Nude*, 1956, Pelican Books, Penguin, London 1960.
10. Gerald Wilkinson, *Turner Sketches 1789-1820*, Barrie and Jenkins, London, 1977.
11. For the best description of this, and other, views of the Marsh, see John Piper, *Romney Marsh*, a King Penguin book, Penguin Books, London, 1950.
12. T. Rice Holmes, *op. cit.*
13. K. M. E. Murray, *op. cit.*
14. Walsingham *Historia Anglican, Vol I*, quoted in Reginald Hargreaves, *op. cit.*

CHAPTER 8

1. Richard Harris Barham, *The Ingoldsby Legends*, J. M. Dent (Everyman's Library), London, 1960.
2. William Lambarde, *op. cit.* 'Rumney, called in Saxon, Rumen-ea, that is to say, The large watry place, or Marish.'
3. Walter J. C. Murray, *Romney Marsh*, Robert Hale, London, 1953 and 1972.
4. John Newman, 'West Kent and the Weald' in *The Buildings of*

England, edited by Nikolaus Pevsner, Penguin Books, London, 1969, page 416. Copyright © John Newman 1969.

5. For this, and other churches on the Marsh, see the authoritative church guides by Anne Roper MBE, FSA. St Mary in the Marsh, published 1929; St Clement, Old Romney, 1938 *et seq*; St Augustine, Brookland, 1932; St George's, Ivychurch (o.p.); All Saints, Burmarsh.

6. E. Nesbit, *The Wouldbegoods*, Ernest Benn, London, 1958.

7. John Piper, *op. cit.*

8. From 'The Little Church in the Marsh' (Fairfield) by Joan Warburg, in *Country Life*, 3 June 1965, and in *The Golden Boy and Other Poems*, The Mitre Press, London, 1966.

9. Kent records, *A Calendar of the White and Black Books of the Cinque Ports, 1432–1955*. Edited by Felix Hull, BA, PHD, HMSO, London, 1967.

10. Extract kept at Dymchurch from document of reign of Queen Mary I, in Lambeth Palace. See Brentnall, *op. cit.*

11. H. G. Wells, *Kipps*, Collins, London, 1905.

12. Letter from Sidonius Apollinaris, quoted in Green's *Making of England*. See Lieut Henry N. Shore RN, *Smuggling Days and Smuggling Ways*, E. P. Publishing Ltd, Cassell, London, 1892.

13. W. S. Gent, *The Golden Fleece*, 1656. See Kenneth M. Clark, *Many a Bloody Affray – The story of Smuggling in the Port of Rye and District*, Rye Museum Publication No. 8, 1968.

14. Keith Spence, *op. cit.*

15. Daniel Defoe, *op. cit.*

16. Edward Hinings, *op. cit.*

17. F. F. Nicholls, *Honest Thieves – The Violent Heyday of English Smuggling*, Heinemann, London, 1973.

18. William Holloway, *The History and Antiquities of the Ancient Town and Port of Rye*, 1847.

19. Anne Roper MBE, FSA (with H. R. Pratt Boorman), *Kent Inns: A Distillation*, Kent Messenger, 1955. Anne Roper MBE, FSA, *The Gift of the Sea – A Short Guide to Romney Marsh*, Redmans, Ashford, 1950.

20. Article by Anne Roper in Lydd Parish Magazine, July, 1978.

CHAPTER 9

1. Copy of a Letter from Oscar Wilde, at Smallhythe Place.

2. 'Ellen Terry' by James Agate, *Radio Times*, 24 February 1928.

3. William Cobbett, *op. cit.* 'Ride through the North east part of Sussex, and all across Kent, from the Weald of Sussex to Dover. 1823'.

4. CTC Handbook, available from the National Headquarters of the Cyclists' Touring Club, Cotterell House, 69 Meadrow, Godalming, Surrey, GU7 3HS.

5. See Michael J. Winstanley, *op. cit.*

6. *Ibid.*

7. A. R. Pickup, 'Industrial Revolution for Dungeness', in *Birds*, the RSPB Magazine, Summer 1978, published by the Royal Society for the Protection of Birds, Sandy, Bedfordshire.

CHAPTER 10

1. Celia Fiennes, *op. cit.*; quoting Ovid, *Heroides* I, l, I, i. 53.
2. The Book of the Wisdom of Solomon (2,v), in the Apocrypha.
3. Geoffrey S. Bagley, *Edwardian Rye* (from contemporary photographs), Rye Museum Association, 1974.
4. Quoted in *Adams' Illustrated Guide to Rye Royal*, Adams of Rye, 1977.
5. St John, XV, 13.
6. Celia Fiennes, *op. cit.*
7. MS in Trinity College Library, Cambridge.
8. Thomas of Walsingham, quoted in William Durrant Cooper, *History of Winchelsea*, 1850.
9. Introduction by Thackeray's daughter, Lady Ritchie, to *Denis Duval* by William Makepeace Thackeray, Smith, Elder and Co., London, 1911.
10. (SRS 65), quoted in Beryl Lucey, *Twenty Centuries in Sedlescombe*, Regency Press, London and New York, 1978.
11. Daniel Defoe, *op. cit.*

CHAPTER 11

1. Charles Lamb, *The Last Essays of Elia*.
2. Letter to Mr Moore, 8 July 1814.
3. John Bratby, *Breakdown*, Hutchinson, London, 1960.
4. *Ibid.*
5. Thomas Stanley Treanor, *op cit.* William's chaplain, William of Poitiers, recorded the facts in *Gesta Guillelmi Ducis Normanorum et Regis Anglorum*, Poitiers, 1071 to 1076.
6. Augustus J. C. Hare, *Sussex*, Allen, London, 1896.
7. Walter H. Godfrey, *Lewes – The Official Guide to the Historic County Town*, edited and revised by L. S. Davey and W. E. Godfrey, Lewes Town Council, 1977.
8. This, and the above quotations, from Thomas Paine, *The Rights of Man*, with an introduction by Arthur Seldon, Dent (Everyman's Library), London, 1969.
9. Ian Nairn and Nikolaus Pevsner, *Sussex*, (*The Buildings of England*), Penguin, London, 1965, page 553. Copyright © Ian Nairn and Nikolaus Pevsner 1965.
10. *Baxter, 175 Years of Progress*, compiled by Lynn Cox, W. E. Baxter Ltd., Lewes.
11. Quentin Bell, *Virginia Woolf: A Biography*, Volume Two, The Hogarth Press, London, 1972.

Select Bibliography

BAGLEY, GEOFFREY S., *Edwardian Rye* (from contemporary photographs), Rye Museum Association, Rye, 1974.

BARHAM, RICHARD HARRIS, *The Ingoldsby Legends*, J. M. Dent (Everyman's Library), London, 1960.

BARKER, A. J., *Dunkirk: The Great Escape*, J. M. Dent, London, 1977.

BEDE, THE VENERABLE, *The Ecclesiastical History of the English Nation*, with an Introduction by Dom David Knowles, Dent (Everyman's Library), London, 1965.

BELL, QUENTIN, *Virginia Woolf: A Biography*, Volume Two, The Hogarth Press, London, 1972.

BONNER, G. W., *The Picturesque Pocket Companion to Margate, Ramsgate, Broadstairs*, William Kidd, London, 1831.

BOYLE, JOHN, *Canterbury Pilgrim's Guide – The Official Guide to the City*; Canterbury City Council, Canterbury, 1968.

BOYS, WILLIAM, *Collections for an History of Sandwich in Kent, with notices of the other Cinque Ports and Members and of Richborough*, Canterbury, 1792.

BRATBY, JOHN, *Breakdown*, Hutchinson, London, 1960.

BRENTNALL, MARGARET, *The Cinque Ports and Romney Marsh*, John Gifford, London, 1972.

BROWN, R. ALLEN, *Dover Castle*, HMSO, London, 1974.

BRYANT, ARTHUR, *The Great Duke*, Collins, London, 1971.

BURNAND, F. C., *The Zig-Zag Guide*, illus. by Phil May, Adam and Charles Black, London, 1897.

CAESAR, JULIUS, *The Conquest of Gaul*, translated by S. A. Handford, Penguin Classics, London, 1951.

CARTER, GEORGE GOLDSMITH, *Forgotten Ports of England*, Evans Brothers, London, 1951.

CHAUCER, GEOFFREY, *The Canterbury Tales*, translated by Nevill Coghill, Penguin Classics, London, 1951.

CHURCH, RICHARD, *Kent,* (The County Books Series), Robert Hale, London, 1948.

—— *Kent's Contribution,* (People of England Series), Adams and Dart, Bath, 1972.

CHURCHILL, WINSTON S., *The Second World War* (6 Volumes), Cassell, London, 1960.

CLARK, KENNETH, *Another Part of the Wood. A Self-Portrait* (Vol. I), John Murray, London, 1974.

—— *The Other Half. A Self-Portrait* (Vol. II), John Murray, London, 1977.

CLARK, KENNETH M., *Many a Bloody Affray – The Story of Smuggling in the Port of Rye and District,* Rye Museum Publications no. 98, Rye, 1968.

CLARKE, H. G., *The Centenary Pot-Lid Book,* Courier Press, London, 1949.

COBBETT, WILLIAM, Rural Rides (in 2 Vols. with an introduction by Professor Asa Briggs), Dent (Everyman's Library), London 1966–7.

COLLARD, A. O., *The Oyster and Dredgers of Whitstable,* Joseph Collard, London, 1902.

COOPER, WILLIAM DURRANT, *History of Winchelsea,* 1850.

CROUCH, MARCUS, *Kent,* Batsford, London, 1966.

DEANESLY, MARGARET, *Augustine of Canterbury,* Nelson, London, 1964.

DEFOE, DANIEL, *A Tour Through England and Wales* (2 Vols.), Dent (Everyman's Library), London, 1948.

DEIGHTON, LEN, *Fighter,* Jonathan Cape, London, 1977.

DUGGAN, ALFRED, *Thomas Becket of Canterbury,* Faber and Faber, London, 1967.

EADE, CHARLES, *The War Speeches of Winston S. Churchill* (in 3 Vols.), Cassell, London (Vol. I, 1951).

EAGLE, DOROTHY and CARNELL, HILARY, *The Oxford Literary Guide to the British Isles,* Oxford University Press, London, 1977.

EMERSON, BARBARA, *The Black Prince,* Weidenfeld and Nicolson, London, 1976.

FOSTER, JIM, *Adams' Illustrated Guide to Rye Royal* (Twentieth edition by Kenneth Clark and Clifford Foster), Adams of Rye, Rye, 1977.

GARDINER, DOROTHY, *Companion Into Kent*, Methuen, London, 1949.

—— *Historic Haven: The Story of Sandwich*, Pilgrim Press, Derby, 1954.

GARMONSWAY, G. N. (Trans.), *The Anglo-Saxon Chronicle*, J. M. Dent, London, 1965.

GIBBS-SMITH, CHARLES H., *Aviation – An historical survey from its origins to the end of World War II*, HMSO, London, 1970.

GODFREY, WALTER H., *Lewes – The Official Guide to the Historic County Town*, edited and revised by L. S. Davey and W. E. Godfrey, Lewes Town Council, Lewes, 1977.

GREEN, JOHN RICHARD, *History of the English People* (Vol. I), Macmillan, London, 1878.

HAMMOND, J. W., *Complete South-East Coast* (Red Guide), Ward Lock, London, 1974.

HARE, AUGUSTUS J. C., *Sussex*, Allen, London, 1896.

HARGREAVES, REGINALD, *The Narrow Seas*, Sidgwick and Jackson, London, 1959.

HASTED, EDWARD, *History and Topographical Survey of the County of Kent* (4 Vols.), Canterbury, 1778–99.

HILL, DEREK INGRAM, *Christ's Glorious Church: the Story of Canterbury Cathedral*, with a Foreword by HRH The Prince of Wales, SPCK, London, 1976.

—— *The Stained Glass of Canterbury Cathedral*, The Friends of Canterbury Cathedral, Canterbury.

HILLARY, RICHARD, *The Last Enemy*, Macmillan, London, 1942.

HININGS, EDWARD, *History, People and Places in the Cinque Ports*, Spurbooks, Bourne End, Buckinghamshire, 1975.

HOLLOWAY, WILLIAM, *The History and Antiquities of the Ancient Town and Port of Rye*, John Russell Smith, 1847.

HOSKINS, W. G., *English Landscapes*, BBC, London, 1973.

—— *The Making of the English Landscape*, Hodder and Stoughton, London, 1955.

HUGHES, PENNETHORNE, *Kent* (A Shell Guide), Faber and Faber, London, 1969.

HULL, FELIX, (Ed.), *A Calendar of the White and Black Books of the Cinque Ports 1432–1955*, HMSO, London, 1966.

HUNTER, ROBERT EDWARD, *A Short Account of the Isle of Thanet*, Burgess, Ramsgate, 1810.

JESSUP, RONALD and FRANK, *The Cinque Ports*, Batsford, London, 1952.

KITTON, F. G., *The Dickens Country*, Adam and Charles Black, London, 1911.

LAMBARDE, WILLIAM, *A Perambulation of Kent* (first published 1570), with an Introduction by Richard Church, Adams and Dart, Bath, 1970.

LONGFORD, ELIZABETH, *Wellington: The Years of the Sword*, Weidenfeld and Nicolson, London, 1969.

—— *Wellington: The Pillar of State*, Weidenfeld and Nicolson, London, 1972.

LUCEY, BERYL, *Twenty Centuries in Sedlescombe*, Regency Press, London and New York, 1978.

MANNING-SANDERS, RUTH, *Seaside England*, Batsford, London, 1951.

MARSDEN, CHRISTOPHER, *The English at the Seaside*, Collins, London, 1947.

MCINTOSH, K. H., (Ed.), *Fordwich, the Lost Port*, McIntosh, Ramsgate, 1975.

MEE, ARTHUR, *Kent (The King's England)*, Hodder and Stoughton, London, (new edition) 1969.

MILLWARD, ROY, and ROBINSON, ADRIAN, *South-East England: The Channel Coastlands* (Landscapes of Britain), Macmillan, London, 1973.

MORAN, LORD, *Winston Churchill. The Struggle for Survival 1940–1965*, Constable, London, 1966.

MORRIS, CHRISTOPHER (Ed.), *The Journeys of Celia Fiennes*, The Cresset Press, London, 1947.

MURRAY, K. M. E., *The Constitutional History of the Cinque Ports*, Manchester University Press, Manchester, 1935.

MURRAY, WALTER J. C., *Romney Marsh*, Robert Hale, London, 1972.

NAIRN, IAN, and PEVSNER, NIKOLAUS, *The Buildings of England. Sussex*. Penguin Books, London, 1965.

NEWMAN, JOHN, *The Buildings of England. North East and East Kent*, edited by Nikolaus Pevsner, Penguin Books, London, 1969.

—— *The Buildings of England. West Kent and the Weald*, edited by Nikolaus Pevsner, Penguin Books, London, 1969.

NICHOLLS, F. F., *Honest Thieves – The Violent Heyday of English Smuggling*, Heinemann, London, 1973.

ORTZEN, LEN, *Famous Lifeboat Rescues*, Arthur Barker, London, 1971.

PAINE, THOMAS, *The Rights of Man*, with an introduction by Arthur Seldon, J. M. Dent (Everyman's Library), London, 1958.

PEARSON, JOHN, *The Life of Ian Fleming, Creator of James Bond*, Jonathan Cape, London, 1966.

PÉQUINOT, C. A., *Chunnel*, C.R. Books, London, 1965.

PIPER, JOHN, *Romney Marsh*, (a King Penguin Book), Penguin Books, London, 1950.

RICE HOLMES, T., *Ancient Britain and the Invasions of Julius Caesar*, The Clarendon Press, Oxford, 1907.

ROPER, ANNE, Church Guides to: *St Mary in the Marsh; St Clement, Old Romney; St Augustine, Brookland; St George's, Ivychurch; All Saints, Burmarsh.*

—— *The Gift of the Sea – A Short Guide to Romney Marsh*, Redmans, Ashford, 1950.

—— with PRATT BOORMAN, H. R., *Kent Inns: A Distillation*, Kent Messenger, 1955.

ROSE, J. HOLLAND, *A Short Life of William Pitt*, G. Bell and Sons, London, 1925.

—— *The Life of William Pitt*, Vols I and II, G. Bell and Sons, London, 1934.

SCOTT, RIVERS, *The Gateway of England*, Dover Harbour Board, Dover, 1965.

SELINCOURT, AUBREY DE, *The Channel Shore*, Robert Hale, London, 1953.

SHORE, LIEUT. HENRY N., RN, *Smuggling Days and Smuggling Ways*, EP Publishing, Cassell, London, 1892.

SPENCE, KEITH, *The Companion Guide to Kent and Sussex*, Collins, London, 1975.

THACKERAY, WILLIAM MAKEPEACE, *Denis Duval*, with an Introduction by Lady Ritchie, Smith, Elder and Co, London, 1911.

The Margate Guide, T. Carnan and F. Newbery jun., London, 1775.

The New Margate, Ramsgate and Broadstairs Guide, The Thanet Press, Margate, 1801.

The Thanet Itinerary or Steam Yacht Companion, Bettison, Garner and Denne, Margate, 1822.

The Wreck of the Indian Chief, Kent Echo Office, Ramsgate, 1881.

TREANOR, REV. THOMAS STANLEY, *Heroes of the Goodwin Sands*, London, 1892.

TURNER, JAMES (with photographs by Edwin Smith), *The Countryside of Britain*, Ward Lock, London, 1977.

VINE, P. A. L., *The Royal Military Canal*, David and Charles, Newton Abbot, 1972.

WHITE, JOHN TALBOT, *The South-East, Down and Weald: Kent, Surrey and Sussex* (The Regions of Britain), Eyre Methuen, London, 1977.

WHITEHOUSE, ARCH, *The Early Birds*, Nelson, London, 1967.

WILKINSON, GERALD, *Turner Sketches 1789–1820*, Barrie and Jenkins, London, 1977.

WINSTANLEY, MICHAEL J., *Life in Kent at the Turn of the Century*, Dawson, Folkestone, 1978.

WOODFORD, CECILE, *Portrait of Sussex*, Robert Hale, London, 1972.

Index

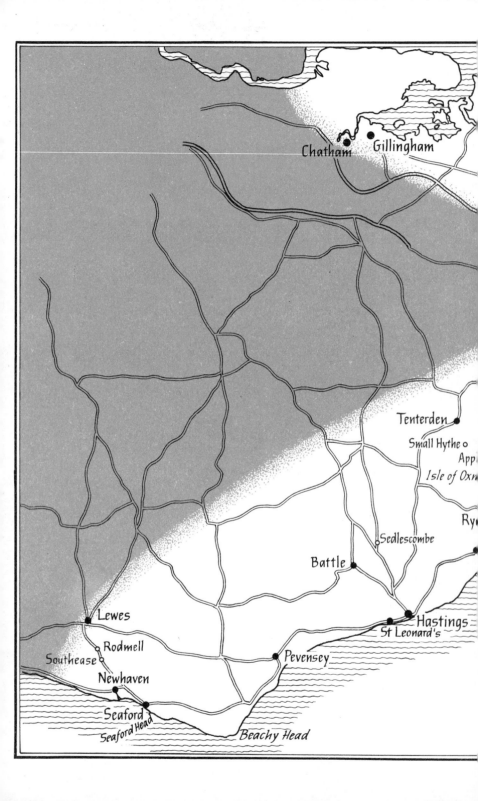